50 Pouches

Putting Your Fabric Scraps to Good Use

4880 Lower Valley Road • Atglen, PA 19310

Introduction

This book gives you your stash-happy key to ongoing pouch happiness! Some are practical, while others are simply cute. Some are made from a creative patchwork (plenty of happy roles for even your smallest stash members!), others from a single fabric.

A pouch is low commitment; it's easier to make than an item of clothing or a bag, so you can just relax, decide which of the 50 you're in the mood for, and casually make the pouch of your choosing. Enjoy using them yourself, give them away as gifts . . . most important, have fun making these pouches your own!

The instructions include step-by-step photos, and you'll notice that the examples use red thread (or another color of thread that's different from the fabric). This is done on purpose to make the instructions clear and easy to understand. When you make your pouch following these visuals, remember to use the color of thread that closely matches your fabric. That will give you a beautiful finish without visible stitches.

For the basics of making pouches, see page 81. Quilting and other techniques are also explained there, so that you can refer to them as needed.

CONTENTS

Basic Shapes

Of course, measurements determine the shape of the pouch but how the corners are boxed will also drastically change the shape of the pouch. Just thinking about the measurements and the overall shape of the pouch for your project can be fun. The pouches introduced in this section are all easy to make.

1 Appliqué Pouch with Boxed Corners

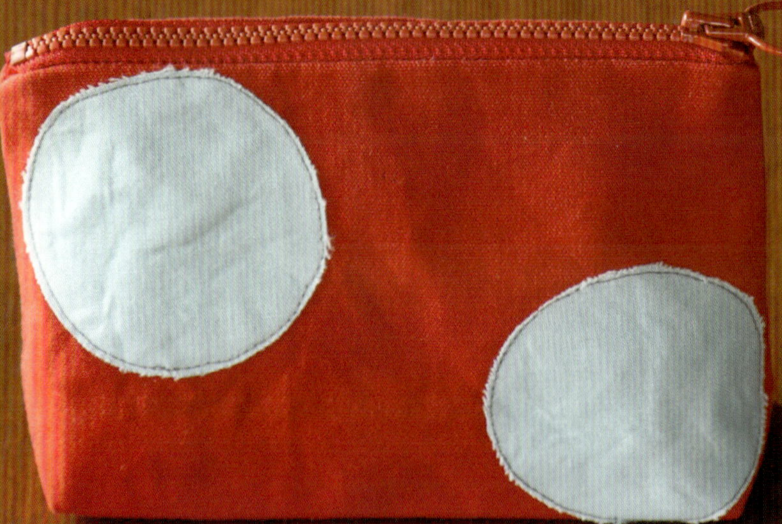

An appliqué is fused onto the outer fabric of the pouch and the raw edges of the appliqué are stitched. Be bold and free with your appliqué. The less-than-perfect look of the appliqué will add playfulness to the pouch. The shape here is quite basic. The bottom corners are sewn by folding the corners into a triangular shape. You've probably already sewn a pouch like this before.

10 x 15 cm (4" x 5⅞") Sakura Yamamoto

How to make ▶ p. 8

How to Make the Appliqué Pouch with Boxed Corners on Page 6

If this pouch is made from a rectangular shaped piece of fabric the finished pouch is going to be trapezoidal, narrowing towards the bottom. If you wish your finished pouch to be a rectangular shape, as seen in this example, just cut your fabric in an oblong hexagon.

Materials

Appliqué

Outer fabric, Lining fabric: 25 x 30 cm (9⅞" x 11⅞")

one 15 cm (6") zipper

Double-sided fusible interfacing

Double-sided fusible interfacing sheets have spiderweb-like fusible adhesive on both sides. Place the adhesive side of the sheet over the fabric that you intend to fuse. Then, iron on the released paper side of the sheet. Cut the fabric any shape you desire and then peel-off the released paper. Place the cut fabric (an appliqué) on the base fabric and then iron to fuse them together.

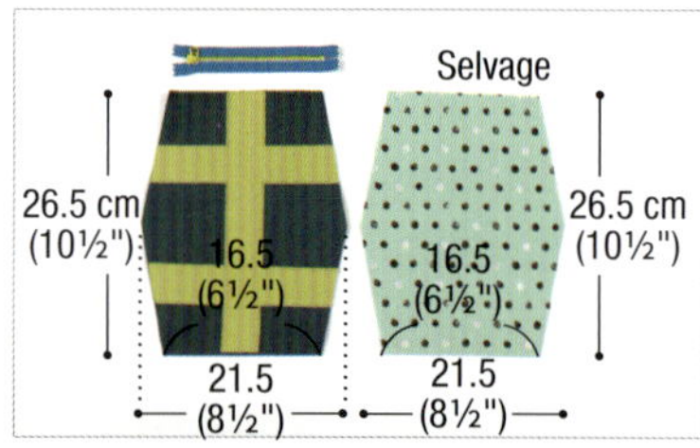

1 1 Prepare the outer fabric, lining fabric, and a zipper. The seam allowance is 0.7 cm (¼"). As for the appliqué, after fusing to the outer fabric using a double-sided fusible interfacing, stitch the raw edges of the appliqué.

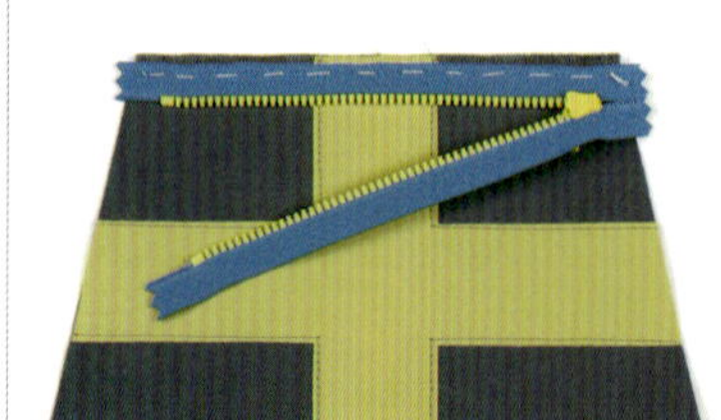

2 With the right sides together, place a zipper along the opening of the outer fabric. Align the zipper and the edge of the outer fabric, then temporarily secure them together with a basting stitch.

3 Place the lining fabric over the outer fabric with both right sides facing together. Secure. We are using clips but you can use pins instead.

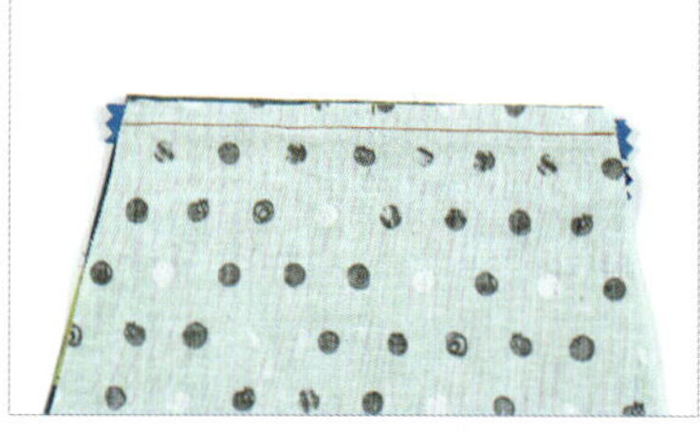

4 Sew the outer fabric, zipper, and lining fabric together. For machine sewing use a regular presser foot (not the zipper presser foot). Move the zipper slider out of the way as you sew.

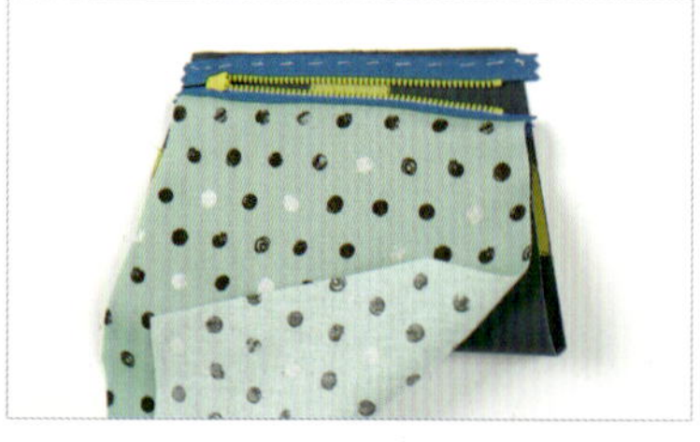

5 Do the same for the other side of the zipper tape. Align the zipper tape and edge of the outer fabric and use a basting stitch in order to temporarily secure them together.

6 Fold the right side of lining fabric up and secure the edge and the zipper tape. This time, leave the zipper unzipped.

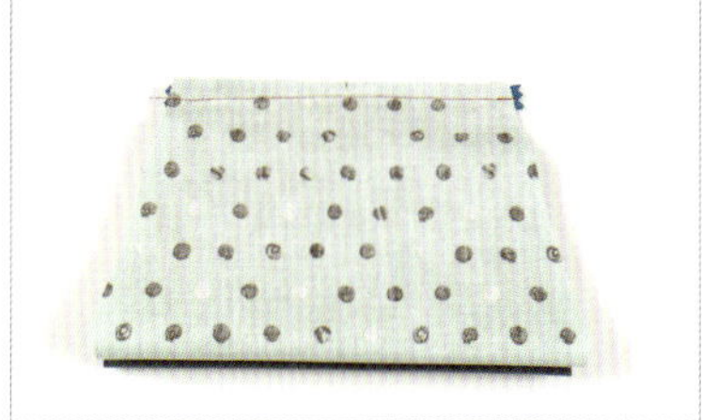

7 Sew as you did in step 4. For machine sewing it is not necessary to mark the sewing line; instead use the width of the presser foot or the feed edge of your sewing machine as your guideline.

8 Now the zipper is installed. The zipper is inside, between the outer fabric and lining fabric.

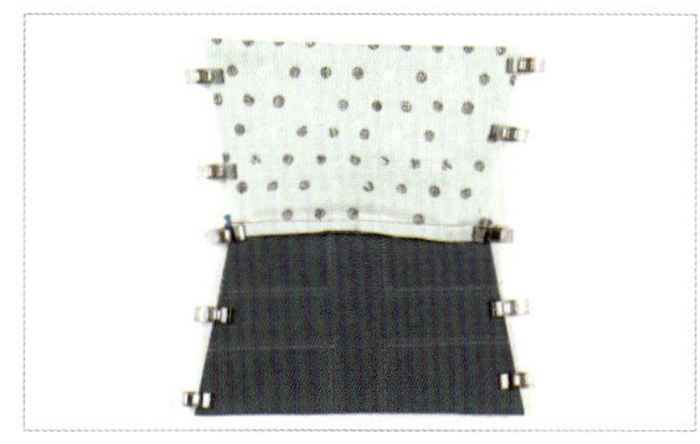

9 Place the zipper between the lining and outer fabrics. Place the lining fabric above the zipper and the outer fabric on the other side. Then secure each side.

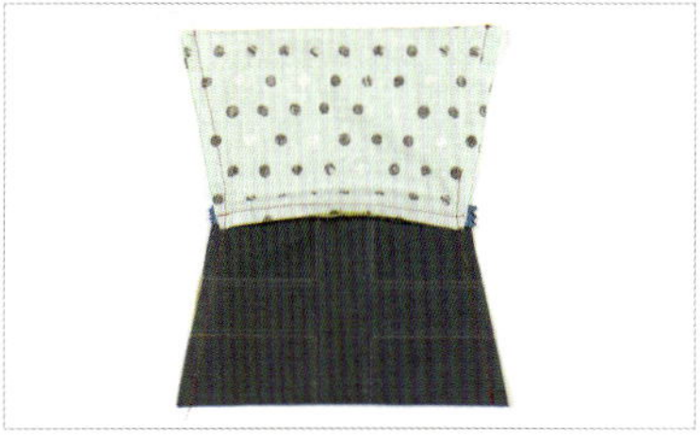

10 Sew both sides. Be sure to leave an opening in the lining fabric for turning the pouch inside out. Be careful when sewing over the zipper to keep your stitches straight.

11 Fold the box corner. Press the corner down into a triangle while aligning the center seam with the side seam. It should look like the corner is pinched together.

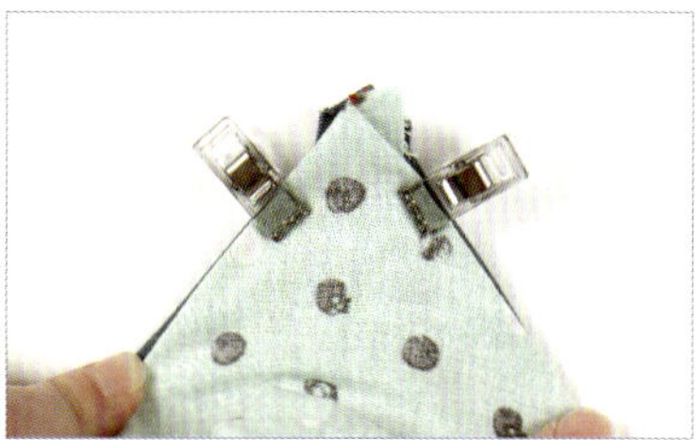

12 Do the same for the corners on the lining fabric. With the side seam facing down, place the lining fabric corner over the outer fabric corner.

13 It should look like the photo above. The corners are small, so it might be hard to match them up. Try your best not to allow misalignment.

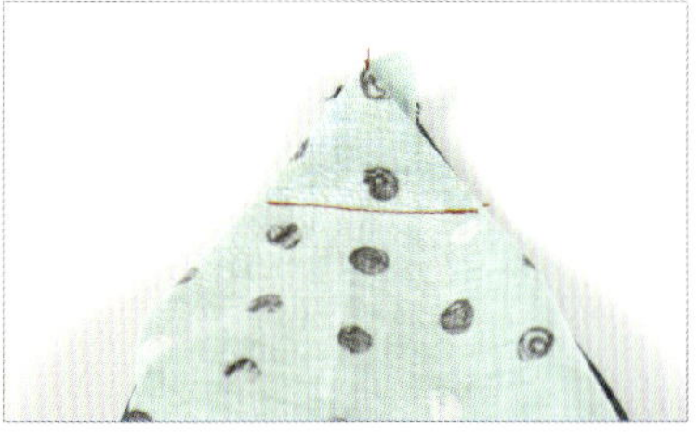

14 Mark the width 5 cm (2"). From the center seam, measure 2.5 cm (1") to the left and right, and mark a line. Then sew over the marked line.

15 Do the same for the other corner.

16 Turn the fabric right side out. Since the opening is facing inward it might be hard to turn it right side out. Just push the fabric through the opening little by little.

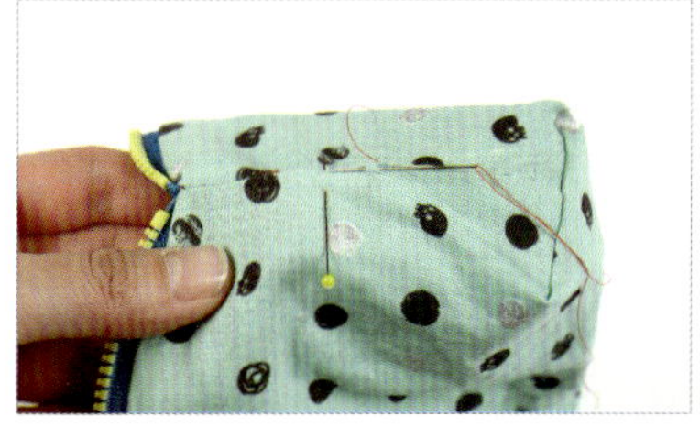

17 Fold the seam allowance of the opening inward and blind stitch the opening. If machine sewing, pinch only the lining fabric and sew using a similar color thread as the fabric.

18 The pouch is complete. Iron and shape it nicely.

2 Compact Emergency Pouch

This pouch carries all the necessary items for an emergency. But at a glance, it just looks cute. This functional pouch has tightly crafted quilting and a hook on the side for convenience.

13 x 18 cm (5⅛" x 7⅛") Sachiko Ishikawa

How to make ▶ p. 84

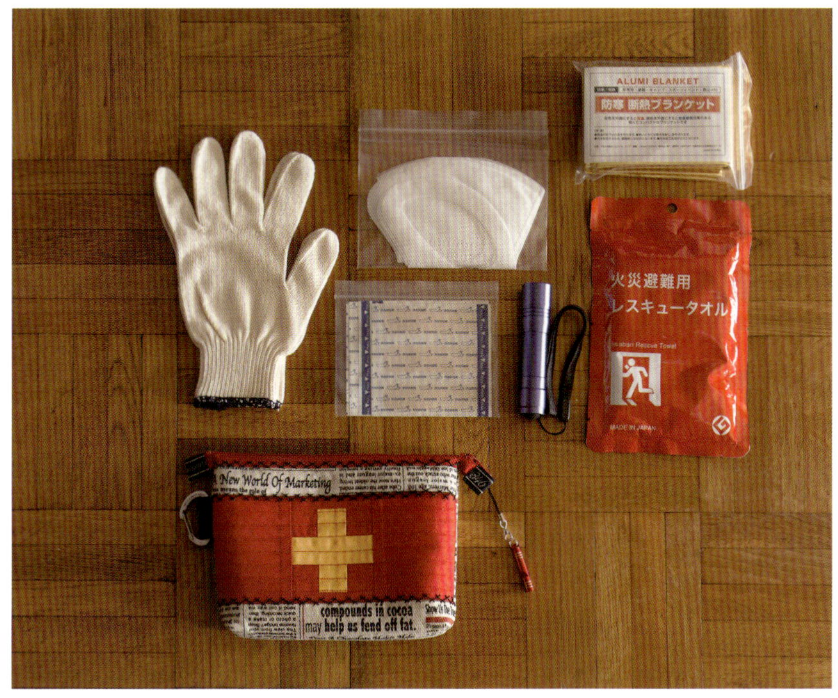

Just the set of items you would want to carry in this pouch: a pair of cotton gloves, a mask, bandages, a flashlight, an emergency thermal blanket, and a Rescue Towel. A small whistle is attached to the zipper tag.

How to Install an Exposed Zipper

1 After sewing the pouch, finish the opening with 0.5 cm (¼") wide piping. Align the edge of the piping and the edge of the zipper tape. Pin to secure. Align the edges to make the installation process easier.

2 Blind stitch along the piped edge of the opening. Looking inside we see that traces of the blind stitch are visible.

3 Both ends of the zipper are longer than the opening of the pouch. Blind stitch just before the side seam of the pouch.

4 Fold excess zipper tape down and stitch. Wrap the end with a ribbon or fabric to conceal.

5 Herringbone stitch over the zipper tape to prevent the zipper tape from bulging out.

3

Boxy Pouch

Each side seam uses a boxed corner to create this cute, cube-shaped pouch. It's best to attach a tab to each end of the bag to make zipping and unzipping easier.

7 x 12 cm ($2\frac{3}{4}$" x $4\frac{3}{4}$") Masumi Sasao

How to make ▶ p. 85

4

Oblong Pouch

This pouch uses the same measurements as the pouch on page 12, but it's sewn a little differently. The boxed corners are wider. This makes the pouch skinny and oblong. Just by changing the width of the boxed corners, your pouch's appearance will drastically change.

10 x 9 cm (4" x 3⅝") Masumi Sasao

How to make ▶ p. 15

5 Shell-shaped, Quilted, Zippered Pouch

The outer edge is bound with a contrasting fabric. The plumpness and petite size of these pouches makes them extra cute. The zipper is hand-sewn because it's installed after the binding strip is sewn on. Let's make a large, medium, and small pouch, just like a set of nesting dolls!

4 x 5.5 cm (1½" x 2¼") Noriko Hosoo

How to make ▶ p. 15

How to Make a Shell-shaped, Quilted, Zippered Pouch

After separately sewing the outer fabric and lining fabric, you just need to put them together to make your pouch.
The steps are simple . . .

Materials

Outer fabric, Lining fabric, Fusible cotton batting – L size: each 15 x 20 cm (5⅞" x 7⅞"),
M size and S size: each 10 x 15 cm (3 15/16" x 5⅞")
Binding strip – L size: 3 x 50 cm (1 3/16" x 19 11/16"), M size: 2.5 x 35 (1" x 13¾"), S size: 2 x 30 cm (13/16" x 11 13/16")
Zipper – L size: 12 cm (4¾") long, M and S sizes: 10 cm (3 15/16") long

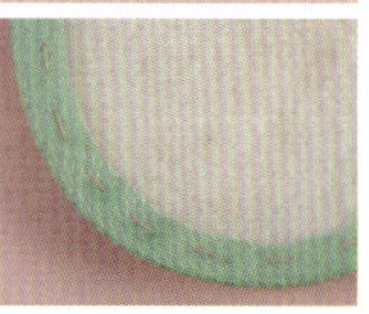

1 Fuse cotton batting to the wrong side of the outer fabric, then quilt as you desire. Attach a binding strip to the right side of the outer fabric. Instead of sewing a binding strip on the backside, just use a basting stitch. The width of the binding is 0.5 to 0.7 cm (3/16" to ¼"). Cut lining fabric the same size as the outer fabric.

2 With the right sides together, sew the lining fabric to the pouch's opening. Seam allowance: 0.5 cm (3/16").

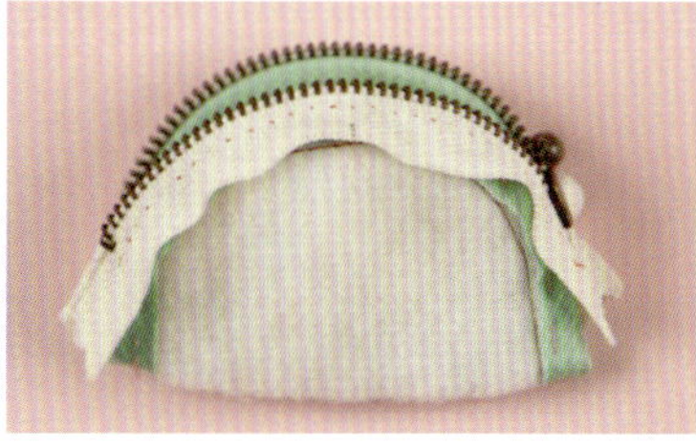

3 Install a zipper on the pouch's opening. See p. 80 for installing a zipper.

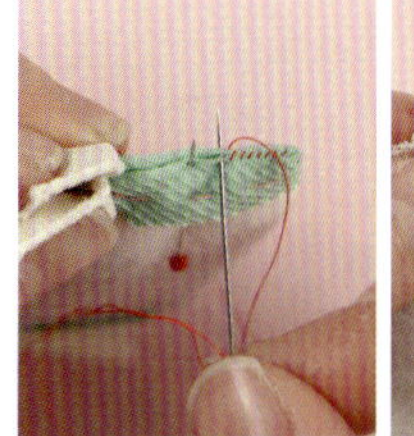

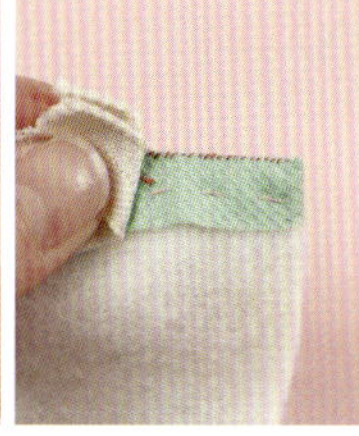

4 With the right sides together, whip stitch on the side of the pouch that is under the zipper.

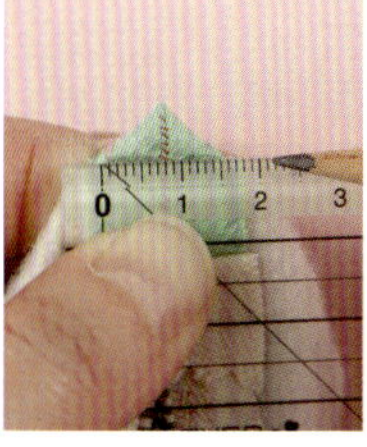

5 Sew boxed corners. Align side seam with bottom crease to make a point. From the corner point measure in:
L: 3 cm (1 3/16"), M: 2 cm (3/16"),
S: 1.5 cm (9/16"), and mark. Then sew.

6 Do the same for the lining.

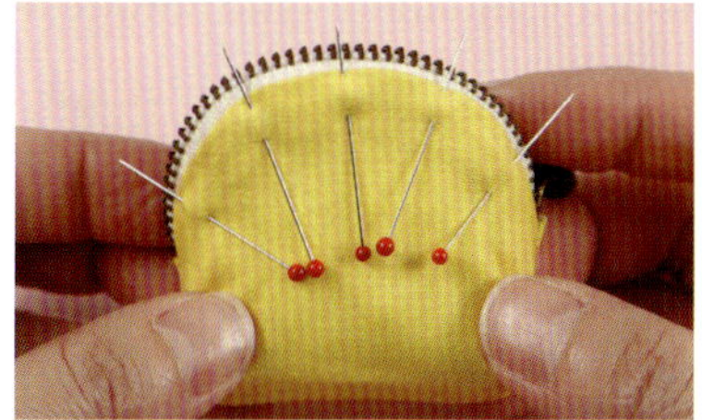

7 Put the outer fabric onto the lining, and pin to secure. Before pinning, tuck the seam allowance of the lining under.

8 Blind stitch along opening of the lining, to the zipper.

9 Once the lining is sewn on, it's complete.

6

Boxy Oblong Pouch

The look of the boxed corners reminds me of gift wrapping. The sewing is very easy. The size of the pouch determines the width of the boxed corner. The side view is square.

8 x 19 cm (3⅛" x 7½") Sakura Yamamoto

How to make ▶ p. 17

How to Make a Boxy Oblong Pouch

Installing the zipper is the same as for the pouch on page 6. Refer to the instructions on page 8.

Materials

Outer fabric 2 pieces 15 x 35 cm (5⅞" x 13¾")

Lining fabric, 30 x 35 cm (11⅞" x 13¾")

One 25 cm (9⅞") zipper

Leather for a tab 10 x 5 cm (4" x 2")

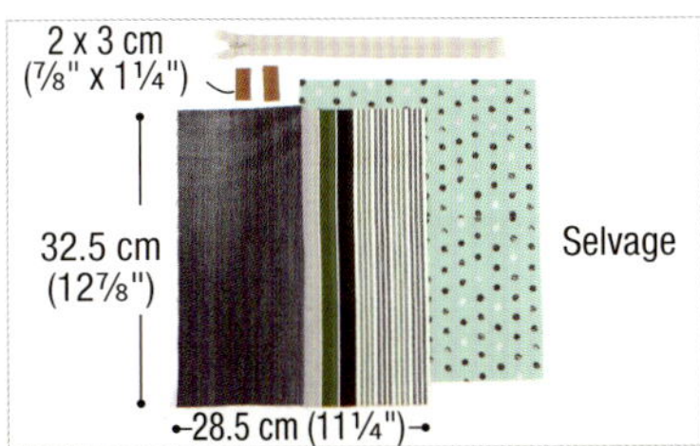

1 Prepare outer fabric, lining fabric, a zipper, and a tab. The outer fabric actually uses two different fabrics joined together. Sew the lining fabric while leaving an opening at the center seam for turning inside out. The seam allowance is 0.7 cm (¼").

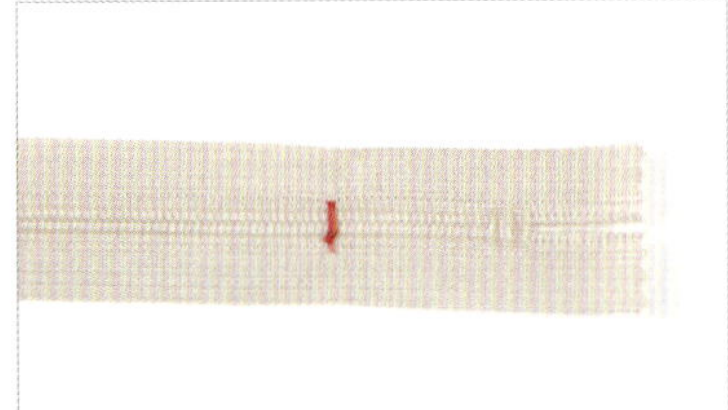

2 The zipper is Flatknit®. The teeth of the zipper are flat, thin, and soft. It's easy to cut, so it's very convenient to adjust the length. If you cut the zipper short be sure to add stitching before the cut line (i.e., create a thread stopper so the zipper doesn't come off).

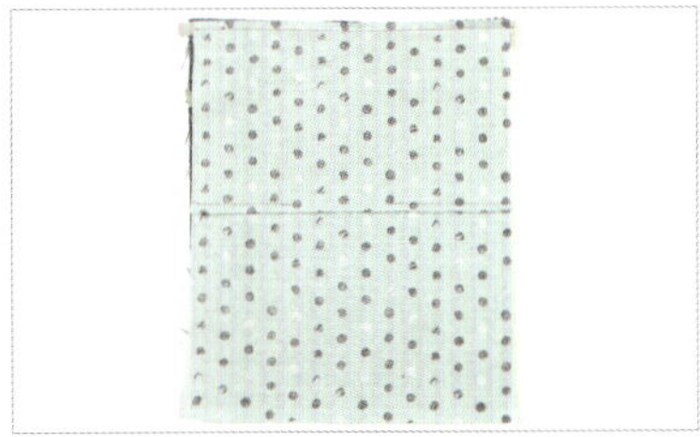

3 Install the zipper. Refer to the instructions on page 8. Align the zipper along the opening of the pouch and lay the lining fabric down with the right side facing down. Then sew together.

4 Next, do the same for the other side of the zipper tape. Up to this point the steps are the same as for the pouch on page 8.

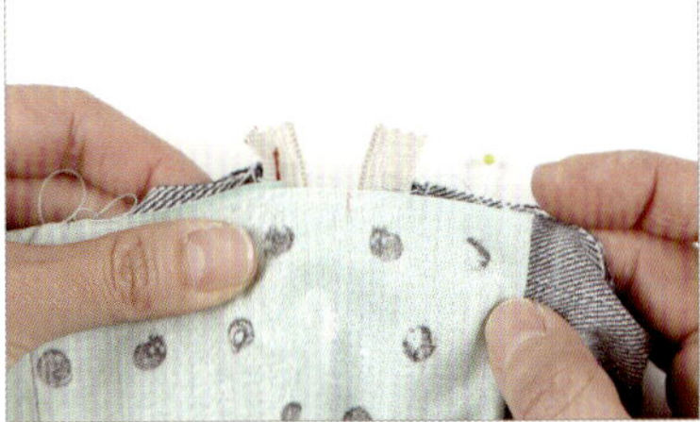

5 Mark the center seam and the halfway point from the center seam to the opening on the side seam (the center of the side seam). Align the center seam with the zipper; refold. Also, align the center of the side seam with the zipper.

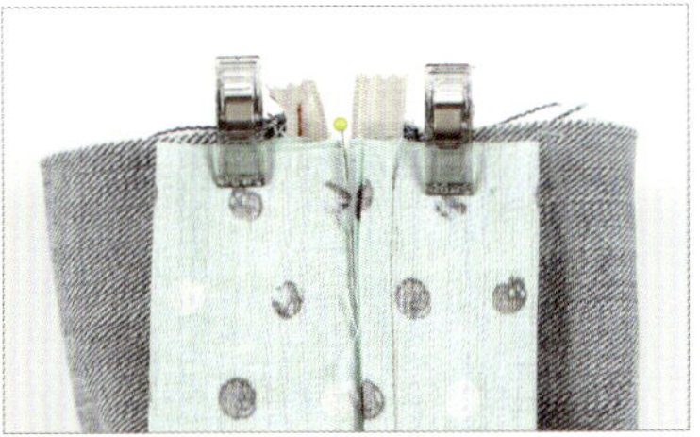

6 Fold the lining fabric. In the above picture (where the yellow-headed pin marks the center seam) the center of both side seams is folded inward like a bellows.

7 Fold the outer fabric in the same manner as the lining fabric. The picture above shows where the outer fabric and lining fabric are folded like a bellows and aligned with the zipper.

8 Insert a tab between the outer fabric and the zipper.

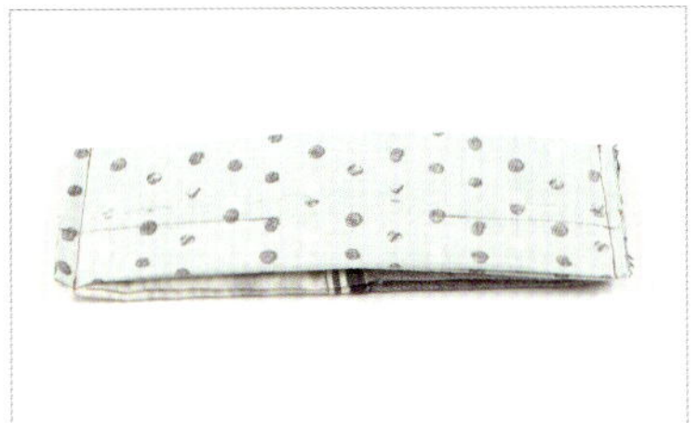

9 Sew both sides. To keep the fabrics aligned, press them together firmly while sewing.

10 Turn the right side out through the opening in the lining fabric.

11 Fold the seam allowance of the opening inward and blind stitch the opening.

12 Adjust the fabric on each side to complete. You can see that the side looks like a wrapped gift.

7 Zippered-gusset Fabric-collage Pouch

We don't sew a zipper directly on the pouch this time. Instead, the zipper is sewn on a gusset and the gusset is then sewn into the pouch. This pouch is a little difficult to put together. It's like a mini-bag with handles.

11 x 22 cm (4⅜" x 8¾") Chizuko Kojima

How to make ▶ p. 86

8 Slim Pen Case with Gusset

The corners are not boxed; instead a gusset is sewn on. When bags are small, sewing tends to be difficult. Once you align the center seam, corners, and opening, sew separately in the order of left side, right side, and bottom to create a beautiful finish.

6.5 x 18 cm (2⅝" x 7⅛") Sakura Yamamoto

How to make ▶ p. 88

9 Appliqué Flat Pouch

A simple shape with round appliqués. This is a great chance to enjoy mixing up different patterns. To add even more playfulness use a colorful zipper with double sliders, and install it so that it's exposed.

18 x 19.5 cm (7⅛" x 7¾") Sachiko Ishikawa

How to make ▶ p. 89

10

Flat Wool Pouch

A tricolor pouch in red, white, and black. Felt, wood beads, needlework, and covered buttons are combined to create motifs. The embellishments steal the show! Don't they look like a flower, or maybe the sun?

17 x 25.5 cm (6¾" x 10") Sachiko Ishikawa

How to make ▶ p. 90

11 A Simple Drawstring Pouch

A drawstring pouch is easy to make. It's also perfect for wrapping small gifts. Since the drawstrings that pass through the opening of the pouch are partially exposed, this pouch is easily opened just by pulling on both sides of the mouth of the pouch.

12.5 x 11.5 cm (4¹⁵⁄₁₆" x 4½") Noriko Sakurai

How to make ▶ p. 23

How to Make a Simple Drawstring Pouch

The outer fabric and lining fabric are sewn at the same time. Sewing the pouch is quite easy because the casing of the drawstring is attached first.

Materials

Outer fabric (including drawstring tag) – 35 x 20 cm (13¾" x 7⅞")
Casing for drawstring (including drawstring tag) – 25 x 15 cm (9⅞" x 5⅞")
Lining fabric – 35 x 20 cm (13¾" x 7⅞")
Diameter 0.5 cm (¼") drawstring 80 cm (31½")

Outer fabric (1 piece)
Opening
Opening
Selvage
Center
Fold
20 (7⅞")
30 (11¾")

Lining fabric (2 pieces)
Opening
Bottom
Opening
Selvage
20 (7⅞")
16 (6¼")

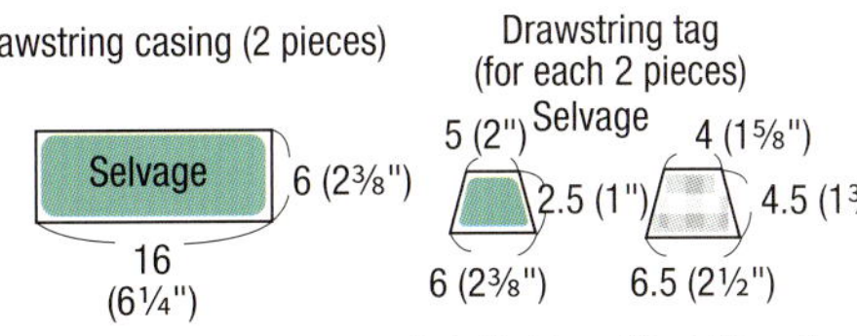

Unit: cm (inch)

Cut all sides with pinking shears for a zigzag finish

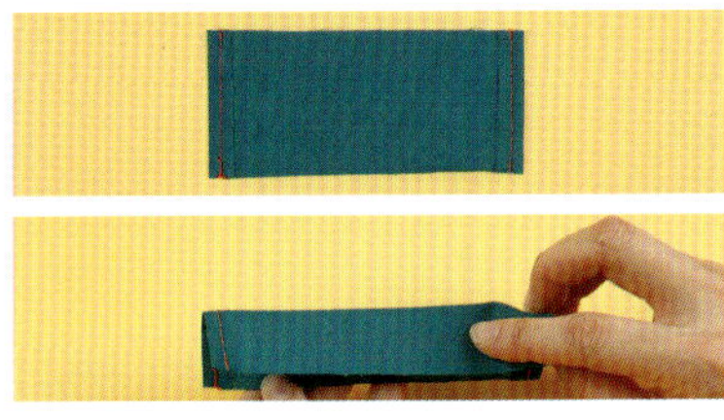

1 For the casing fabric just crease both sides along the seam allowance and sew about 0.7 cm (¼") in from the creased edge. Fold the casing fabric lengthwise in half with the wrong sides together. Seam allowance is all 1 cm (⅜").

2 Place the outer fabric (facing up) and lining fabric (facing down) on the outer fabric. Sandwich the drawstring casing. For the drawstring casing, place the folded edge facing inward and align the outer edge with the outer fabric edge. Sew each side (seam allowance: 1 cm (⅜")).

3 Unfold the lining fabrics. The place where the casing is attached will become the opening of the pouch.

4 Fold the outer fabric in half so that half of the outer fabric and each piece of the lining fabric is facing the other.

5 Sew the side of the lining, but leave an opening around 10 cm (4") so that you can turn the fabric right side out later. Sew the top and bottom of the outer fabric and lining fabric.

6 Cut the corners so we can make them into boxed corners. On each corner, measure 2 cm (¾") from the stitch and mark. Then, cut accordingly.

7 Turn the fabric to align the side and top seam of the outer fabric and lining fabric. Then sew the boxed corners of both fabrics together. Do the same for the other corner. For machine sewing, press the seam open. In the case of hand-sewing, press the seam to one side.

8 Turn the fabric around and sew the opening closed. Now the pouch is formed.

9 Thread a drawstring into the left and right side of the casing. Attach a tag to the end of the drawstring as desired. Here, two kinds of fabric are used. Place one on top of the other and wrap the drawstring, then stitch together.

Small and Cute

These pouches snugly fit in the palm of your hand. Tiny and lovely items make us want to create as many as we can. Luckily, they don't take much time to make.

12 Hat-shaped Pouch Made from Six Fabric Scraps

Six small pieces of fabric scraps are sewn together to make a semicircular pouch. The top pouch on the opposite page is a four-gored type. Since they're quite small it's not necessary to fuse the fabric with an adhesive interlining. However, a very thin fusible cotton batting is used here to add firmness to the pouch.

5.5 x 12 cm (2⅛" x 4¾") Naomi Sato

How to make ▶ p. 91

When unzipped, the pouch's mouth opens wide, making a circle. However, once zipped up this pouch becomes slim and compact.

These are even smaller in size. They can hold about five coins and make for really cute key chains.

13

Oval-shaped Mini Pouch

This is a slim and chic shaped pouch, but it also holds plenty because it has a gusset. If you attach a strap to the loop, you can conveniently attach it to your bag. For the quilting, just use variegated thread and quilt as you like.

8.5 x 11 cm (3 3/8" x 4 5/16")
Design: Shigeyo Nakayama / Sewing: Tamayo Kubo

How to make ▶ p. 92

14 Whip-stitched Easy-to-Make Coin Purse with a Key Case

This pouch is small, but it can certainly carry some coins and your keys. In the front is a zippered coin purse, while in the back there's a key case with a loop and magnetic buttons. Prepare the outer fabric and gusset separately, then sew together. Doing this creates a beautiful finish with simple sewing.

6.5 x 10 cm ($2\frac{9}{16}$" x $3\frac{15}{16}$") Noriko Hosoo

How to make ▶ p. 94

This pouch securely holds keys with a loop and magnetic buttons, so there are no worries regarding keys.

15 Shell-shaped Coin Purse

A shell-shaped coin case that fits in the palm of your hand! The key point about making a shell shape is installing the zipper crosswise to the binding of the outer fabric. Looking from the bottom, we see a diamond shape. The opening of the case is quite wide because of its shape.

6.5 x 11 cm (2⅝" x 4⅜") Hiromi Imoto

How to make ▶ p. 29

How to Make a Shell-shaped Coin Purse

Full-size patterns are on page 87. The round shape is created from the curve of the coin case. Depth is created by changing the direction of the center seam.

Materials

Outer fabric 2 types (including a zipper decoration)
20 x 10 cm (7⅞" x 4")
Backing fabric 35 x 20 cm (13¾" x 7⅞")
Fusible cotton batting 15 x 20 cm (5⅞" x 7⅞")
3 cm (1¼") width piping fabric 35 cm (13¾")
one 12 cm (4¾") zipper
two 1.5 cm (⅝") diameter covered button

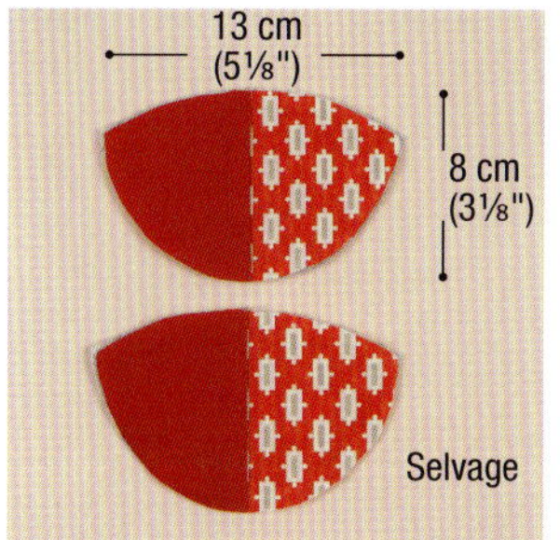

1 Add a seam allowance to the pattern, then cut the fabric to make two pieces of outer fabric. Fuse cotton batting on the wrong side of the outer fabrics and lay backing fabric over the batting right side up. Quilt as desired.

2 Put the outer fabric together with the right sides facing each other. Align the edge of the bias tape along the curve of the center seam and sew them together. Wrap the center seam with bias tape and blind stitch the raw edge of the bias tape. When you manually sew, use a half-back stitch.

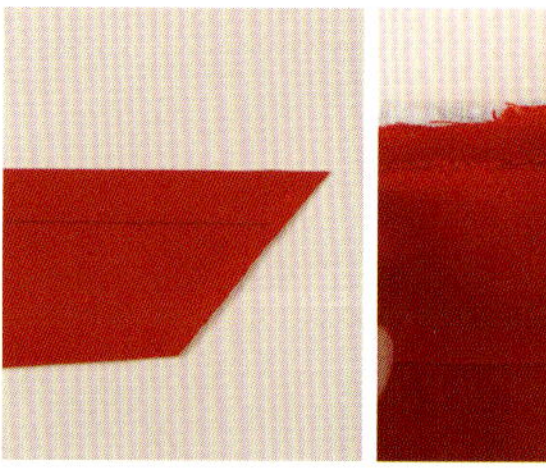

3 Treat opening with piping. Mark 0.7 cm (¼") on the bias tape. Place the bias tape right side down along the opening and sew it on.

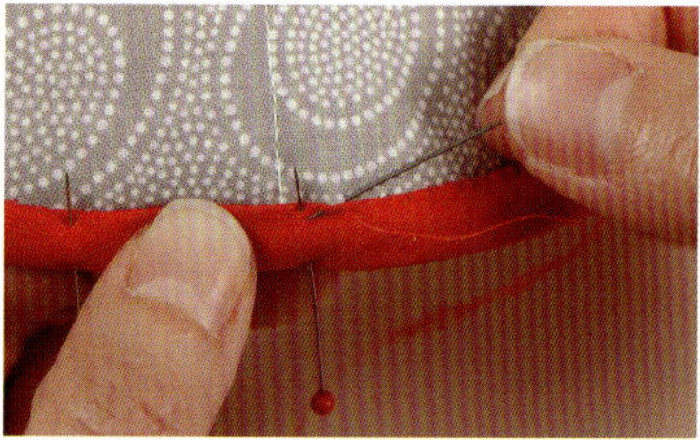

4 Turn the coin case inside out. Then wrap the untreated edge and blind stitch the bias tape to the backing fabric.

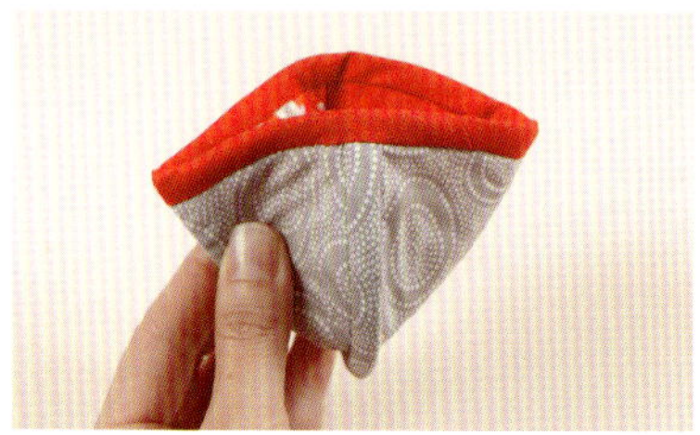

5 Now the piping around the opening and along the center seam is complete. Hold the coin case so the center seam runs vertically.

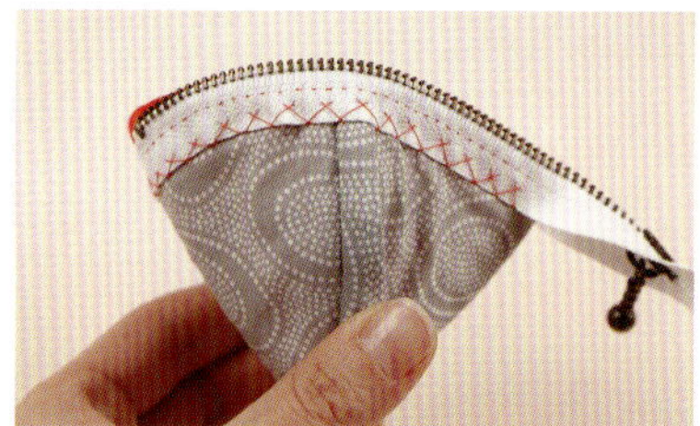

6 Install a zipper on the opening with a blind stitch and a blind zigzag stitch. See p. 80 for detailed instructions.

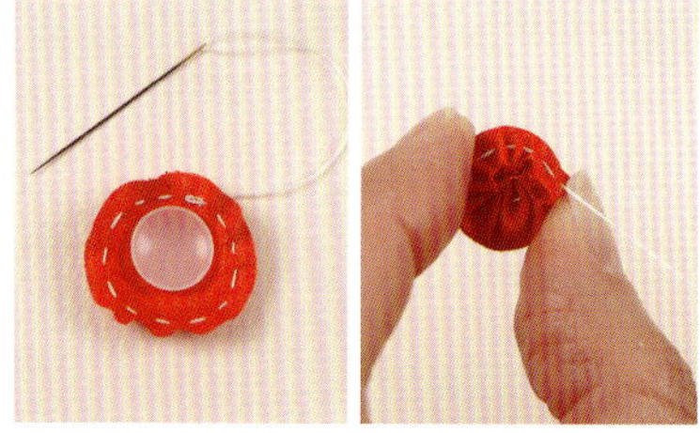

7 Make a zipper tape decoration. Cut fabric into a 3 cm (1¼") diameter circle. Running stitch the circumference of the fabric and add a button. Then pull the stitches to hold the button.

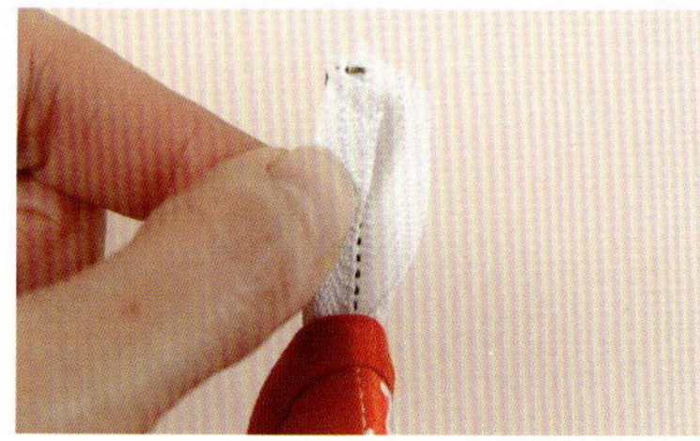

8 Fold the end of the zipper tape to match a the size of the covered button. Be sure to cut the bottom of the tape extensions off.

9 Sandwich the ends of the zipper tape with the covered button. Blind stitch around the circumference of the buttons to secure.

10 Complete!

16 Plump Petite Pouch

Gathered fabric creates the plumpness of this pouch. Its roundness, gathered fabric, and volume of the basting create a distinctive softness—it's very comforting to touch. Even without quilting you can enjoy softness!

7 x 12 cm (2¾" x 4¾") Akemi Takahara

How to make ▶ p. 31

How to Make a Plump Petite Pouch

The gathered edge of the circular fabric forms the shape of the pouch. Gather the fabric evenly.

Materials

Outer fabric (including piping)
40 x 20 cm (15¾" x 7⅞")
Quilt cotton batting, backing fabric
20 x 20 cm (7⅞" x 7⅞")
one 12 cm (4¾") zipper

1 Cut the outer fabric, batting, and backing fabric to make a 19 cm (7½") diameter circle.

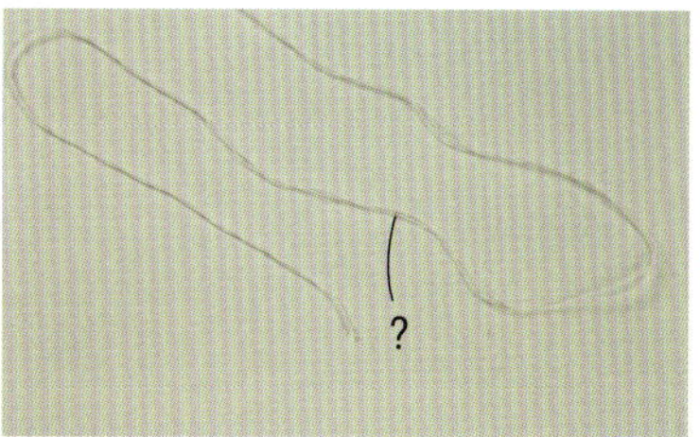

2 Double up your thread and knot the end. Make a mark 26 cm (10¼") from the knot.

3 Make a running stitch (using the thread you prepared in step 2) 0.3 cm (⅛") from the raw edge all around the circumference. Then pull the thread to the 26 cm (10¼") mark to create gathers.

4 Place bias tape (length: 28 cm (11"), width: 3.5 cm (1⅜") on right side along the opening, then sew it on.

5 Turn the bias tape right side up. Wrap the seam allowance around the opening, then blind stitch onto the backing fabric. Now, the opening is piped.

6 Install the zipper. Align the seam and the end of the opening, then pin the zipper to secure. Refer to instructions on page 80.

7 Make sure the teeth of the zipper align with the edge of the piping.

8 Stitch the zipper tape with a half-back stitch to install the zipper.

9 Fold down the top tape extensions and sew them on with a blind stitch. It's not necessary to sew on the bottom tape extensions. Just stitch at end of the teeth.

10 Turn the pouch inside out to complete.

17 Create a Drawstring Pouch by Folding Fabric

This drawstring pouch is created simply by folding and sewing a square-shaped piece of fabric. This pouch can be made using a handkerchief. Since the lining fabric is visible from the outside, using different colored fabrics can be more fun. Enjoy making these with a child as an arts and crafts project!

9 x 11 cm (3⅝" x 4⅜") Fumiko Sasaki

How to make ▶ p. 33

How to Make a Drawstring Pouch by Folding Fabric

Materials

Outer fabric, Lining fabric each 25 x 25 cm (9⅞" x 9⅞")
0.3 cm (⅛") diameter cord 90 cm (35½")

Fold a square shape as if you were making origami, then just sew three sections and the corners to complete.

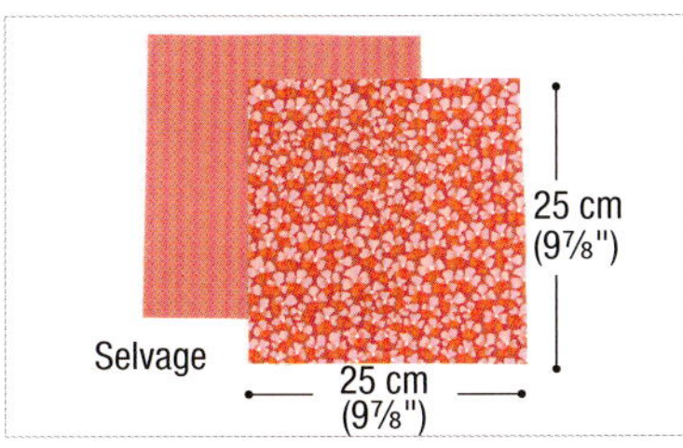

1 Prepare pieces of 25 cm x 25 cm (9⅞" x 9⅞") outer fabric and lining fabric.

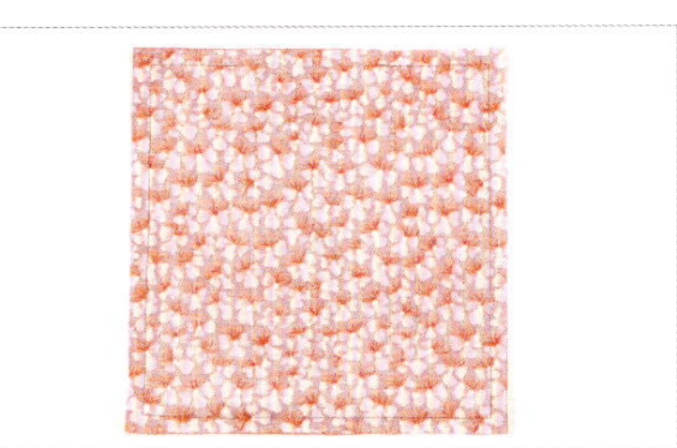

2 With the right sides facing together, sew along the circumference of the outer fabric and the lining fabric leaving an opening for turning the pouch inside out. Seam allowance is 0.7 cm (¼").

3 Turn the fabric right side up. Fold the seam allowance along the inside of the opening, and stitch circumference of the square.

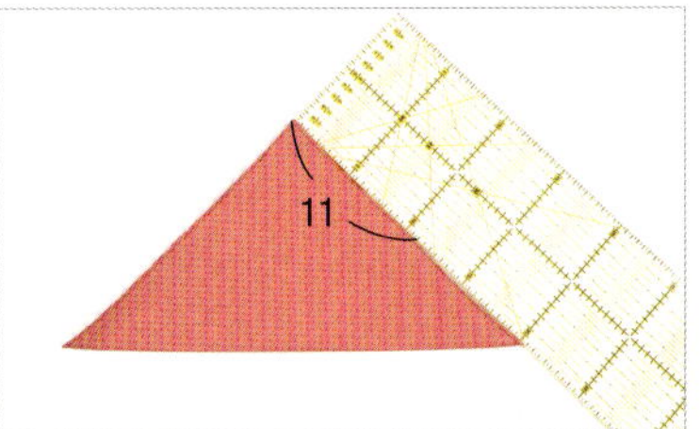

4 Place the inside faces together and fold the fabric into a triangle. Mark 11 cm (4⅜") from the vertex of the triangle.

5 From the mark, sew straight down. Do the same for the other side.

6 Fold the bottom corners inward from the stitch.

7 Sew for about 2 cm (⅞") where the two corners overlap.

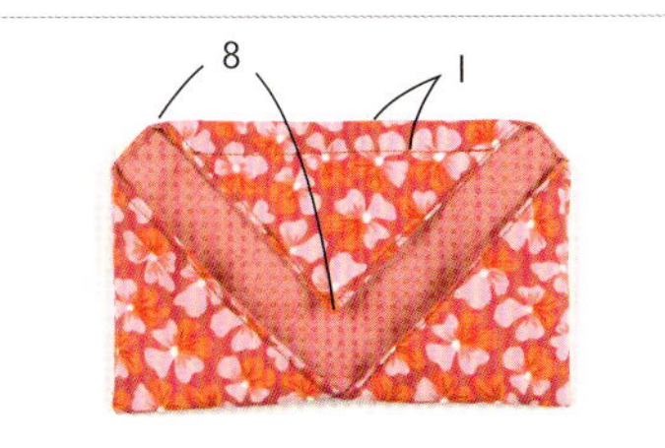

8 Fold the top corners down on each side. Stitch 1 cm (⅜") down from the edge of the top to make a drawstring casing.

9 Sew the corners. Turn the lining fabric outward and align the side seam and the center seam. Sew the corners at 3 cm (1¼") width.

10 Now we have the boxed corner shape.

11 Thread a 44 cm (17⅜") cord from each side and knot the end of the cord. It's complete!

Large and Practical

This is a little large for a pouch, but the size allows us to experiment with shapes and designs. This pouch is big enough to be a mini-bag or a clutch.

18

Colorful Hexagon Patchwork Pouch

Connect hexagon-shaped pieces of fabric to create the exterior of the pouch. It looks complicated but it's easy to make. The size of the pouch can be adjusted depending on the size of the hexagonal pieces. Make a few to find your favorite size!

15 x 25 cm (5⅞" x 9⅞") Chizuko Kojima

How to make ▶ p. 93

19 Hexagonal Flower Pouch

This pouch uses a hexagonal piece to make a flower appliqué. Even though it's slim, this pouch is slightly on the large side. It's as easy to carry around as a bag-in-bag or a clutch. Firmly bind the pouch by attaching a zipper to the front pocket and the opening.

31.5 x 21.5 cm (12$\frac{3}{8}$" x 8$\frac{1}{2}$") Sachiko Ishikawa

How to make ▶ p. 96

20 Easy-to-Make Duffel Bag Shaped Pouch

This is a duffel bag shaped pouch that you'll want to make at least once. You might think that the duffel-like shape is difficult to make, but it's as simple as making a boxy pouch. This pouch can even be used as a lunch sack!

11 x 20 cm (4⅜" x 7⅞") Yasuko Hara

How to make ▶ p. 98

Discover Unique Large Pouches

P. 34

This pouch is made by connecting large hexagonal pieces. It's a ton of fun to connect the 26 hexagonal pieces and compete your own pouch! Use 3 hexagonal pieces on each side to add width.

The mouth opens wide. Installing a zipper is easy because it's sewn externally.

From the side, it's clear that the triangular shape has ample width.

P. 35

This is the pouch that will make you think bigger is better. It is slim, but it can store many things. It even has a pocket and can be used as a clutch. The paper-piecing method is used to connect the hexagonal flowers.

The backside is a cute polka dot meshed fabric. The transparency of the meshed fabric brings a certain lightness to this large pouch.

How to Paper Piece

1 This set of paper-piecing shapes is commercially available. You can also make your own patterns.

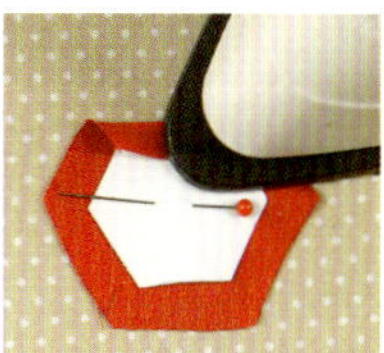

2 Cut the fabric to include a seam allowance. Place the paper-piecing shape on the fabric and fold the seam allowance down while ironing.

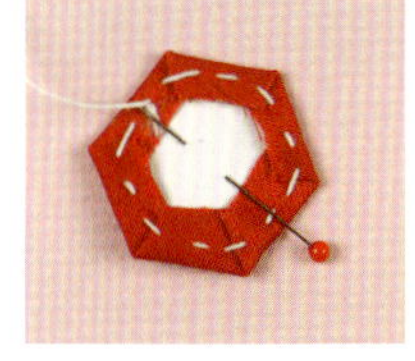

3 Baste around the seam allowance. Do not sew the paper piecing shape, just stitch the fabric.

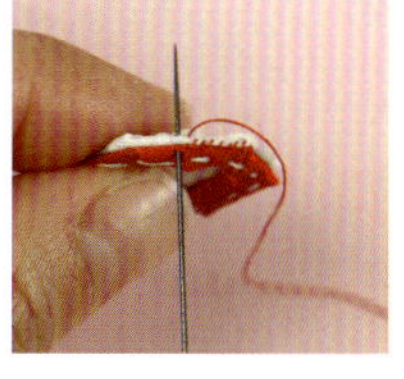

4 With the right sides together, whip stitch the edge. Connect as many as you need, then pull the paper piecing shape out at the end.

P. 36

The major plus of making this pouch is that it can be constructed quite easily despite its being shaped like a duffel bag. Using geometric patchwork-like patterns gives the pouch an intricate look.

The side view shows the folded out corners.

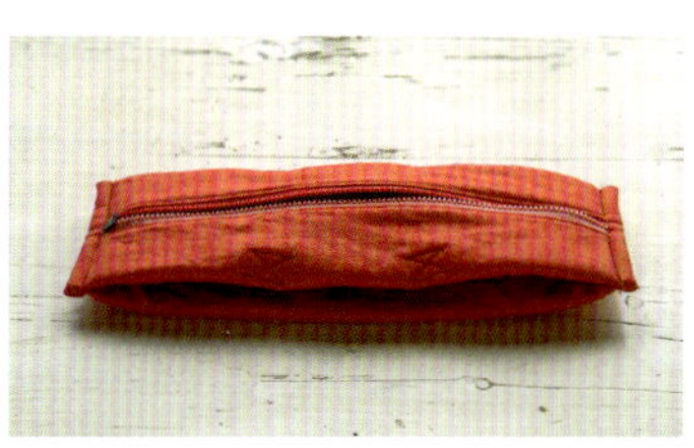

Since the side seams are piped the pouch can be folded flat by turning it inside out.

Patchwork Quilting

If you enjoy sewing, you know that you need to have plenty of fabric scraps. Every fabric scrap is precious so we need to hang on to even the tiniest piece. A brilliant patchwork project made with such scraps only increases our crafty satisfaction!

21

V-shape Quilt Zippered Boxed Corner Pouch

Narrow band-like fabric is sewn in a V shape. As a general rule, when multicolored fabric scraps are used, a pouch becomes colorful and cute. If you limit color use, it becomes chic. The round shape with the sharpness of the V creates a nice contrast here.

13 x 16 cm (5⅛" x 6⅜") Noriko Hosoo

How to make ▶ p. 99

22 Chic Log Cabin Quilt Modern Pouch

Encase the square piece at the center within a rectangular-shaped piece. This pattern is called a "log cabin." The amusing thing about this design is that the pattern will look different depending on the color of the fabric and how it is placed. At a glance the pattern looks intricate. However, it is simply constructed by folding one piece of quilt together and sewing the edges.

11 x 24 cm ($4\frac{3}{8}$" x $9\frac{1}{2}$") Masayo Otsuka

How to make ▶ p. 100

Fold the quilt making two compartments and simply sew the edges together.

23 Flower Drawstring Pouch

A fluffy opening and chubby shape make this drawstring pouch super cute. The edge of the opening is scalloped, so when the string is drawn it looks like a flower bud. When opened, it looks like a blooming flower. Feel free to enjoy a mix of unique fabrics on this pouch.

9 x 11 cm (3⅝" x 4⅜") Noriko Hosoo

How to make ▶ p. 101

It opens wide and round.

Cut the fabrics in such a way that you can make the best use of their patterns.

24 Flat Drawstring Pouch

Using of fabric scraps at the center can be fun. Pieces that are about 2.5 x 5 cm (1" x 2") are used for the center–small scraps that are usually thrown out! When you match up fabric scraps, be sure to use related colors or patterns so that the overall look will be uniform.

16 x 23 cm (6⅜" x 9⅛") Sachiko Ohara

How to make ▶ p. 102

25 Girly Pouch with Yo-yos and Wooden Beads

Combinations of soft and gentle colors give this pouch a pretty look. The long ribbon and lace attached at the side add sweetness. Modest plumpness suits the pouch's cute style.

14.5 x 19 cm (5⅞" x 7½") Sachiko Ishikawa

How to make ▶ p. 103

How to Make Yo-yos

Fabric scraps are really useful for making yo-yos. When you store leftover fabrics, cutting them all the same size helps make future yo-yos easy!

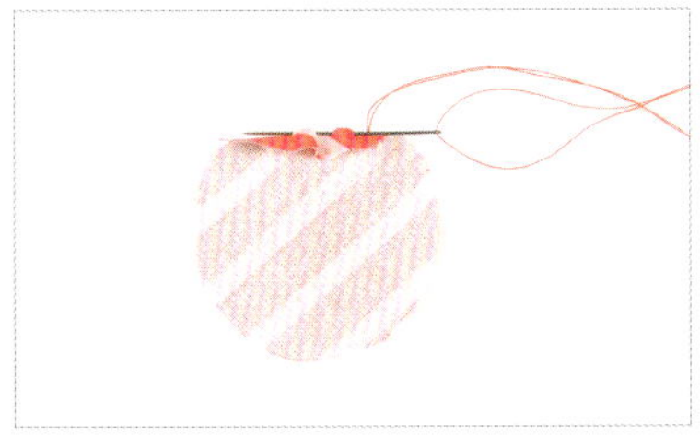

1 Cut the fabric in a circle of about 0.5 cm (½") including the seam allowance. Use a running stitch along the edge as you fold down the seam allowance. Use doubled thread.

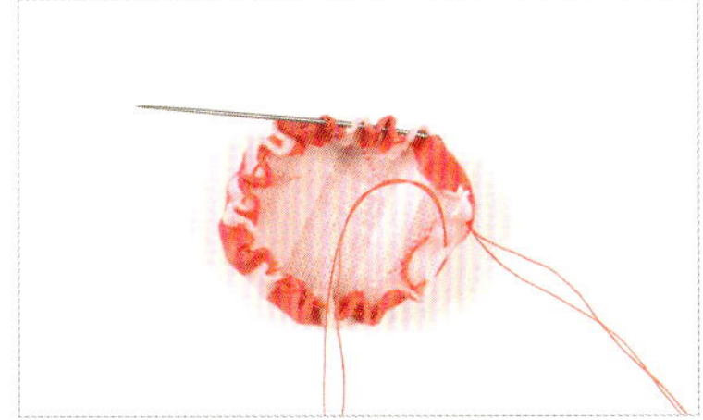

2 Once you have stitched the entire edge, inset the needle into the first stitch. Adjust your stitching in order to meet the first stitch.

3 Pull the thread tight to draw in the fabric. Adjust the shape as you pull the thread.

4 Put the needle through the center of the gathered fabric and pull it through.

5 Tie off the thread with a knot. Instead of pulling the thread through you can tie off the thread at the edge of the gathered fabric with a knot.

6 The yo-yo is complete. To link two yo-yos you need to stack them so that they have their right sides together and make a couple of whip stitches on the edge that you intend to link.

When making yo-yos, fine running stitches around the edge make the center of the yo-yo large. Instead, do the opposite: use a large running stitch to make the center of the gathered fabric small. To decorate this pouch, make as many yo-yos as you desire and enjoy linking them together.

Simply Flat

These are simply enjoyable!

Flat pouches are easy to adjust according to their use or according to your favorite shape of the moment. They're surprisingly handy and don't take up much space in your bag.

This pouch will carry a small-sized tablet like an iPad mini. This envelope-like design is easy to make and (of course) it's cute. Ready to make your first one?

16 x 22 cm (6⅜" x 8¾") Masayo Otsuka

How to make ▶ p. 104

26 **Sturdy and Soft Tablet Case**

These are envelope-shaped pouches. The heart patterned fabric is made into an envelope shape, so I would call this the Love Letter Pouch. It is the perfect size for carrying small items like lipstick, a small mirror, etc. Of course, you can put a love letter inside too.

Large: 11 x 13.5 cm ($4\frac{3}{8}$" x $5\frac{3}{8}$") Mutsuko Tanino

How to make ▶ p. 105

27 Love Letter Pouch

28

Rabbit Pouch

The silhouette of a rabbit is made into a cute pouch. The red pouch here uses wool, and the gray one uses a knit fabric. Use cute patterned fabrics when making these for kids. Using chic and textured fabrics creates a more mature, but still cute, pouch.

20 x 15 cm (7⅞" x 5⅞") Ryoko Matsumoto

How to make ▶ p. 106

29 Bird Pouch

Compared to the rabbit pouch, this shape is simple and easier to make. As for the attached yo-yo decoration (see page 43), make a circle out of cut ribbon and stitch the edges. Then pull the thread.

14 x 20 cm (5½" x 7⅞") Ryoko Matsumoto

How to make ▶p. 106

There's an opening at the back side, secured by hooking a loop over a button. The closure suits the simple and retro style of the pouch.

30 Pouch with Pocket Tissue Case

A pocket tissue case is attached to the front side of the zippered flat pouch. As always, you can choose among many combinations of fabric to guarantee that each of the pouches you make in this style is original.

12.5 x 16.5 cm (5" x 6½") Yasuko Hara

How to make ▶ p. 108

31

These pocket tissue cases have small pockets on the backs. To make them you just fold long pieces of fabric and sew both sides at the end. Since they're so quick and simple to make you can just go on creating you own fun designs forever.

9.5 x 12.5 cm (3¾" x 5") Sakura Yamamoto

How to make ▶ p. 50

How to Make the Pocket Tissue Case on Page 49

Materials
Fabric 75 x 20 cm (29½" x 7⅞")

You need a long piece of fabric. However, if you don't have a piece that is long enough you can use different pieces for the cover or the lining. Fold your fabric carefully in the same manner as the diagram below.

One piece

A B C D E F G H I

Opening Opening

Outward fold Inward fold Selvage

1 1

9 (3⅝") 4.5 (1¾") 4.5 (1¾") 9 (3⅝") 4.5 (1¾") 4.5 (1¾") 18 (7⅛") 18 (7⅛")

15 (5⅝")

74 (29⅛")

How to Fold

G F C D E A B

Right side

Wrong side

I H

Unit: cm (inch)

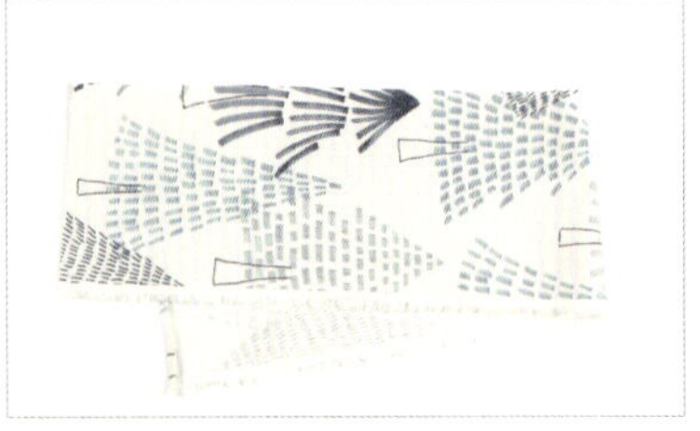

1 Prepare a piece of fabric 74 cm (29⅛") long and 15 cm (5⅞") wide. If your fabric has a pattern that needs to face in a certain direction, be careful that the pattern on the cover doesn't end up backwards. As shown in the above photo, place the right side up at the left so that the pattern on the cover won't be backwards.

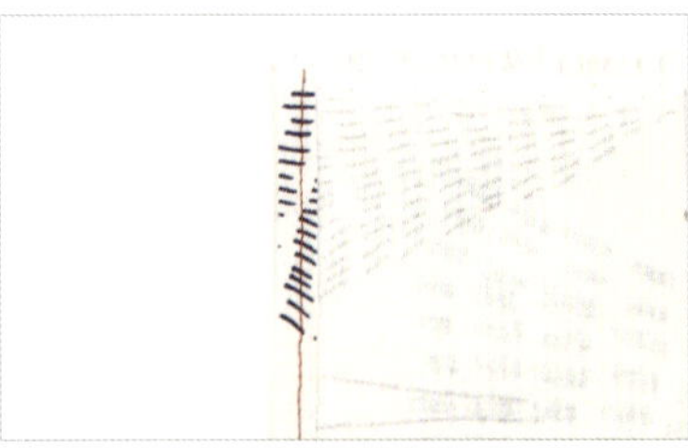

2 Fold down the fabric along the seam allowance (1 cm / ⅜") and then sew on the side.

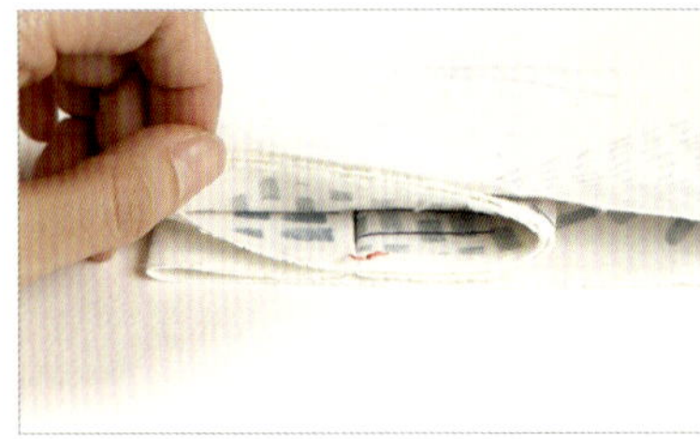

3 Fold the fabric according to the diagram above. Pin or running stitch where F and C meets so that it doesn't come apart.

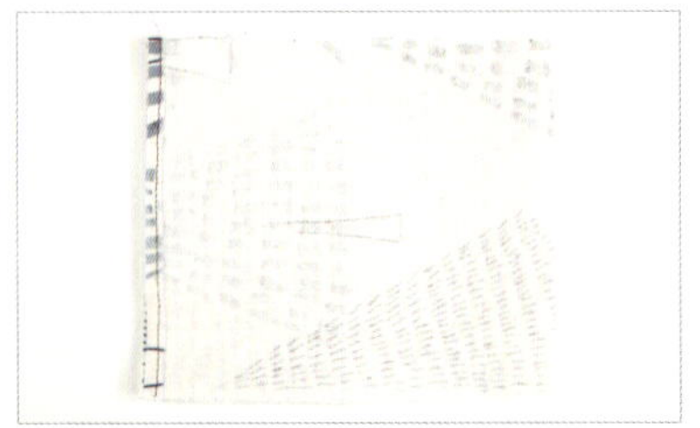

4 Iron the fabric to form a shape.

5 Seen from the side. The backside of the pouch and the pocket encase the opening of the pouch.

6 Sew lengthwise. The seam allowance is 1 cm (⅜").

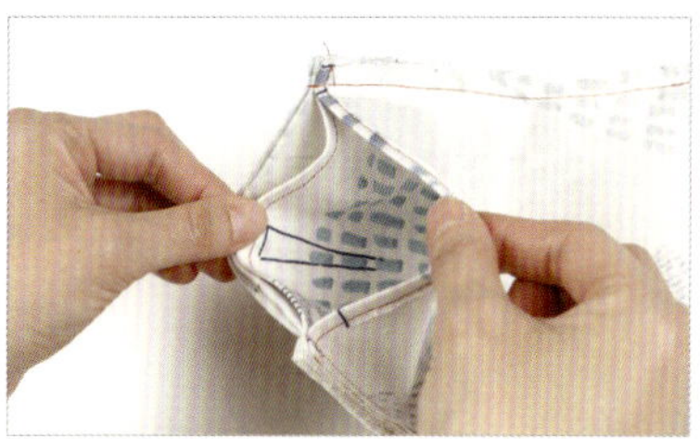

7 Beginning with the I on the diagram, turn the pouch inside out.

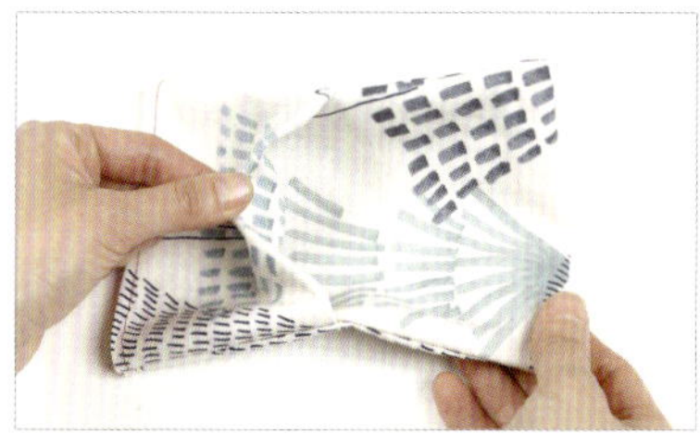

8 Also, turn the pouch from the pocket.

9 The opening faces out. Now it's complete.

Inside a Flat Pouch

The flap on the tablet case seen on page 44 is secured by wrapping a ribbon around a button. The combination of these outer and lining fabrics, visible when the flap is open, is fun.

A magnetic button is sewn on the pouch (as seen on page 45) to secure the flap.

Be Careful!
If you intend to use this pouch for carrying your credit cards make sure you DON'T use a magnetic button!

The pouch on page 48 has an inner pocket. You can arrange the features of your pouch to make it the most useful for your needs.

Lots of Pockets for Easy Storage

The large number of partitions and pockets in these pouches allow you to better organize your favorite items. When compared to other pouches the sewing of these pouches is more complex because they have more added parts. However, pouches in this section are also very convenient and useful.

32

Fashionable Envelope Shaped Case

This slightly large pouch is sturdy and solid – you can neatly organize receipts and cards within its confines. It's slim but the sides expand like a bellows so it is easier to look inside and to remove whatever you want.

13.5 x 22.5 cm (5⅜" x 8⅞") Yuko Nishijima

How to make ▶p. 110

33 Sewing Case Bag

This is a sewing case that can carry six spools of thread. The bottom is wide and flat so there is no problem carrying other sewing tools as well. There are pockets inside where you can store scissors and zippers.

8 x 20 cm (3⅛" x 7⅞") Noriko Hosoo

How to make ▶ p. 109

34

Case with Fabric Flap

This thin and slim case can hold all your valuables in one place. Credit cards, bank books, etc., you can store all your valuables inside the zippered pocket. That way you always know where they are.

16.5 x 11.5 cm (6½" x 4½") Yumi Ishida

How to make ▶p. 112

35

Oblong Passport Case

Keep everything you need for your travels, like passports and airline tickets, in this lovely case. It has five pockets and the fabric is reinforced with an adhesive interfacing so you can put items in and take them out smoothly. The top two cases in this photo use laminated fabric.

22 x 11 cm (8¾" x 4⅜") Yuko Nishijima

How to make ▶p. 114

36 Bellowed Card Case – Easy to Find, Easy to Remove

When you carry a bunch cards in your wallet, don't you find it hard to dig out the one you want? This card case holds your cards vertically so you can remove them easily. And since it folds so flat, it looks really slim. But, even though it looks slim, it opens like a bellows and the pockets are actually quite wide.

10 x 15 cm (4" x 5⅞") Mitsuko Ito

How to make ▶ pp. 57, 115

How to Make Bellowed Pockets

This section will explain how to make the bellowed pockets that are the main feature of the card case seen on page 56. See p. 115 for instructions on making the body as well as measurements for each of the components of the bellowed pockets and how they are folded.

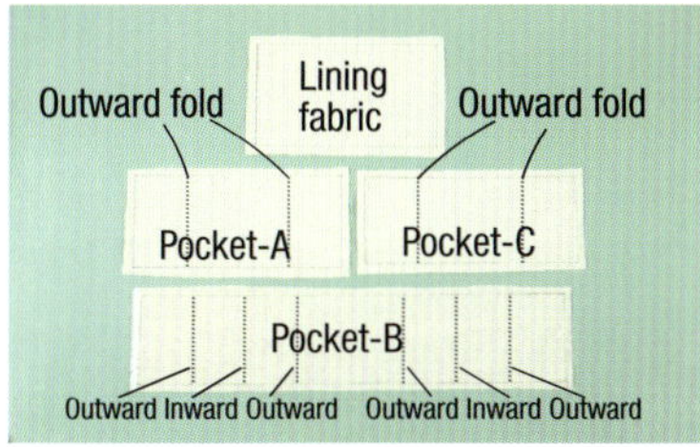

1 Including 1 cm (⅜") seam allowance, cut the lining fabric and pockets, A, B, and C. See p. 115 for the measurements. As for pocket-B, fold outward and inward following by (---).

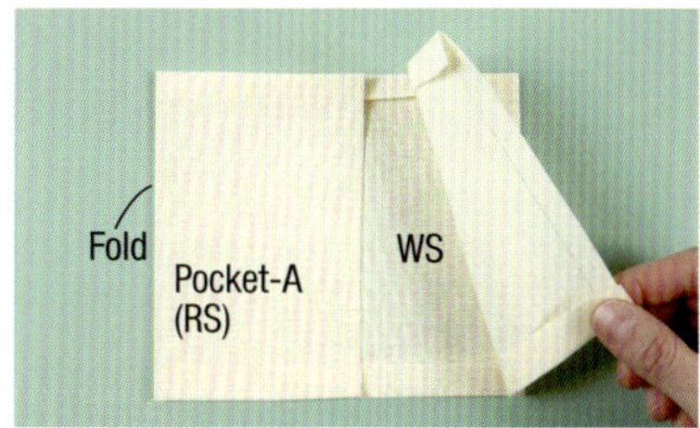

2 Fold down the seam allowance lengthwise for pocket-A. Fold pocket-A while aligning both raw edges at the center. See the diagram on page 115.

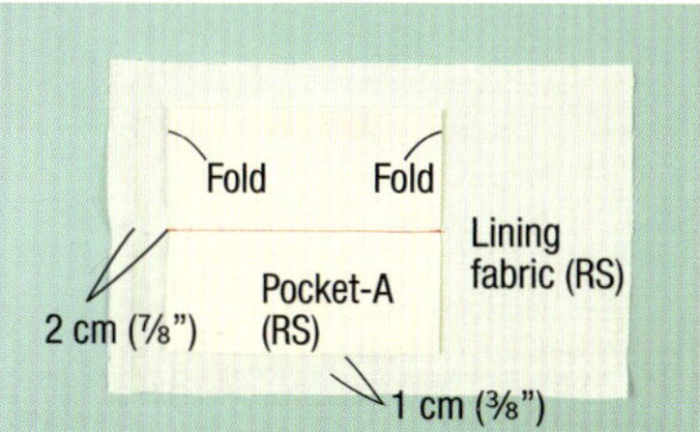

3 Place the overlapped edge down. Place pocket-A on the lining fabric. Sew pocket-A lengthwise along the center. See diagram on page 115 for position of pocket-A on the lining fabric.

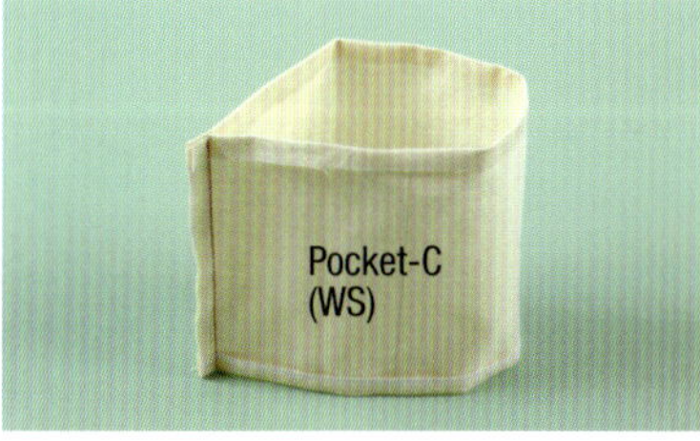

4 Fold down the seam allowance lengthwise for pocket-C. Fold pocket-C with the right sides together and sew the side edges together so that pocket-C makes a tube.

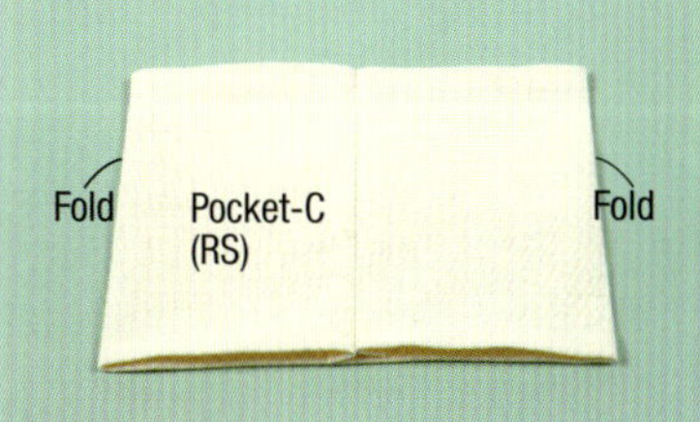

5 Press open the seam on each side and flip the fabric right side out. Refold the fabric so that the side seam and center of the fabric align.

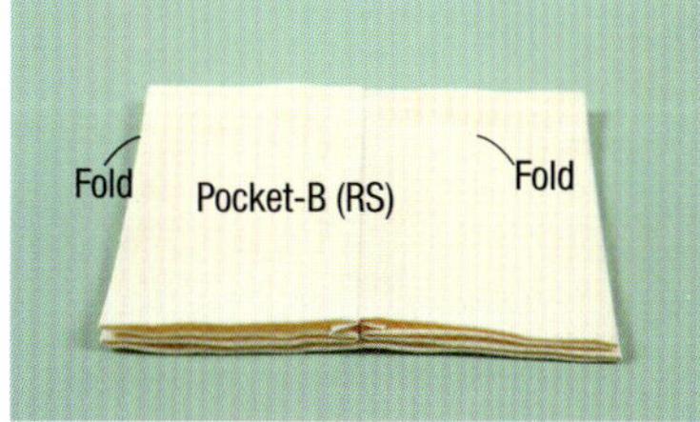

6 Do the same for the pocket-B and fold it according to the diagram on the page 115.

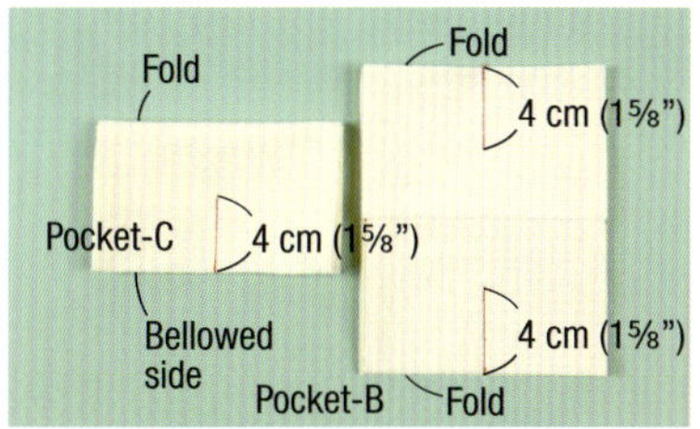

7 Fold pocket-C in half from the side seam. For pocket-B, sew the center.

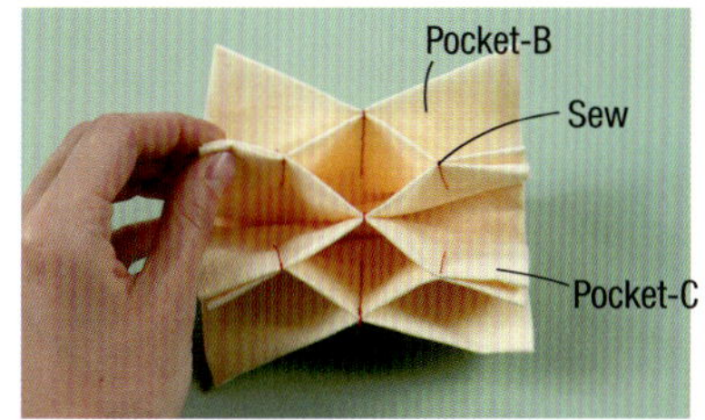

8 Fold pocket-B in half and insert pocket-C. Align both pockets and sew in four places that are about 4 cm (1⅝") apart.

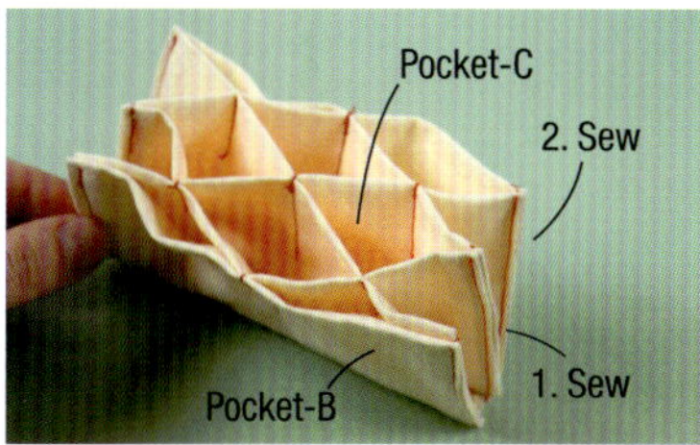

9 For pocket-B and pocket-C, sew the loose edges together. The pockets expand and hold fourteen cards. Even if you put two cards in one pocket you can still quite easily find the one you are looking for.

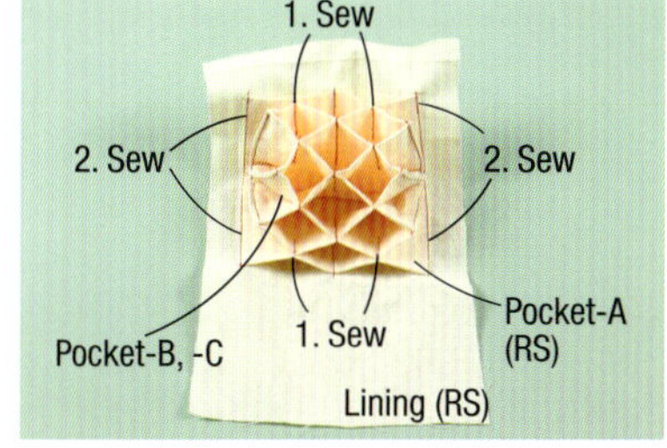

10 Place the pockets (B and C sewn together) on pocket-A. Sew them together on each side (see photos). Lastly, sew the edges of pocket-A on the lining fabric.

The pockets expand to hold fourteen cards.

37

Simple Compact Pouch with a Flap

These are cute trapezoidal shaped pouches. The flap is made by folding the outer fabric down. Under the flap is a pocket that snugly holds a pack of tissue. These are compact and well-balanced pouches.

9 x 14 cm (3⅝" x 5½") Hiroko Fukuda

How to make ▶ p. 116

38 Triple Pocket Pouch

A flat pouch with three zippered pockets. It is handy for carrying different sized objects. Just use the pockets accordingly. This flat pouch holds plenty.

17.5 x 25 cm ($6\frac{7}{8}$" x $9\frac{7}{8}$") Yasuko Hara

How to make ▶ p. 117

39 Flower Appliqué Small Wallet

This is a square shaped small wallet. Despite its compact size, it can carry both coins and bills. The key point is to bring out a rustic, but cute, aesthetic using textured fabric like wool.

10 x 11.5 cm (4" x 4½") Chizuko Kojima

How to make ▶ p. 118

The pocket at the center carries coins and you can put bills and cards beside the pocket.

Bragging about Pockets

The pouch seen on page 52 has a bellows-like shape. It has a pocket at the back and inside there is a separate zippered pocket. Since the edge of the pouch is slightly lower, taking things in-and-out is easy.

The sewing case bag seen on page 53. Half of the scissor holder opening at the back is sewn to prevent the scissors from accidentally popping out. At the front, there is a zippered pocket. The case is oblong and there are magnetic snaps on both sides to prevent the lid from bulging.

The flap of the compact pouch seen on page 58 is secured by a snap ring. Installing the ring is quite simple, so please give it a try at least once.

At a glance, the triple pocket pouch seen on page 59 seems to be flat. But, it can hold more than you would think. The depth of each pocket differs. They are convenient for storing small items of varying size.

How to Install Snap Rings on the Compact Pouch on Page 58

This type of snap is secured by inserting its prongs into the fabric and clamping the prongs. They are relatively easily installed compared to other types of hooks and snaps.

1 Prepare a ring snap and press tool.

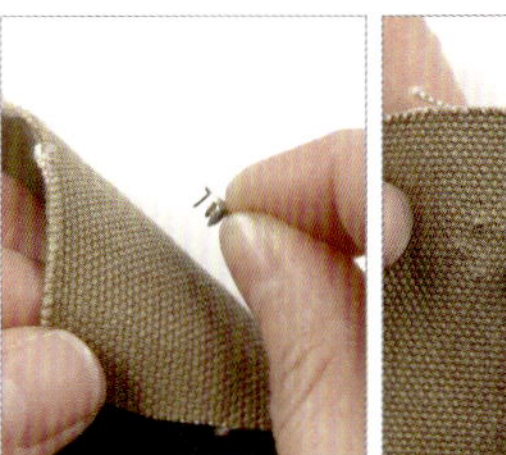

2 Insert the bottom prong from wrong side of the fabric, and inset the socket above the prong from right side of the fabric.

3 Align the press tool with the socket on a solid surface (in the photo, a rubber mat) and hammer the tool.

4 Do the same for the stud. Insert the colored top prong from the right side of the fabric, and inset the socket above the prong from the wrong side of the fabric.

5 Align the press tool with the stud and hammer the tool.

6 Now, the snap is installed. Match the socket and stud and make sure it snaps.

Upgrade the Pouch with Zippers, Snaps, and Clasps

New types of sewing supplies, such as metal clasps, zippers, etc., are readily available nowadays. Pouches that are introduced in this section use sewing supplies to make them more useful or to create pouches with interesting shapes. The sewing supplies used in this section will surely become your go to materials.

40 Square-shaped Coin Case with a Freestyle Zipper

This is a flat zippered coin case. The zipper is installed diagonally. The freestyle zipper is made by attaching zipper tape to a slider. The slider is detachable, and the left and right zipper tape comes apart to make installing the zipper easier.

9.5 x 9.5 cm (3¾" x 3¾") Fumiko Sasaki

How to make ▶ p. 64

This tetrahedron-shaped pouch also uses the freestyle zipper. The zipper position is different from the coin case seen on the facing page. The tetrahedron shape seems to be somewhat nostalgic, no? Feel free to make as many of these as you want, as if you were just playing around with your sewing.

A 10 x 11 cm (4" x 4⅜") B 10 x 11.5 cm (4" x 4½") Fumiko Sasaki

How to make ▶p. 65

41 Tetrahedron-shaped Pouch with a Freestyle Zipper

B

A

The mouth opens wide diagonally.

They are almost identical in size. However, the one on the right looks slightly bigger due to the piping.

How to Make the Square Coin Purse with a Freestyle Zipper on Page 62

Since a freestyle zipper is used, installation is easy.
It doesn't take much time to make, either—that's the charm of this coin case!

Materials

Outer fabric (including zipper decoration), Fabric A, Lining fabric, Adhesive interfacing: each 25 x 25 cm (9⅞" x 9⅞")

One freestyle zipper: 37 cm (14½")

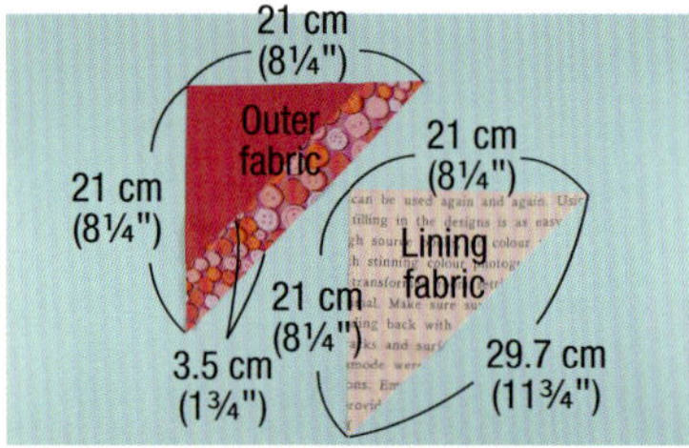

1 Cut both the outer fabric and the lining fabric to the same size. Join the pieces of the outer fabric, then fold the seam allowance down to the A side and stitch. Fuse adhesive interfacing on the wrong side of the lining fabric.

2 Place the zipper on the table face down and, with the right sides facing each other, overlay the lining fabric. Stitch together (seam allowance: 0.7 cm (¼"). These are bias fabrics, so be careful not to stretch them.

3 Flip over and iron along the zipper.

4 Put the slider through the zipper and zip it up (see p. 80). Now the shape should resemble a square.

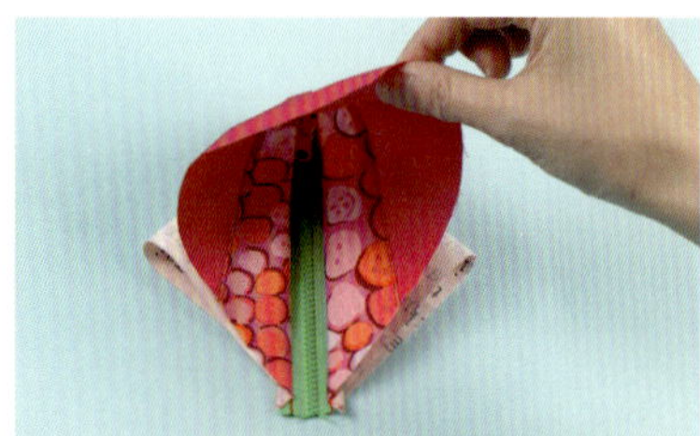

5 Turn the outer fabric inside out. Fold the right sides together to make a square.

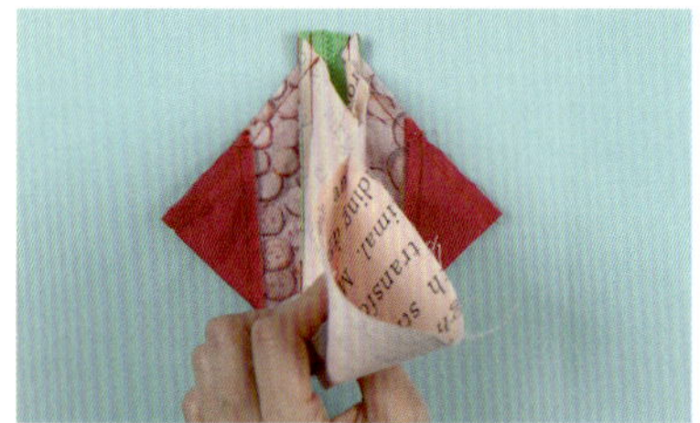

6 Sew two sides of the outer fabric down. Leave the zipper teeth out. Then unzip.

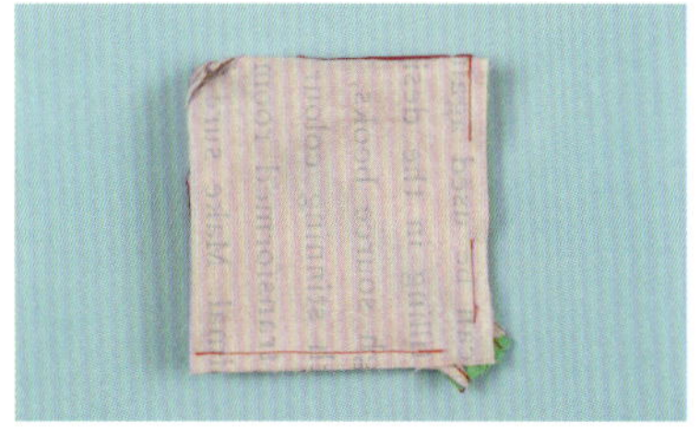

7

8

9 Now the coin case is complete. Next, make the zipper decoration.

10 Fold fabric tape (1.5 x 20 cm / ⅝" x 7⅞") three times and zig-zag stitch using a sewing machine. The width of the zig-zag stitch is about 2.5 cm (⅞").

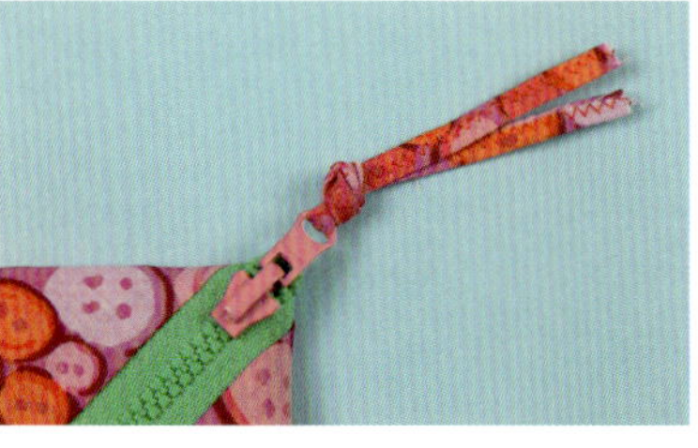

11 Thread the fabric through the zipper slider and knot once. Done!

How to Make the Tetrahedron-shaped Pouch with a Freestyle Zipper on Page 63

This pouch also uses a freestyle zipper like the one used on page 64. The shape is different but the sewing method is basically the same as page 64's.

Materials
Outer fabric, Lining fabric
Adhesive interfacing: each 25 x 15 cm (9⅞" x 5⅞")
One freestyle zipper: 30 cm (11⅞")
For B type: one 30 cm (11⅞") long 3.5 cm (1⅜") wide bias tape
A piece of fabric for a zipper decoration, as required

Type A Tetrahedron-shaped Pouch

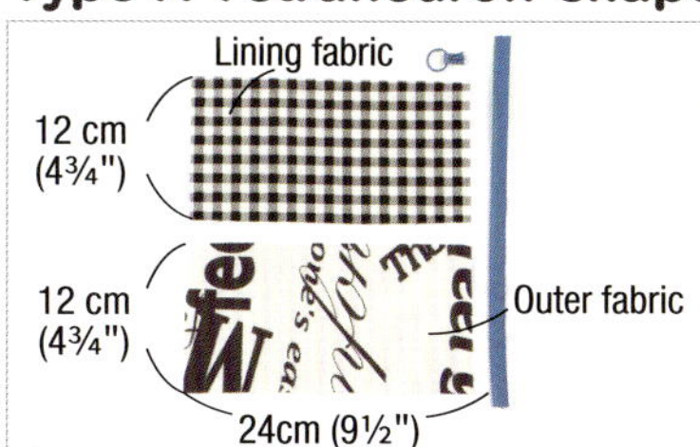

1 Cut both outer fabric and lining fabric to the same size. Fuse adhesive interfacing on the wrong side of the lining fabric.

2 Place a zipper between the fabric with right sides facing together. Stitch together (seam allowance: 0.7 cm (¼"). These are bias fabrics, so be careful not to stretch them.

3 Turn the fabric right side out and iron along opening edge. Cut off excess zipper and slip on a zipper slider (see p. 80).

4 Fold the outer fabric with the right sides and lining fabric together. Then sew down the side seam. Leave the zipper unzipped and don't sew on the teeth of the zipper.

5 Refold the fabric placing the side seam from step 4 at the center. Then sew the bottom seam of both the outer fabric and the lining fabric. Do not sew bottom seam of the lining fabric all the way. Be sure to leave an opening for turning inside out.

6 Turn the fabrics right side out. Fold the seam allowance of the opening inward and blind stitch the opening. Attach a zipper decoration as per instructions on page 64.

Type B Tetrahedron-shaped Pouch

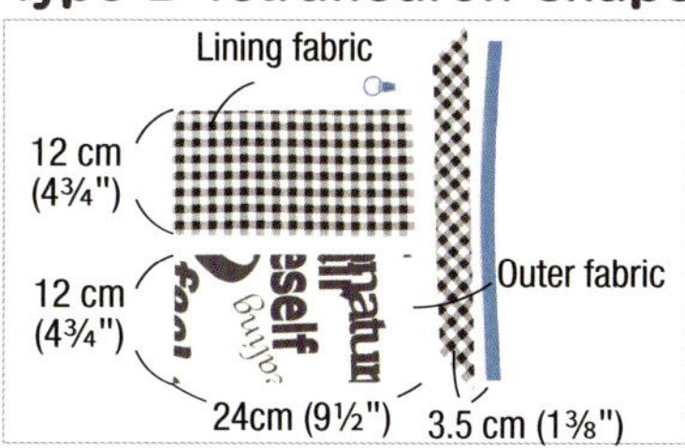

1 Cut both the outer fabric and lining fabric to the same size. Fuse adhesive interfacing to wrong side of the lining fabric. Prepare 3.5 cm (1⅜") wide bias tape.

2 Cut the zipper in half. Align on each side seam of the outer fabric with the right sides together. Then put the lining fabric over, right side down. Sew both side seams together (seam allowance: 0.7 cm (¼")).

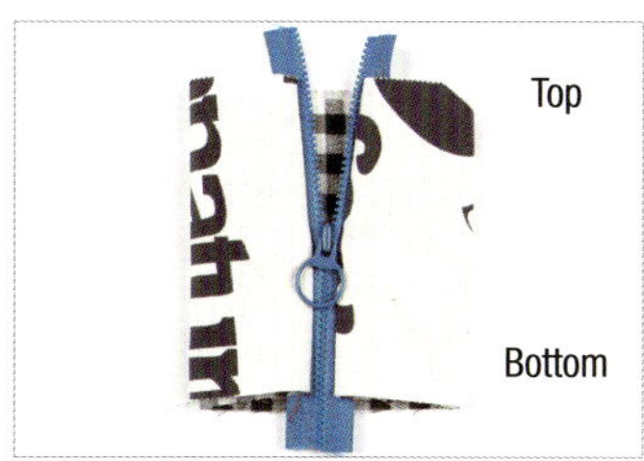

3 Slide the zipper slider over the zipper teeth. Make sure the fabric is not misaligned.

4 Refold the fabric, placing the zipper on top. With the right side facing down, align the bias tape along the right side edge and sew. Cut off excess zipper tape.

5 Fold the bias tape down as you wrap the seam, then blind stitch all around. Be sure to wrap the ends of the zipper tape.

6 Refold the fabric with the zipper at the center. Apply piping to the other side in the same way to complete.

42

Plastic Snap Pouch

This colorful square block quilt creates the cuteness of the pouch. The snap on the flap is plastic. You can install it by pressing the stud and base together with your fingers. Standard snaps are nice but this type comes in handy when you desire quick-and-easy installation.

9 x 11.5 cm (3⅝" x 4½") Fumiko Sasaki

How to make ▶p. 67

How to Make a Plastic Snap Pouch

The body of the pouch uses only two panels of fabric. They're cut from a single quilting block.

Full size pattern is on page 87.

Materials

Various fabrics for the pouch
Quilt batting, Backing fabric: each 20 x 25 cm (7⅞" x 9⅞")
One 60 cm (23⅝") long 3.5 cm (1⅜") wide bias tape
A set of plastic snaps, diameter 1.5 cm (⅝")

1 Add seam allowance to a 2 x 2 cm (⅞" x ⅞") square and cut the fabric. Join the squares as desired and create a block of 10 rows and 8 columns. Layer backing, batting, and quilt top, then baste. Quilt a diagonal checkered pattern.

2 Place the patterns of the pouch on the quilt. Add seam allowance and cut accordingly.

3 Bind the front edge of the pouch with piping fabric. Piping width is 0.7 cm (¼").

4 With the right sides facing out, put the front and back of the pouch together. With the right side down, align the bias tape and bind along the pouch's circumference. Fold the beginning of the bias tape diagonally.

5 Overlap the ends of the piping and bind stitch them together so they won't become misaligned.

6 As you wrap the seam with the bias tape, fold and pin to secure. Blind stitch all around to secure the bias tape to the pouch.

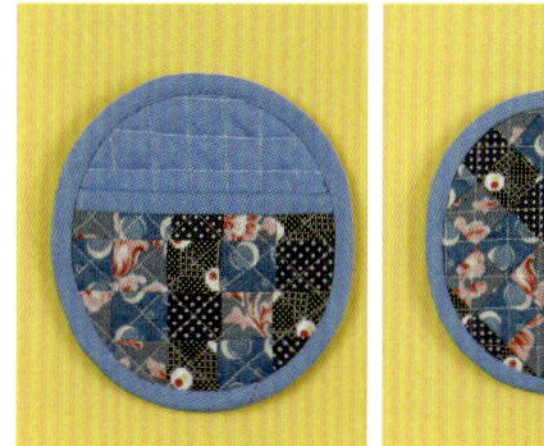

7 Now the circumference is piped.

8 Install a plastic snap at the center of the flap. First, place a snap just below the piping on the front. Then pierce a hole using an awl.

9 From the inside, insert a stud through the pierced hole and put a socket over the stud. Pinch the back and front until it snaps.

10 Confirm the position of the other set of snaps on the flap. Install in the same manner as the first set.

11 Complete!

If you use this as a coin case, you can slide the coins onto the flap to sort them and take the ones you want.

43

Timeless Standard, Metal Clasp Pouch

This oblong metal clasp pouch is useful as a pouch or a wallet. This particular metal clasp, with a width of 11.5 cm (4½"), is quite handy and compliments the patchwork quilt. The cute shape and snapping sound of the clasp are specific to metal clasps. It is worth your while to try and make this pouch at least once.

9 x 13 cm (3⅝" x 5 ⅛") Mariko Hayasaki

How to make ▶pp. 69, 120

How to Install a Metal Clasp

There are quite a few people who have trouble installing metal clasps or maybe they just aren't quite satisfied with their attempts.
Once you master a few tricks, though–and try to install a few clasps–you'll improve, so just stick with it.

1 Prepare a metal clasp. The metal clasp and paper cord make a set.

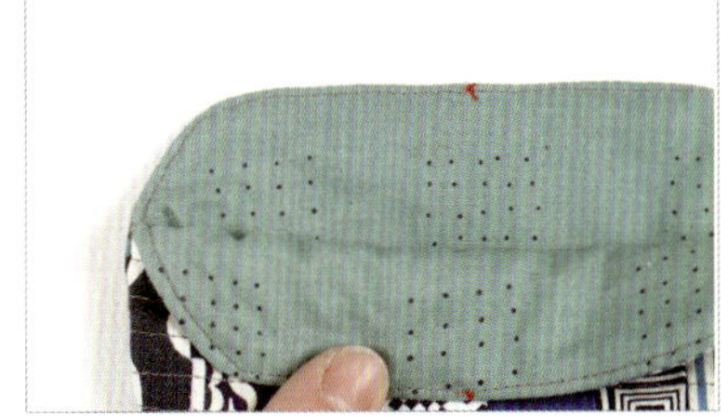

2 Make a pouch. After you have finished, stitch all around the opening of the pouch. This is for reinforcing the opening and to prevent it from becoming twisted. Mark the center with thread.

3 Coat the channel of the clasp with glue. If your glue bottle has a small mouth, you can apply glue directly from the bottle. You can also use a toothpick to apply glue little by little. Be sure to coat thoroughly, but be careful not to use too much glue.

4 While aligning the center of the pouch and the metal clasp, feed the pouch into the clasp. Open the clasp wide and slide the pouch inside. That way the pouch is secure and it makes easier to align the pouch with the clasp

5 Secure with clips to maintain alignment.

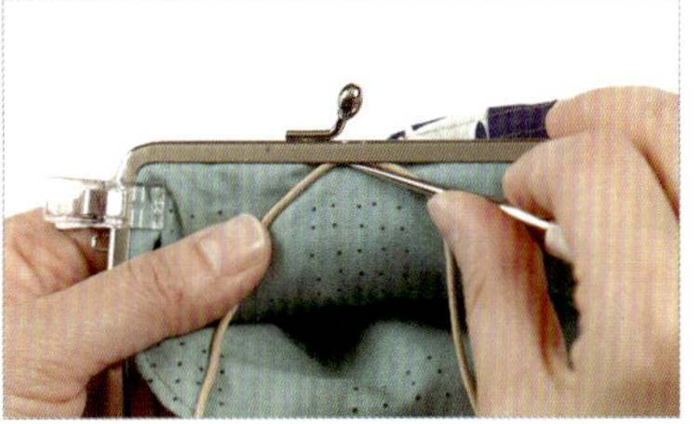

6 Feed the paper cord in from the enter. Use an awl to insert the paper cord under the clasp. Hold the awl at an angle along the paper cord.

7 Tightly insert the paper cord into the corner. Make sure the paper cord is not inserted too deep. Do the same for the other side.

8 Pinch the corners of the metal clasp with pliers to reinforce. Hold the pliers at a 45-degree angle and try to press only on the inside. In the photo the jaws of the pliers are coated with resin. When you use metal-jawed pliers be sure to cover the clasp with cloth so you don't scratch the clasp.

9 Once the glue is dry, it's complete.

44 Log Cabin Quilted Shoulder Pad Pouch

The plump, curved, cute shape is produced by using a shoulder pad as batting. Sew strips of fabric along the curve of the shoulder pad to create the pattern of a log cabin quilt. If you use a single piece of fabric, instead of a log cabin quilt pattern, be sure to tuck your fabric in according to the curve of the shoulder pad.

11 x 12.5 cm (4⅜" x 5") Sachiko Ishikawa

How to make ▶ p. 71

How to Make a Log Cabin Quilted Shoulder Pad Pouch

This pouch uses 10mm (⅜") thick raglan-type shoulder pads. Use craft glue to put two shoulder pads together.

Materials
Various strips of fabric for log cabin quilting
Backing fabric: 15 x 40 cm (5⅞" x 15¾")
One 85 cm (33½") long 3.5 cm (1⅜") wide bias tape (includes loop)
One 15 cm (6") zipper
A set of 11 x 13 cm (4⅜" x 5⅛") shoulder pads

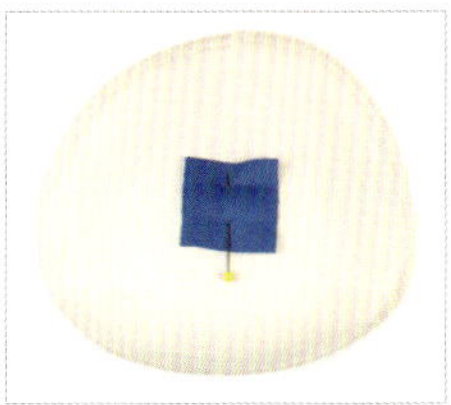

1 Place a 3 x 3 cm (1¼" x 1¼") piece of square fabric at the center of the shoulder pad and secure with a pin.

2 With the right side facing down, place another 3 x 3 cm (1¼" x 1¼") square piece of fabric on the square piece you secured in step 1 and stitch them together with a 0.7 cm (¼") seam allowance. After stitching, turn the fabric right side out. You don't need to stitch all the way through the shoulder pad, you can just stitch part of it.

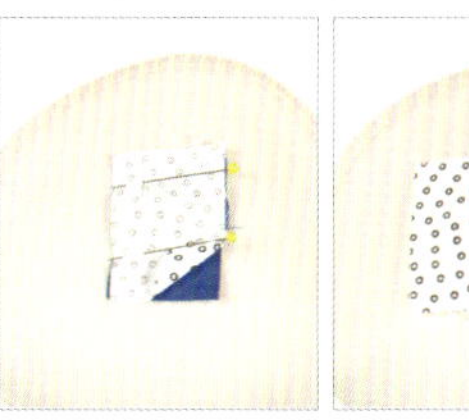

3 In a similar manner, with the right side facing down, place the next strip of 3 x 4.6 cm (1¼" x 1⅞") fabric over the piece sewn on in step 2. Stitch them together. After stitching, turn the fabric right side out.

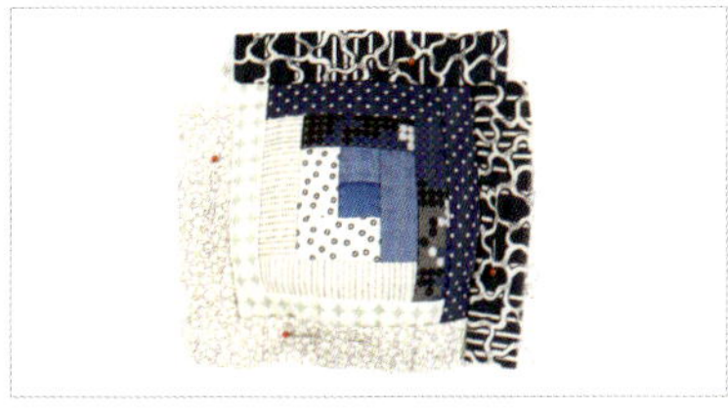

4 Stitch 3 cm (1¼") wide strips of fabric as you fill the surface of the shoulder pad. All the while adjusting the length of the strips. Cut off excess fabric according to the size of the shoulder pad.

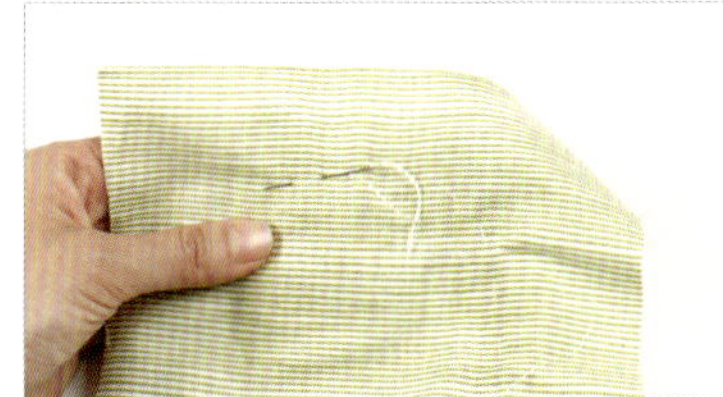

5 With the right side facing up, place the backing fabric on the backside of the shoulder pad, then baste. Spray fabric glue on the wrong side of the backing fabric and lightly glue the backing onto the shoulder pad to make it easier to work.

6 Cut off excess backing along the circumference of the shoulder pad.

7 With the right sides facing together, bind bias tape along the circumference of the shoulder pad. Then stitch. Flip the shoulder pad and wrap the circumference with bias tape. Blind stitch to the backing. Do the same for the other shoulder pad.

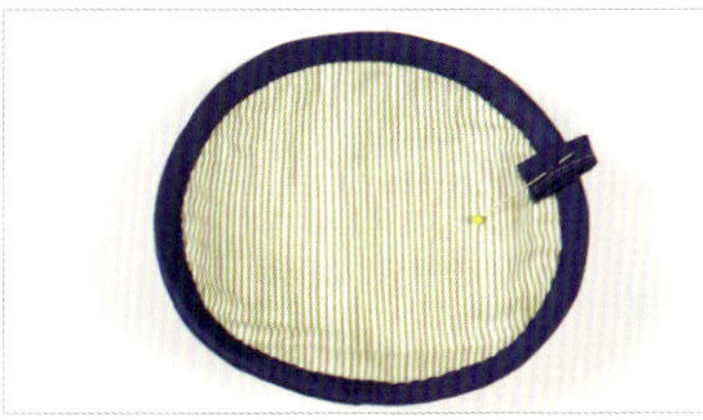

8 Fold a 4 x 3.5 cm (1⅝" x 1⅜") piece of bias tape in four and sew down the end to make a loop. Fold the loop in half and sew both edges onto the inside of the shoulder pad where the end of the zipper will be.

9 Align the center of the shoulder pad and the zipper, plus the edge of the piping and the teeth of the zipper. Blind stitch the zipper tape onto the shoulder pad. Baste the end of the zipper tape to the shoulder pad to secure.

10 Do the same for the other zipper tape.

11 Apply fabric glue inside the shoulder pad starting below the end of the zipper tape. Go all the way to the other end. You can whip stitch the shoulder pads together instead of gluing.

12 Put the shoulder pads together and glue them on. Be sure that the teeth of the zipper are not out of position. Secure the circumference with clips. Once the glue has dried, it's complete.

45

Soft Flex Frame Pouch with a Tacked Fabric

A flex frame is installed on the mouth of the pouch. The tacked fabric creates a soft and gentle appearance. The neat embroidery of white clovers makes a statement.

9 x 13 cm (3⅝" x 5⅛") Design: Mika Ohatake, Sewing: Kazue Murata

How to make ▶p. 121

46

Modern and Pop-style Flex Frame Pouch

The curved shape makes this flex frame pouch fun and interesting. After finishing the front and back panels, put them together by sewing along the circumference. This pouch is quick and easy to make.

12 x 13.5 cm (4¾" x 5⅜") Chizuko Kojima

How to make ▶p. 122

If you push on both ends at the same time, the mouth will open.

47

Wide Mouth Pouch

Narrow wire frames are installed in the mouth of the pouch. Both ends are folded downward and the mouth of the pouch opens really wide. This beautiful pouch also has machine embroidery. Be sure to have fun with your needlework and quilt designs while making this pouch.

7 x 12 cm (2¾" x 4¾") Noriko Sakurai

How to make ▶ p. 123

The mouth opens really wide so you can see inside very clearly.

48 Metal Snap Button Pouch with Design Showcasing Materials

The color combination of black and vivid green will catch anyone's attention. The shallow but wide shape of this pouch, along with its rustic materials, make it look really cool. A metal hook with texture is used.

8.5 x 16 cm (3⅜" x 6⅜") Noriko Sakurai

How to make ▶p. 124

49 Pouch with a Wave Tape Flower 1: Zippered 2: Pocket Pouch

This is a unique pouch with a large flower. The flower is made by sewing together a piece of wave tape. The large flower and polka-dot fabric is eye-catching. But, you must pay attention to the overall shape of the pouch. It makes a butterfly-like shape when spread out and there are two pockets separated by the zipper.

10 x 22 cm (4" x 8¾") Noriko Hosoo

How to make ▶ p. 125

When spread out, it looks like this.

The inside is partitioned into two compartments.

This is for those people who are not good at installing zippers but still prefer pouches that close securely. This pouch uses hook-and-loop fasteners. Pull both sides of the opening and it will open. Lightly pinch the sides together and it will close. A very practical pouch indeed!

17.5 x 23 cm (6⅞" x 9⅛") Noriko Sakurai

How to make ▶p. 126

50 Hook-and-loop Fastener Pouch

Attach hook-and-loop fasteners along the opening of the mouth but leave out fasteners on each end.

If you use wide fasteners you will need to pull them forcefully to open the pouch. Therefore, using slightly narrow fasteners is recommended.

Useful Parts List

These sewing supplies are used for the pouches shown from page 62 to 77. Each item can be purchased at a craft supply store or on the Internet.

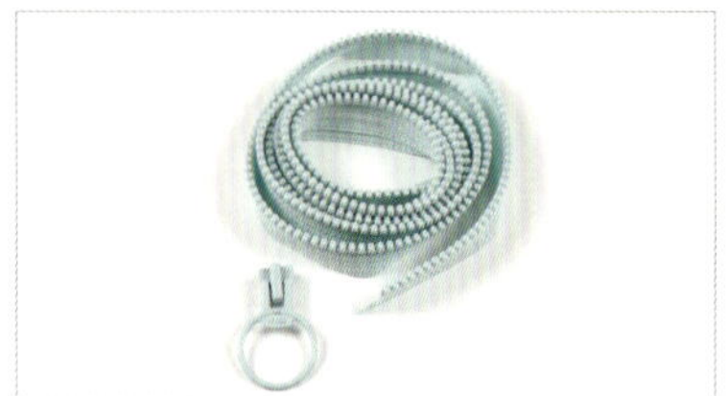

Freestyle Zipper

Used on the pouches on page 62 and 63. There are no top and bottom stops. A zipper slider and one-sided zipper tape makes a set. Use after cutting to the desired length.

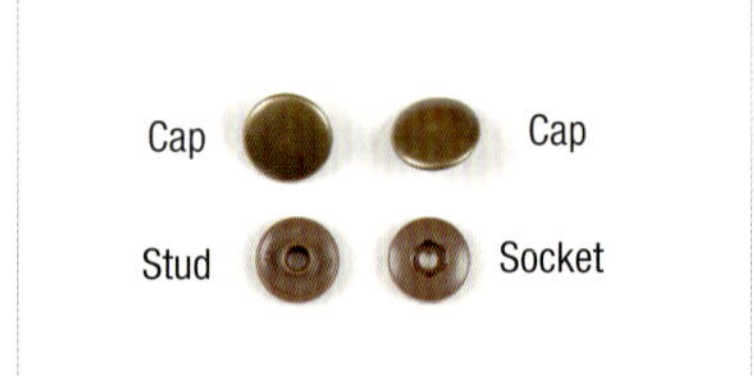

Plastic Snap

Used on the pouches on page 52 and 66. Easily installed. After piercing a hole in the fabric, insert the necessary pair of pieces and pinch them together with your finger. 2 caps, a stud, and a socket make a set.

Metal Clasp

Used on the pouch on page 68. There are glue-on types and sew-on types. The glue-on type is used in this book.

Shoulder Pads and Craft Glue

Used on the pouch from page 70. The raglan-type shoulder pad used for the base of the pouch is approx. 11 x 13 cm (4⅜" x 5⅛"), with a thickness 1 cm (⅜"). Craft glue is used to put two shoulder pads together to make the body of the pouch. Craft glue is a strong adhesive so you don't have to worry about the pads coming apart.

Flex Frame

Used for the pouches on page 72 and 73. Made of two thin metal strips. Used with a set of pins. There are a variety of widths and lengths; just pick one that fits your project.

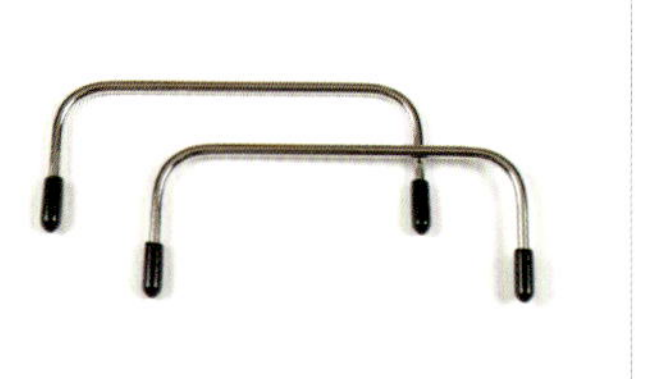

Internal Wire Clasp

Used for the pouch on page 74. This is a narrow wire frame. Lengths and widths vary. These clasps come in handy when you want to make a set of pouches that vary in size.

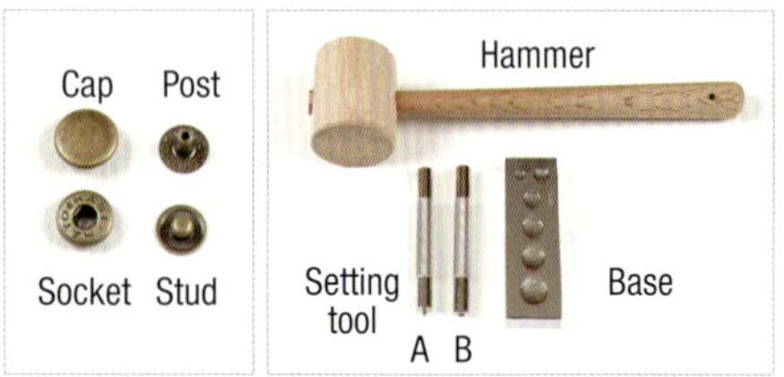

Metal Snap and Setting Tool

Used for the pouch on page 75. Metal snaps are installed by hammering them in with a setting tool. You need to have the necessary tools, but snaps allow your finished product to look professional.

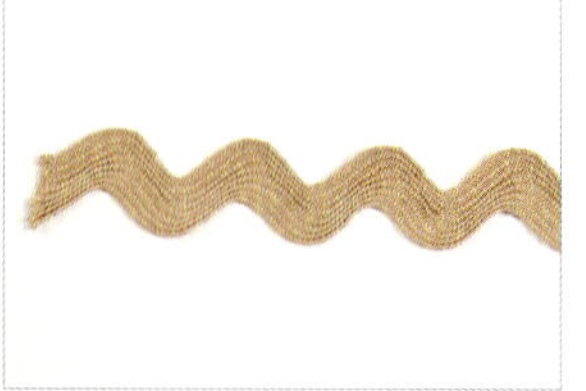

Large Rickrack

Used for the pouch on page 76. This large rickrack makes the flower. The width of the tape is approx. 2.3 cm (⅞").

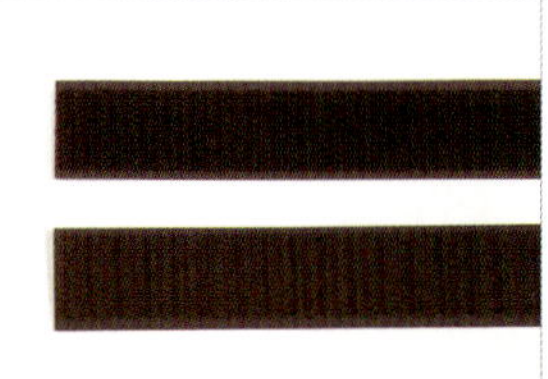

Hook-and-loop Fasteners

Used for the pouch on page 77. Magic Tape® and Velcro® are types of hook-and-loop fasteners. They work by forcing tiny hooks to catch loops on the opposing surface.

How to Make the Flower Using Rickrack on Page 76

Depending on the width and length of the tape of your choice, the size of the flower will vary.

1 Stitch the top fifteen waves together.

2 Align the beginning and end. Then stop stitching and pull the thread.

3 Tie off the thread and adjust the shape of the flower. Sew the flower to the pouch.

How to Install the Flex Frame on Pages 72, 73

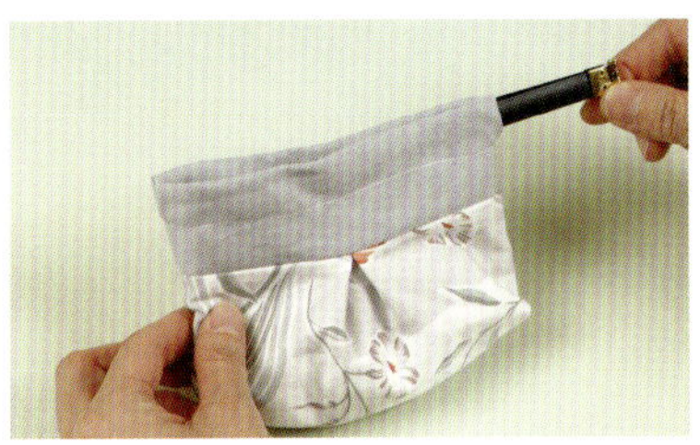

1 Push the flex frames through the openings.

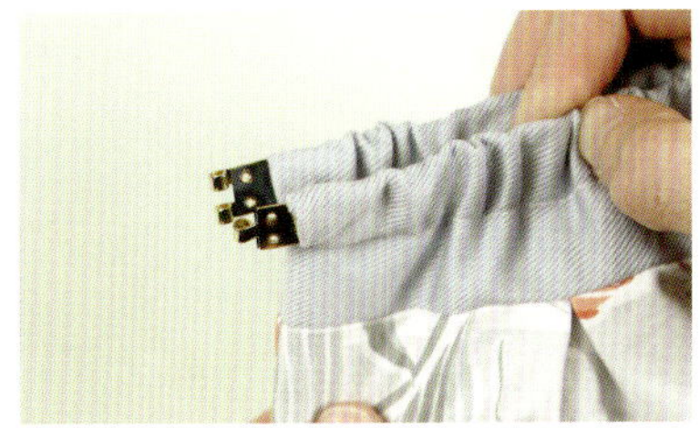

2 Align the ends after fishing them through the openings.

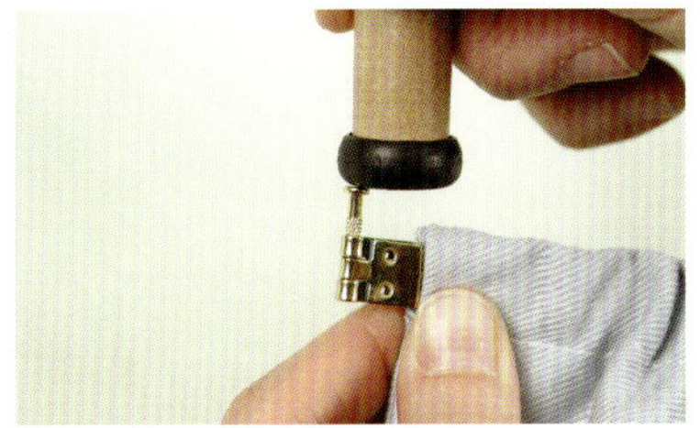

3 Put in a pin to secure the ends. Inset the pin securely by hammering with the handle of an awl on a solid surface. Now, it's complete.

How to Install the Metal Snap on Page 75

You need some tools to install these snaps. However, some packages of metal snaps include the setting tools.

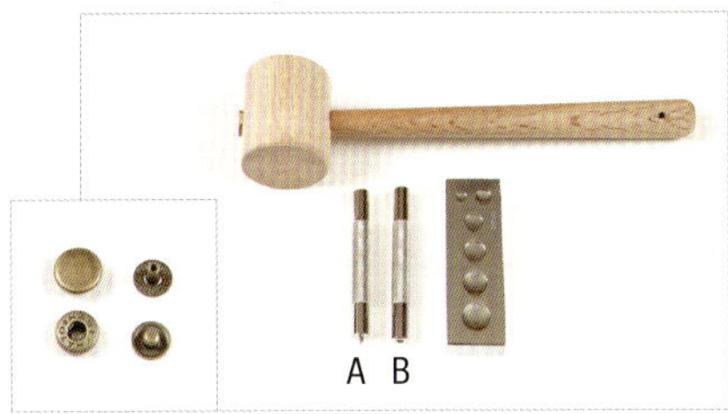

1 Prepare a cap, a socket, a post and a stud. We see a hammer above two setting tools (A, B) and a base.

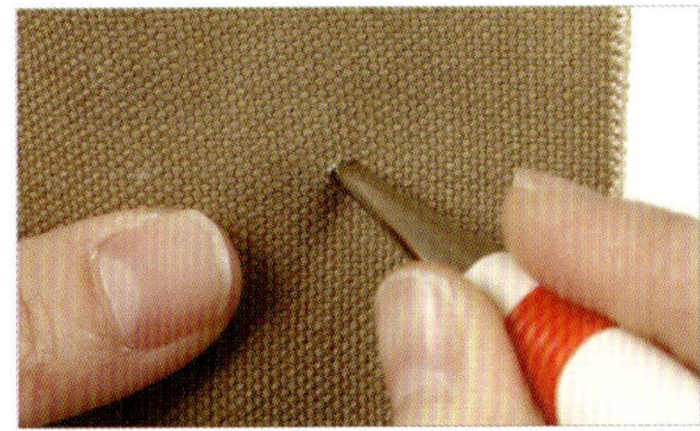

2 Pierce a hole with an awl where you intended to install a snap.

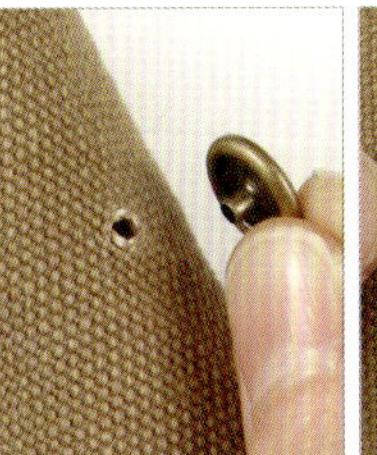

3 Insert a cap from the right side of the fabric and align the socket from the wrong side.

4 Match the indentations of the base and the size of the cap, then place the cap over the indentation. Align setting tool A with the socket.

5 Hammer perpendicular to the surface.

6 The prongs of the cap are inset by securing the cap and the socket.

7 Similarly, insert a post from the wrong side of the fabric and align the stud from the right side.

8 Place on the flat part of the base and then use setting tool B to hammer together.

9 Now, the post is set in the stud. Check that the snap is secured properly.

How to Install a Hand-sewn Zipper

If piping covers the mouth of your pouch, consider installing a zipper manually for a beautiful finish.

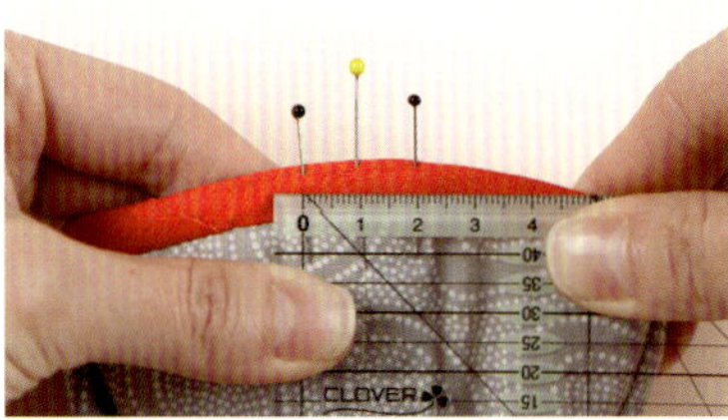

1 Begin by sewing on a zipper 1 cm ($\frac{7}{8}$") (black pins) from the side seam (yellow pin) on both the left and right.

2 Secure the zipper tape with pins, while making sure to begin slightly lower than the edge of the pouch. Align the teeth of the zipper with the edge of the piping or slightly higher than the piped edge.

3 Stop stitching the zipper tape about 1 cm ($\frac{7}{8}$") before the side seam.

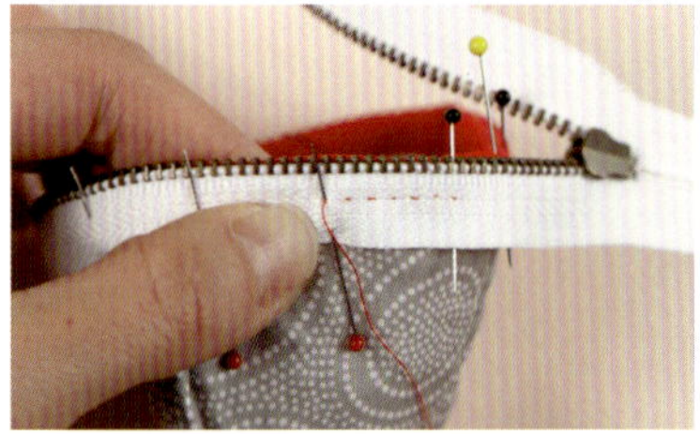

4 The blind stitch of the zipper tape is 0.5 cm ($\frac{1}{4}$") below the teeth.

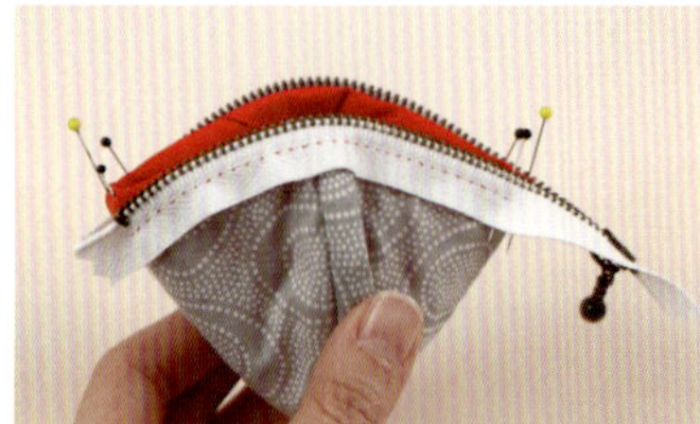

5 Do the same on the other side.

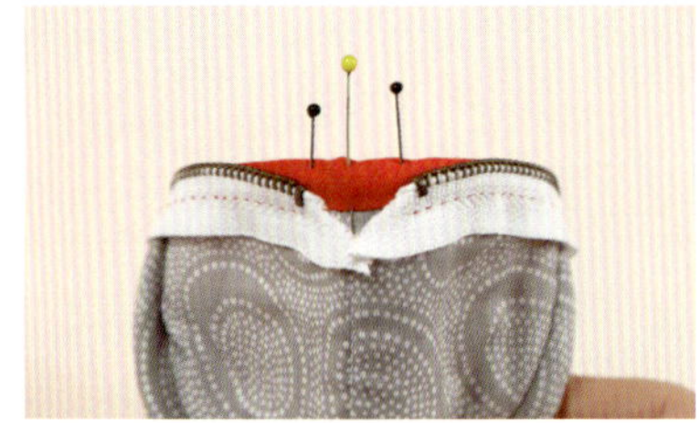

6 As for the top zipper tape extensions, fold them at an angle and blind stitch down.

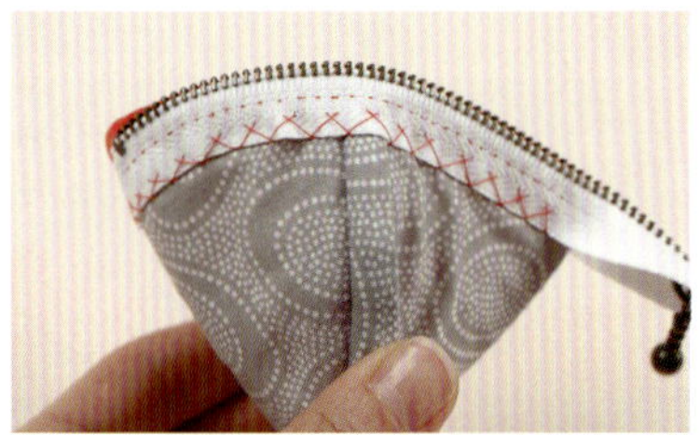

7 Cross stitch along the edge of the zipper tape to press it down. You can use a blind stitch or running stitch instead.

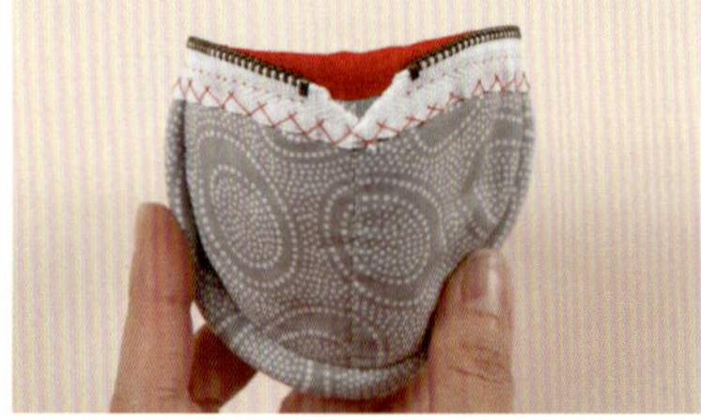

8 Now it has a cross stitch all the way around. Also, securely sew down the top zipper tape extensions.

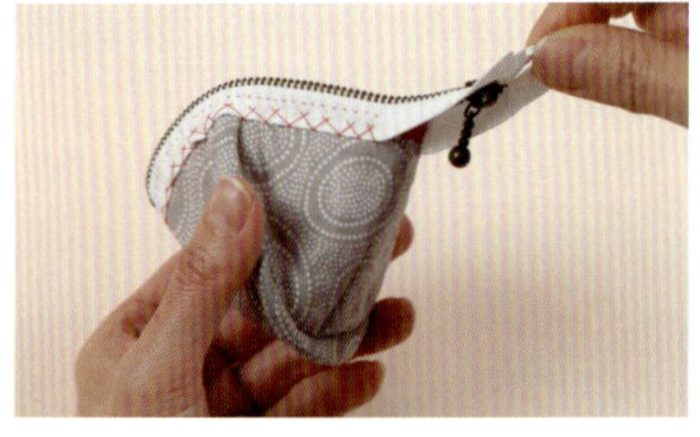

9 If you want the bottom tape extension to be outside the pouch, cross stitch the zipper tape down to where the blind stitch ends.

How to Put a Slider on a Freestyle Zipper

Make sure the zipper teeth don't become misaligned.

Cut to the desired length.

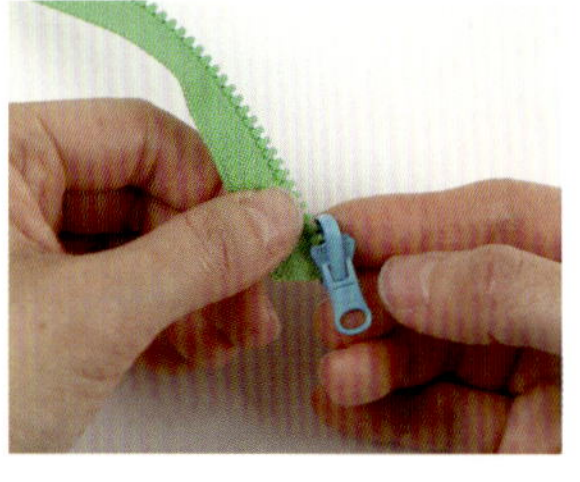

1 Put a zipper slider through the end of the zipper teeth. Do not push it through too far.

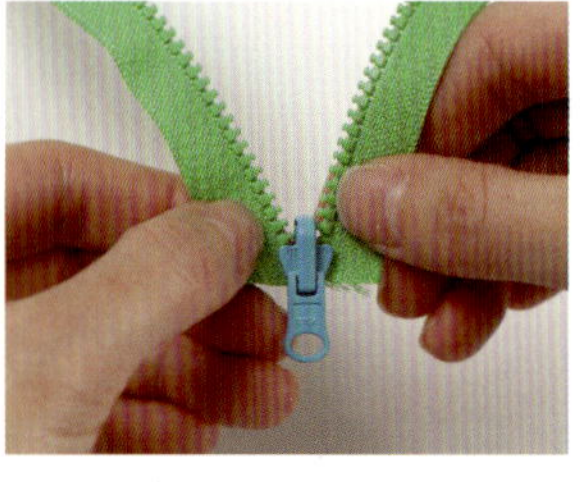

2 Do the same for the other side.

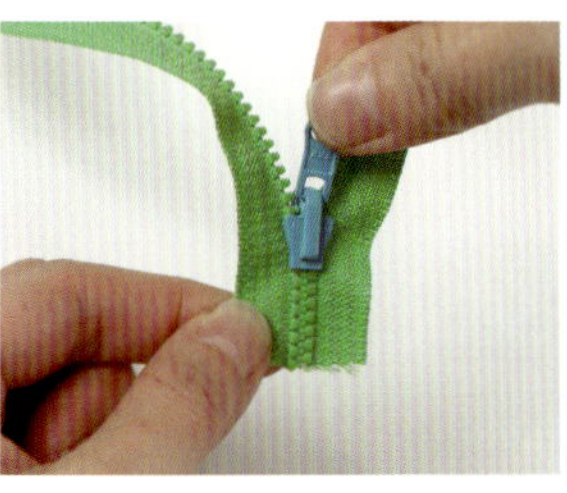

3 The teeth will mesh by pulling the zipper slider up.

The Basics of Making Pouches

Many of the pouches introduced in this book are made by sewing scraps together into larger patchwork quilts. Here are the basics of patchwork quilting. Even if you use plain fabric, instead of your own pieced-together creations, the sewing method is the same. The directions for making this pouch begin on page 83. Also, don't forget to refer to the pages with the step-by-step instructions and photographs.

Quilting Flow

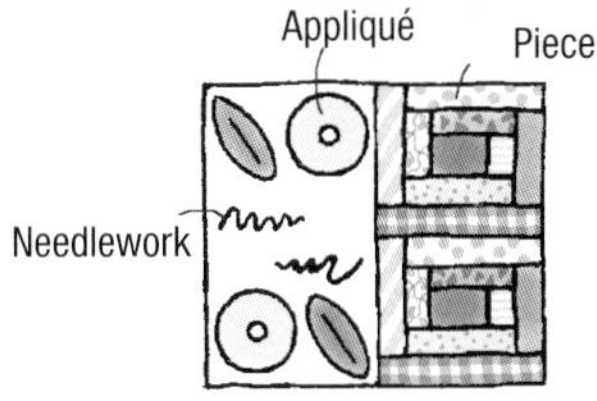

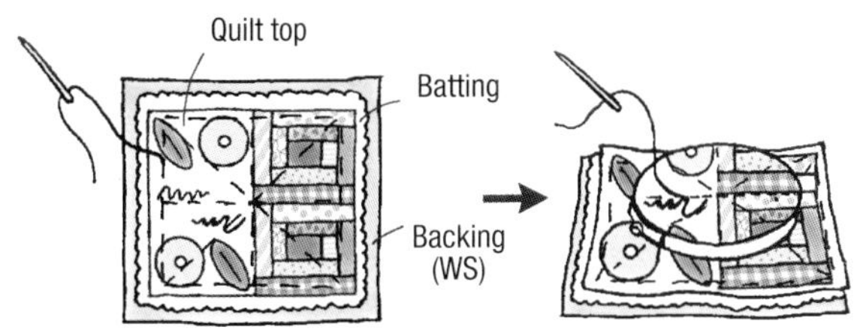

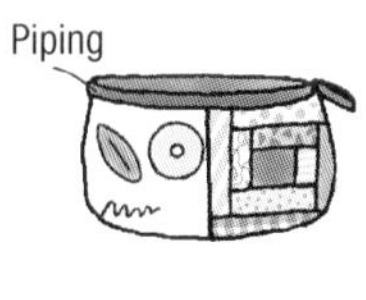

1 **How to Make the Quilt Top**
A quilt top is created through piecing, appliqué, or needlework.

2 **Baste then Quilt**
Layer a backing, a batting, and a quilt top and then baste. Be sure the layers don't become misaligned.

3 **Making a Pouch**
Sew the seams together, create box corners, and bind bias tape along the opening or the edge of the pouch.

Making a Quilt Top

Put fabric pieces together or sew on appliqué or plain fabric.

1 Cutting

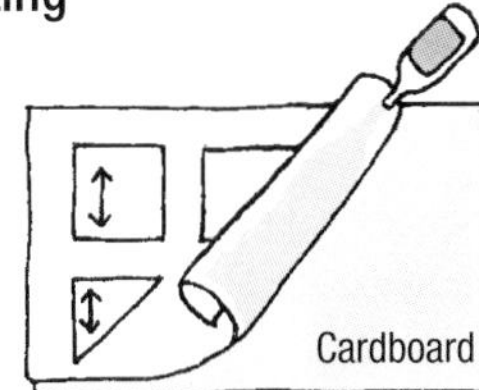

Making Templates
Copy the full-sized patterns on a piece of paper. Glue the paper onto a piece of cardboard to reinforce. Cut out each pattern.

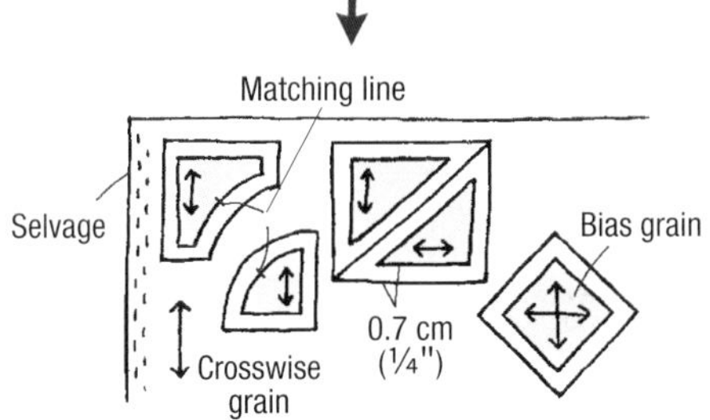

Marking
Place your templates on the wrong side of the fabric. Match selvage and fabric grain either lengthwise or crosswise. Trace the templates onto the fabric with a soft (no. 2) pencil. While eyeballing 0.7 cm (¼") for the seam allowance (check directions for seam allowance), cut the fabric along the mark.

2 Put fabric pieces together (connecting pieces)

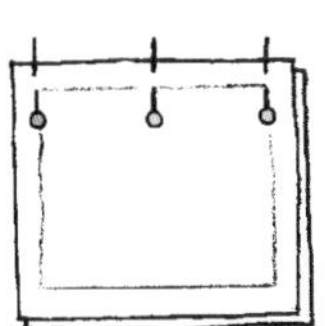

❶ With the right sides facing each other, put two fabric pieces together while aligning the marked line. Secure with pins. Pin the corners first then the center.

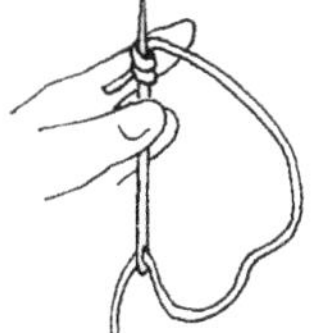

❷ Tie a knot in the thread: Wrap your thread a few times around the needle, then pull the needle through while holding the thread.

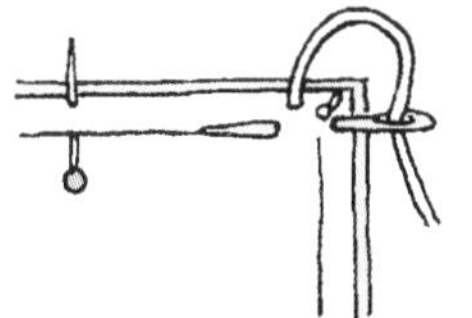

❸ First, back stitch once. Then use a running stitch along the edge.

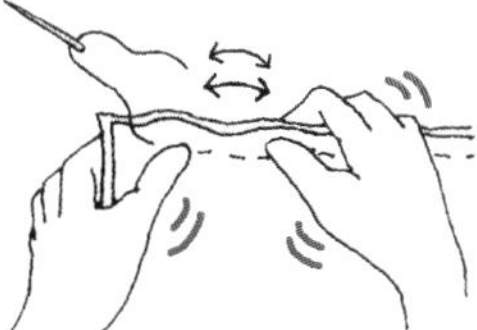

❹ After stitching the edge, smooth out the stitches so they don't pull the fabric.

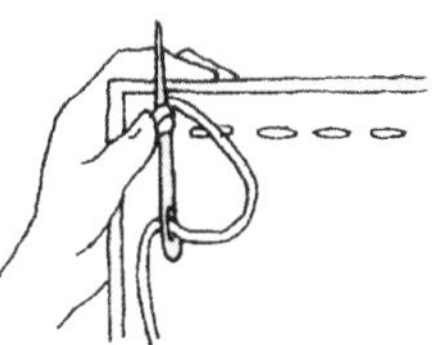

❺ Stroke the stitches with your fingernails and lightly straighten the fabric. Back stitch once at the end. Hold down the needle with your thumb, and wrap the thread a few times around the needle. Then, pull the needle through to tie off.

Three Ways of Stitching Pieces Together

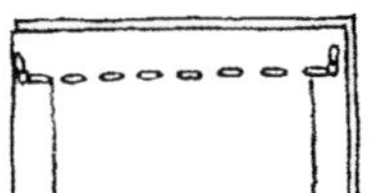

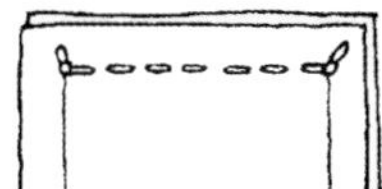

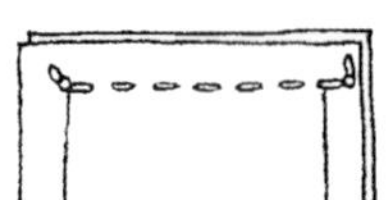

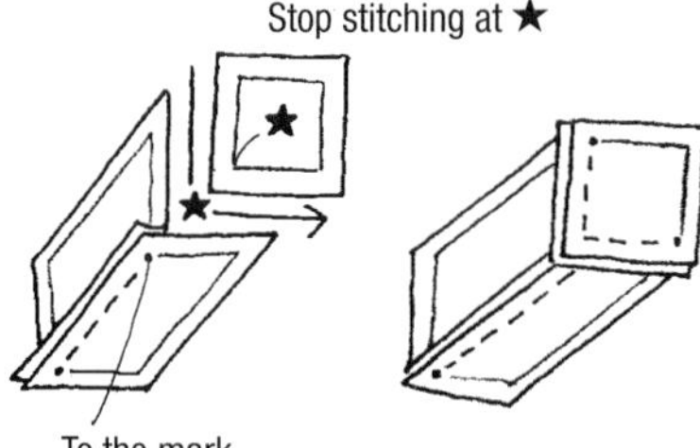

From Edge to Edge
When making a strip.

From Mark to Mark
When both sides have inset seams.

From Edge to Mark
The inset seam is on the side sewn from the mark.

What Is an inset Seam?
After stitching two fabric pieces together, with the right sides together, join another piece of fabric at the corner.

How to Press a Seam

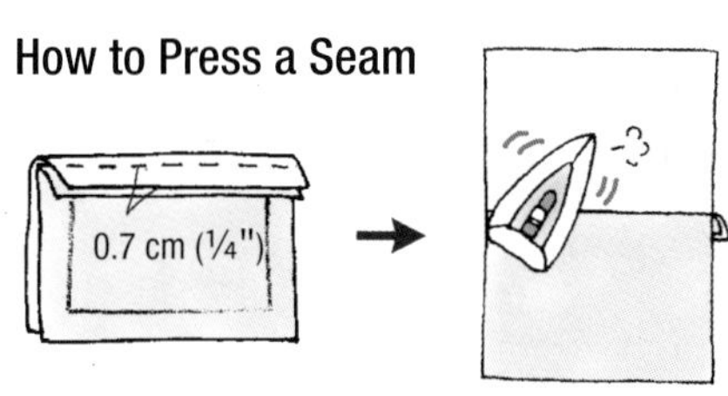

Cut a 0.7 cm (¼") seam allowance. Then press the fabric down to the side you intend to have a curve, or toward the darker colored piece. Iron to set the stitches.

Needles and Threads
There are different types of needles and thread. Use the list below to select the items you're most comfortable with. There are also many special types of thread and needles.

• Piecing	General sewing needle size 8–9. Machine sewing cotton thread #40.
• Appliqué	Sharps, #50–#60 cotton thread
• Basting	Milliner's size 3–9
• Betweens	Quilting Between size 9–12 #50–#60 waxed cotton thread
• Pins	Narrow and short pins

---

3 Appliqué

Blind Stitch after Adjusting Shape
Mark the wrong side of the fabric. Then, running stitch the seam allowance and make sure the fabric is the same size as the template. Pull the thread to gather fabric, then iron on the fabric along circumference of the template. Take the template out and blind stitch circumference of the fabric onto the base fabric.

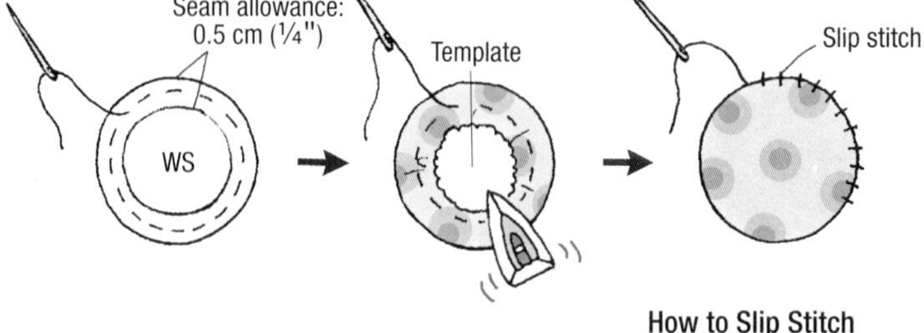

Adjust a Shape of the Appliqué as you Blind Stitch
Trace a template on the right side of the fabric, and clip the seam allowance where indented or curved. As you tack the seam allowance under, whip stitch along edges.

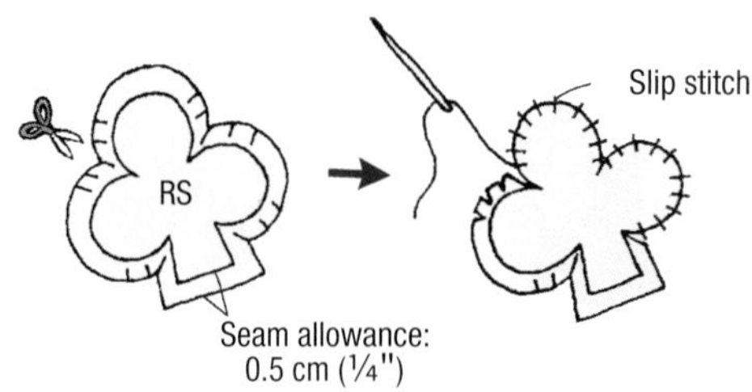

How to Slip Stitch

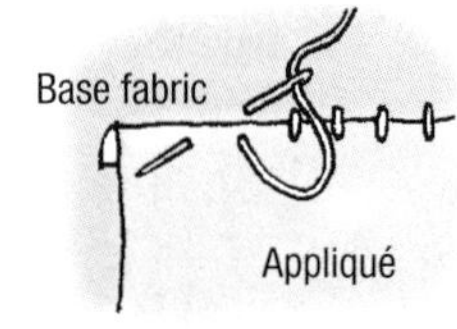

Stitches are visible on the outside. Used for vertically binding two pieces of fabric.

---

3 Transfer Quilting Designs

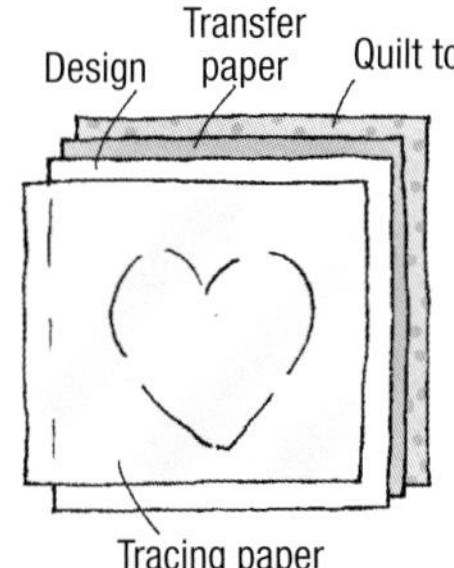

After assembling the quilt top, use a soft (no. 2) pencil or a marking pen to lightly draw quilting designs on the quilt top. Use a ruler to draw lines in grid patterns. If the lines are not straight, just place the quilt top on the design and trace. If your fabric is a darker color, layer the quilt top, the transfer paper, the design, and tracing paper, and trace the design onto the paper.

Baste and Then Quilt

Assemble quilt top, batting, backing fabric.

1 Baste

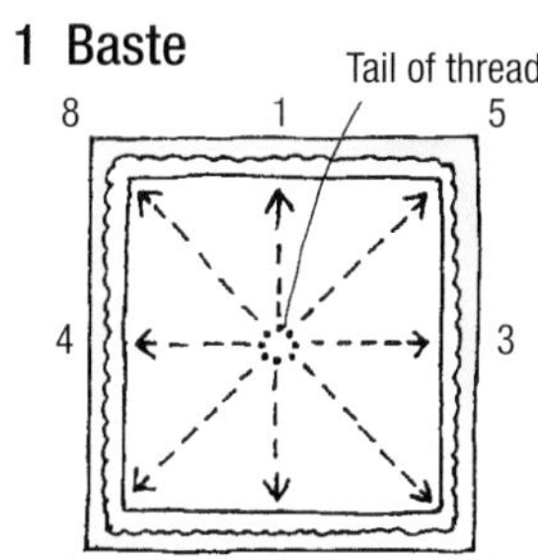

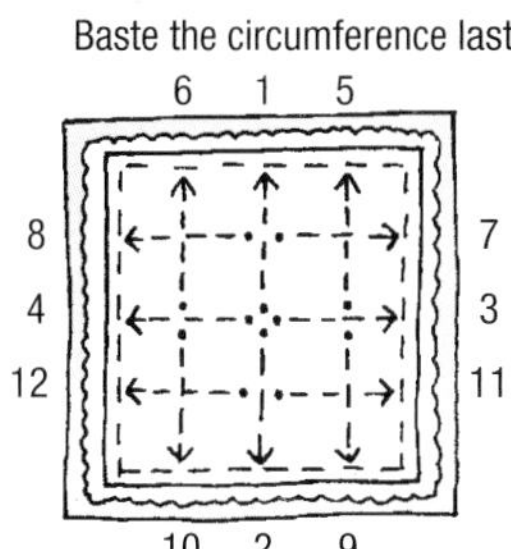

Layer the backing, batting, and quilt top on a flat surface, then smooth out the quilt top from the center out in order to remove air between layers. Baste while keeping the layers in place. Hold the fabric down and make small stitches at intervals of 1–1.5 cm (3⁄8"–5⁄8") in a diagonal direction or grid pattern. When the layers are fused together using fusible batting or interfacing, basting is not necessary.

2 Quilt

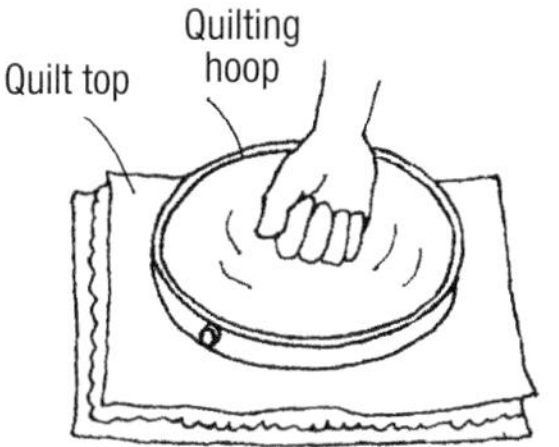

❶ Hoop your quilt. Leave it a bit loose. You don't need a hoop if your item is small.

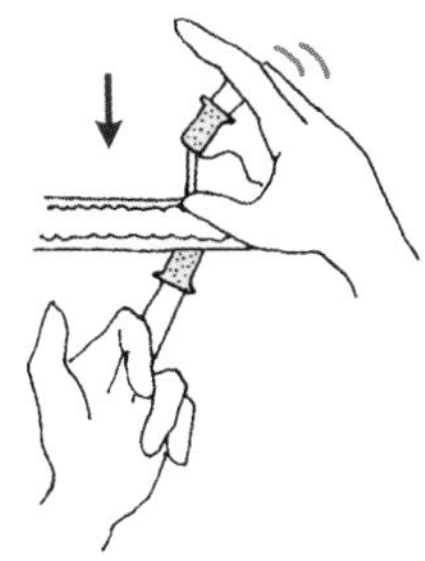

❷ Stabilize the hoop between a working surface and your tummy. Start to quilt from the center out. Insert your needle perpendicular to the cloth. Use your preferred thimble.

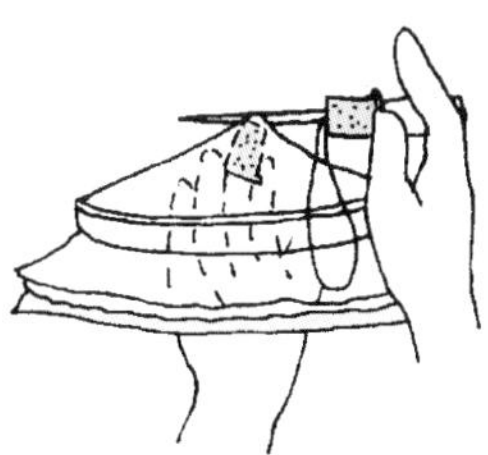

❸ Push the fabric up using a thimble from the back side. Lay the needle down and push it in a little before standing the needle up again. Repeat this motion for three to four stitches, then pull the thread through. Finer stitches make for a more beautiful quilt, but the most important thing is to make your stitches uniform. When you quilt the outline of a quilt block or an appliqué, it's called "outline quilting."

Making a Pouch

There are a variety of ways to put fabric together and sew a pouch. The methods for making pouches begin on page 84.

Basic Stitches that are Used Frequently

Cross stitch

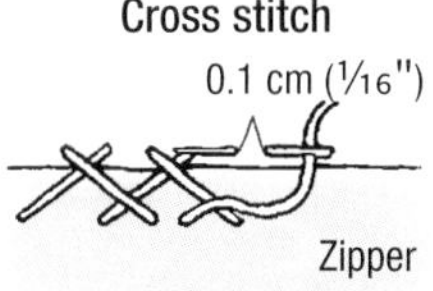

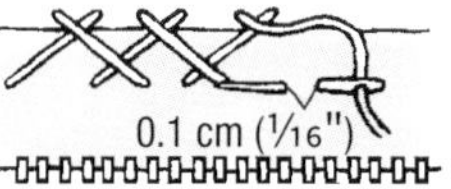

Hold the edge of the zipper tape down.

Whip stitch

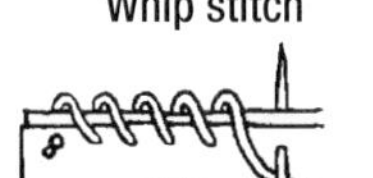

Place the right sides together and bind the edge.

Ladder stitch

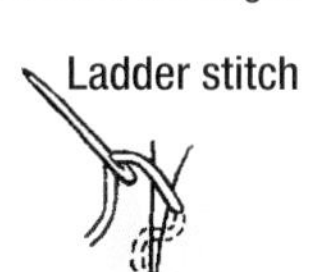

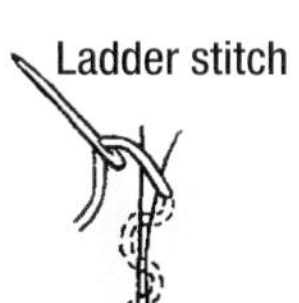

Match edges with the right sides faced out. Stitch left and right alternately.

Blind stitch

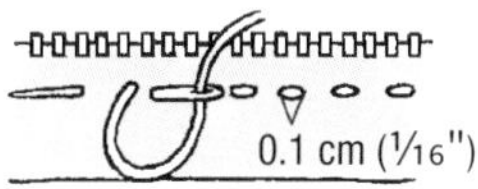

A type of invisible stitching used for manually installing zippers.

Back stitch

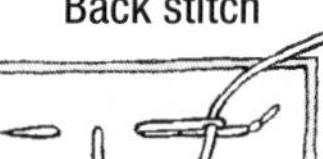

Reinforces stitches when hand stitching.

Binding Bias Tape

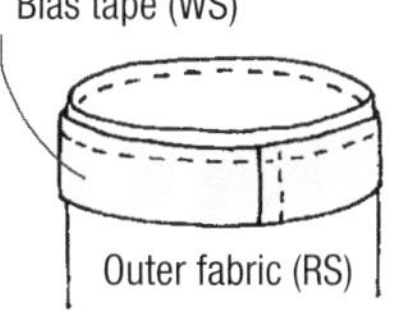

❶ With the right sides facing down, align bias tape along the circumference of the opening or seam allowance. Then sew.

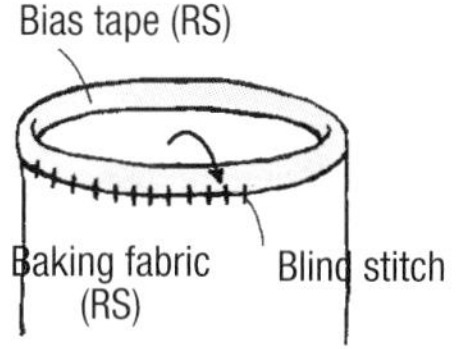

❷ Fold the bias tape right side out, then wrap seam allowance with the bias tape. Sew the bias tape along the edge of previous stitches.

How to Make Bias Tape

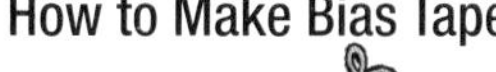

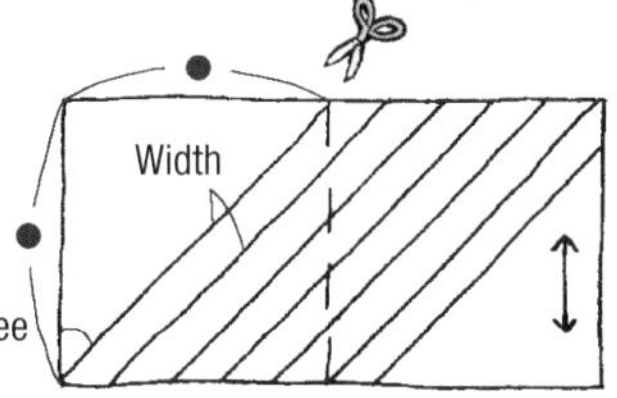

Spread out a piece of fabric, then cut pieces one at a time. When connecting two pieces of tape, place the right sides together. Spread the strip open and cut excess seam allowance.

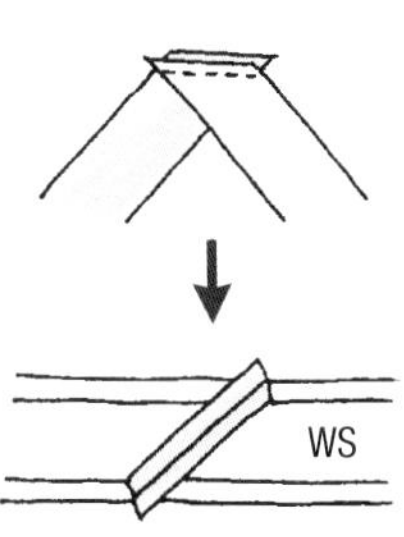

Instructions

- Units of measure are shown in centimeters and (inside parentheses) inches.
- If not specifically noted, measurements do not include seam allowances. Usually the seam allowance for piecing is 0.7 cm (¼"), appliqué is 0.5 cm (¼"), and sewing is 1 cm (⅜"). Cut the fabric without adding seam allowance when designated as seam.
- A dotted line without any other indication is a quilting line.
- The letter S in diagrams is an abbreviation for stitch.
- The abbreviation RS stands for Right Side, and WS stands for Wrong Side.
- The dimensions of a completed work may differ from measurements given on the patterns.

2 Compact Emergency Pouch

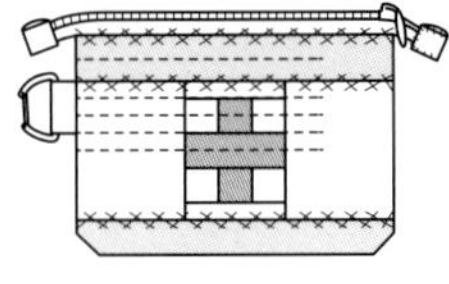

13 x 18 cm
(5⅛" x 7⅛")
Design: Sachiko Ishikawa

Materials
10 x 10 cm (4" x 4") squares / Fabric A (includes piping): 30 x 30 cm (11⅞" x 11⅞") / Fabric B: 25 x 30 cm (9⅞" x 11⅞") / Lining fabric, Fusible batting: 25 x 30 cm (9⅞" x 11⅞") / One zipper: 20 cm (7⅞") / One carabiner hook: 4 x 2.5 cm (1⅝" x 1") / 3 cm (1¼") wide tape: 5 cm (2") / 1.6 cm (⅝") wide ribbon / #8 needlework thread

Key points
- Add seam allowance: opening 0.5cm (¼"), side seams 0.7cm (¼").
- Refer to instructions on page 11 to install the zipper.

Instructions
1 Assemble the quilt top.
2 Fuse batting to the quilt top and quilt as desired.
3 Fold the outer fabric in half with the right sides together. Inside, place tape that has a carabiner hook attached. Sew both side seams and boxed corners.
4 Do the same for the lining fabric.
5 Put the lining inside the outer fabric and add piping along the mouth of the pouch.
6 Install a zipper by binding its tape externally on right side of the pouch and wrap both ends of the zipper with a ribbon.
7 Herringbone stitch the edge of the zipper tape.

Outer fabric: one piece

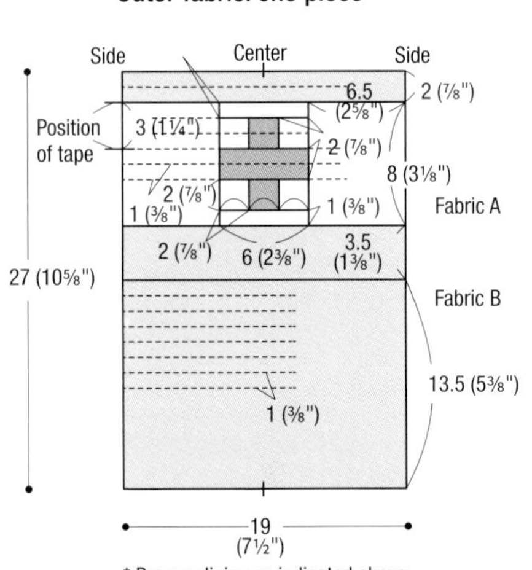

* Prepare lining as indicated above.

Instructions

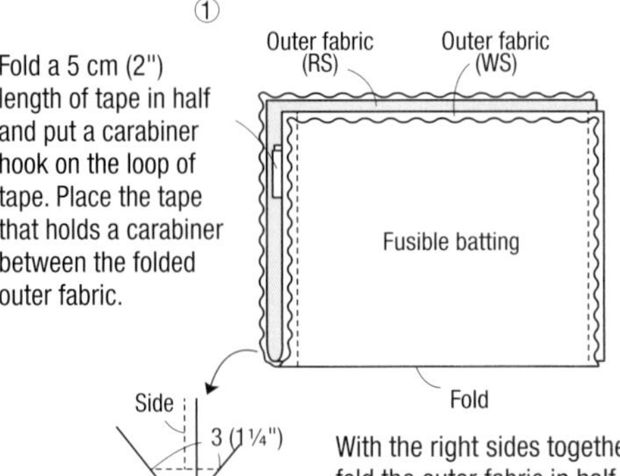

With the right sides together, fold the outer fabric in half. Sew both side seams. Sew a boxed corner. Do the same for the lining fabric.

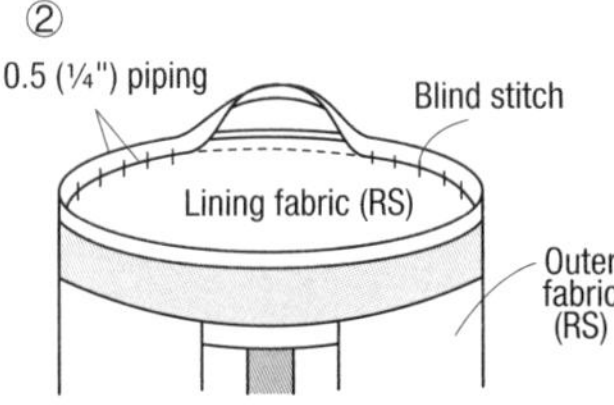

Put the lining inside the outer fabric, sew piping along mouth of the pouch.

How to Herringbone Stitch

①

②

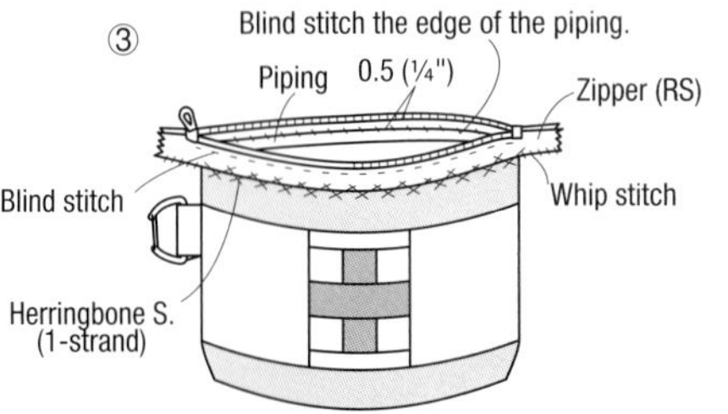

Align the edge of the piping and the zipper tape and install the zipper. Whip stitch the edge of the bottom tape extension.

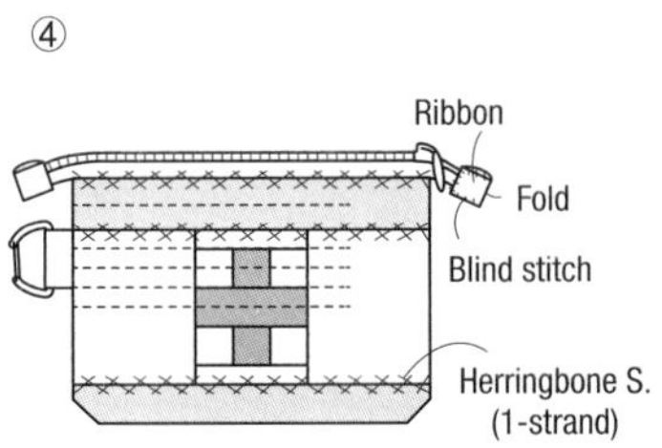

Wrap both end of the zipper tape with a ribbon and bind.

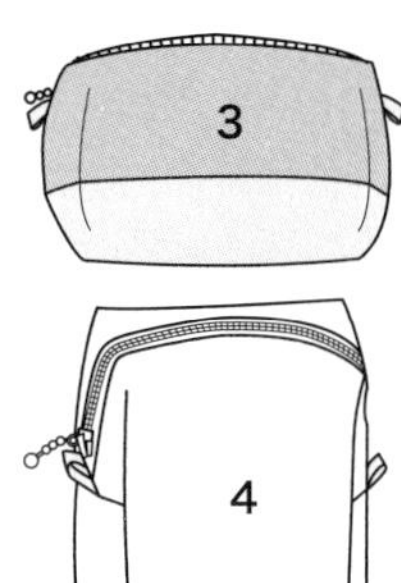

3 Boxy Pouch denoted as α
4 Oblong Pouch denoted as β

α: 7 x 12 cm (2¾" x 4¾")
β: 10 x 9 cm (4" x 3⅝")

3, 4 Boxy Pouch, Oblong Pouch

Materials
Outer fabric, Lining fabric, Adhesive interfacing: each 25 x 35 cm (9⅞" x 13¾") / 1 cm (⅜") Wide tape: 10 cm (4") / One zipper: 18 cm (7⅛") / (When α is patchworked, as in the diagram below, you will need Fabrics A and B: 20 x 25 cm (7⅞" x 13¾"))

Key points
- Add 1 cm (⅜") seam allowance.
- When the outer fabric is a patchwork, fuse the interfacing on Fabrics A and B first, then connect them.
- Drawing guidelines on the interfacing, as shown on the diagram below, will help you fold the fabric and create a beautiful finish.

Instructions
1. Fuse interfacing on the outer fabric.
2. Temporarily secure a tab on each side of the outer fabric and install a zipper.
3. Sew both side seams and make each bottom corner a boxed corner.
4. Do the same for the lining fabric.
5. Put the lining inside the outer fabric and sew the lining on the zipper tape.

α outer fabric: one piece

Draw guidelines
Side
Center
Side
6.5 (2⅝")
3 (1¼")
3.5 (1⅜")
3.5 (1⅜")
14 (5½")
7 (2¾")
3.5 (1⅜")
3.5 (1⅜")
6.5 (2⅝")
3 (1¼")
3.5 (1⅜")
3.5 (1⅜")

β outer fabric: one piece

Side
Center
Side
1.5 (⅝")
5 (2")
5 (2")
27 (10⅝")
4 (1⅝")
5 (2")
5 (2")
1.5 (⅝")
5 (2")
5 (2")
19 (7½")

* Fuse interfacing on the wrong side.
* Prepare lining as indicated above.

Tab: two pieces

Tape
1 (⅜")
5 (2")

How to Make a Tab

Fold

Fold the tape in half with the right side out.

Instructions (α, β common)

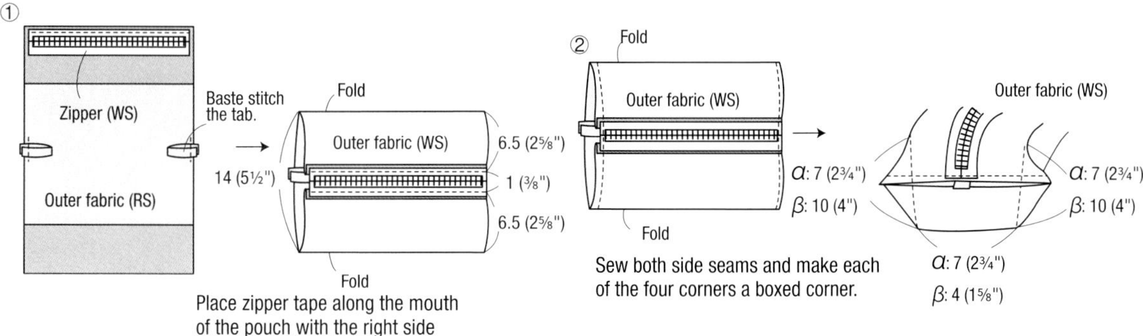

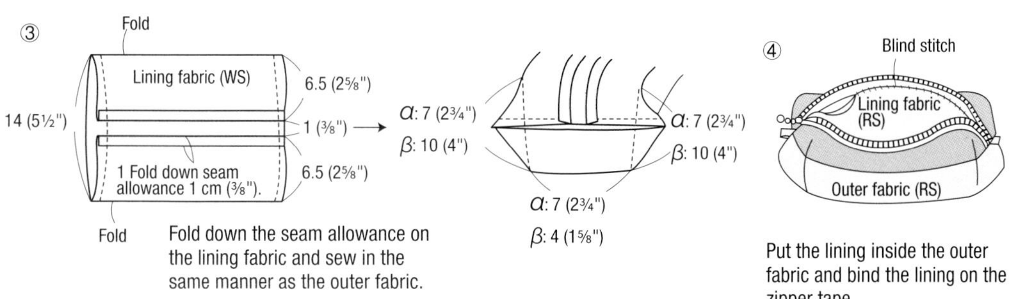

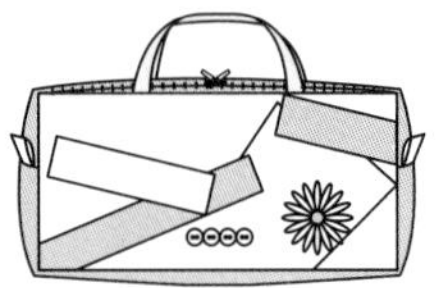

11 x 22 cm (4⅜" x 8¾")
Design: Chizuko Kojima

7 Zippered-gusset Fabric-collage Pouch

Materials

Outer fabric: 25 x 25 cm (9⅞" x 9⅞") / Bottom gusset: 35 x 10 cm (13¾" x 4") / Zipper gusset 2 pieces: each 35 x 5 cm (13¾" x 2") / Handle fabric 2 pieces: each 20 x 5 cm (7⅞" x 2") / Fusible batting: 35 x 30 cm (13¾" x 11⅞") / Thin fusible batting: 35 x 10 cm (13¾" x 4") / Backing fabric (including inside pocket): 80 x 30 cm (31½" x 11⅞") / 1.5 cm (⅝") wide grosgrain tape: 15 cm (5⅞") / One double slider zipper: 30 cm (11⅞") / Double-sided iron-on / Tape, lace, motif, and buttons for collage, as needed

Key points

- For the collage, fuse your choice of materials on the fabric using double sided iron-on. Zig-zag stitch on appliqué.

Instructions

1 Collage your choice of materials and assemble quilt top.
2 Sew the bottom gusset to the quilt top. After fusing the batting, layer backing, and quilt top together, quilt as desired.
3 Make a pocket. Sew it on the backing.
4 Make zipper gussets.
5 Make handles.
6 Sandwich the handles between the body of the pouch and the zipper gusset. Then sew the zipper gusset to the body.
7 Align the ends of the zipper gusset with the ends of the bottom gusset (right sides together) and put a tab in between. Then sew the seam together.
8 Sew side gussets to the body with the right sides facing together.
9 Attach buttons to embellish.

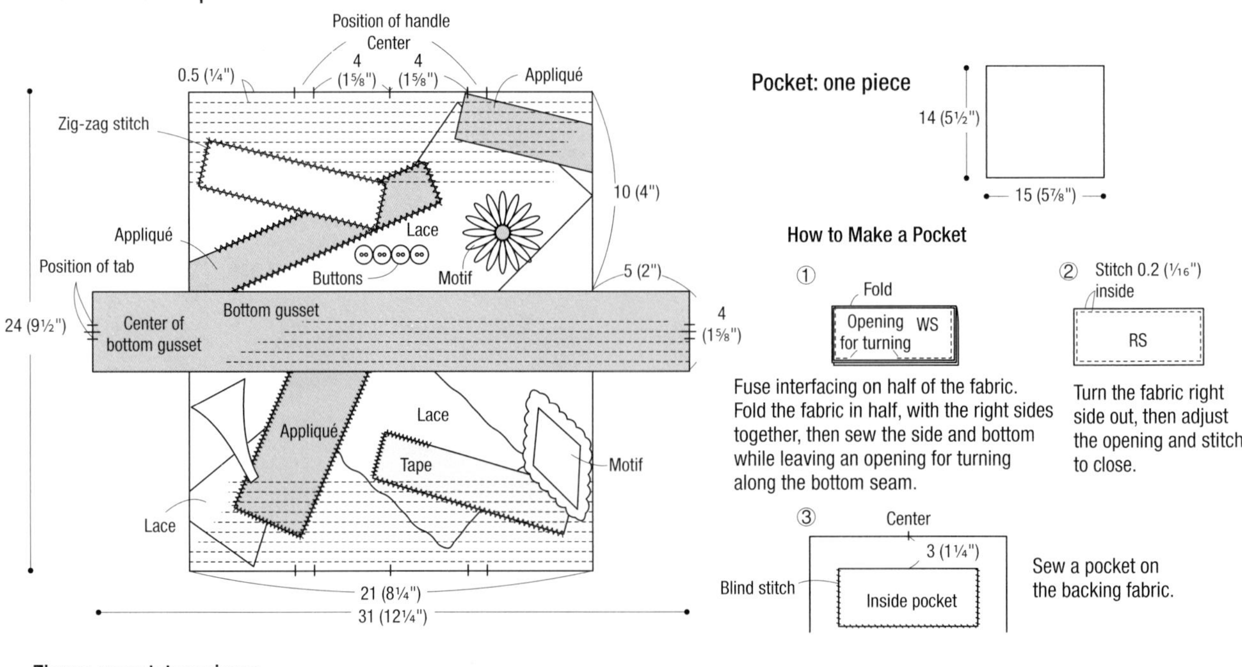

Zipper gusset: two pieces

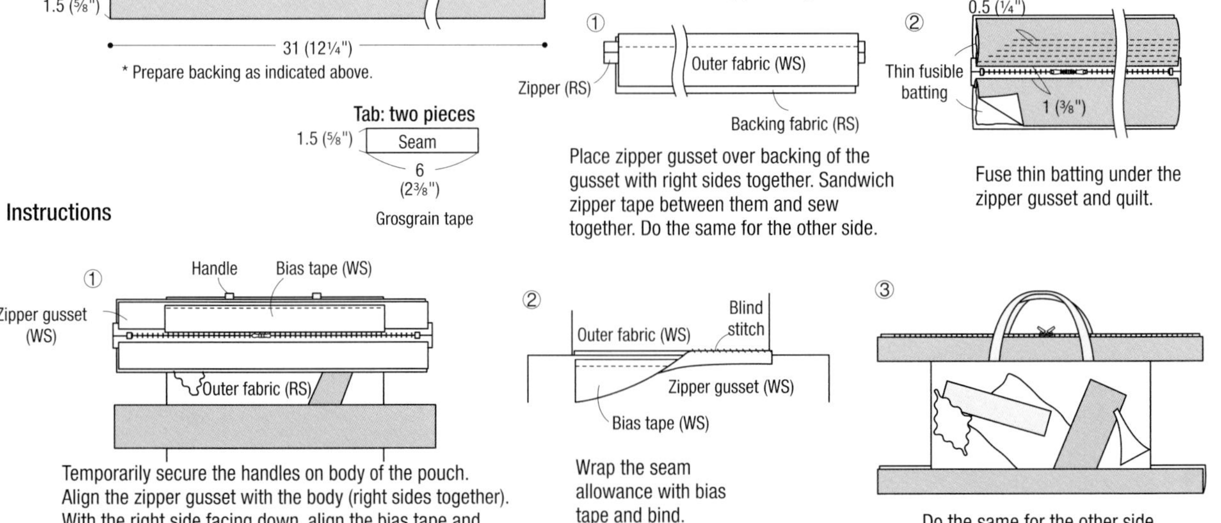

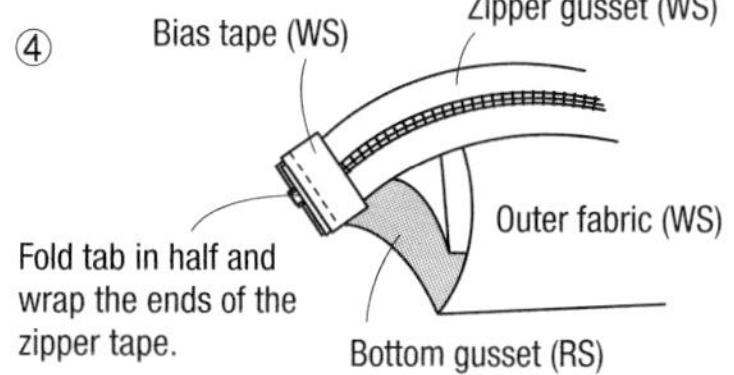

Place the side seam of the zipper gusset over the side seam of the bottom gusset (right sides together). Insert a folded tab between the two and align bias tape along the side seam. Sew them together. Wrap the seam allowance with bias tape and bind.

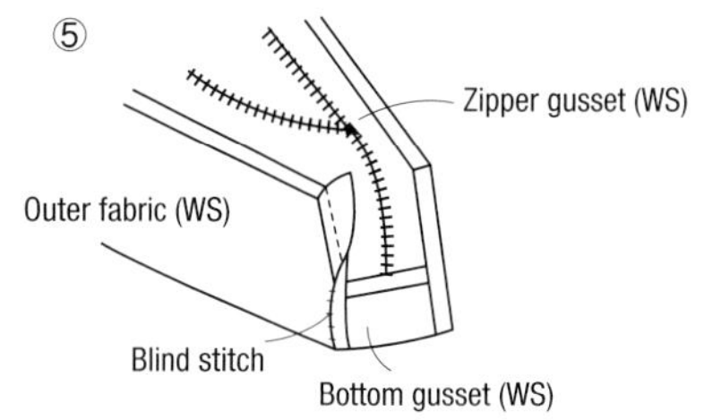

Attach the zipper gusset and the bottom gusset - which were sewn together in ④ - to the body of the pouch. Align bias tape with the seam and sew together. After attaching the gussets to the body of the pouch, wrap the seam with bias tape and bind.

Handles: two pieces

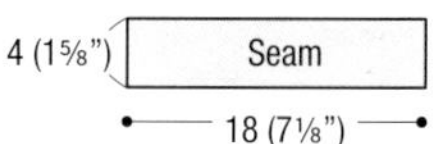

How to Make a Handle

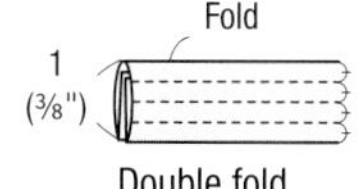

Double fold lengthwise and sew.

Full size patterns

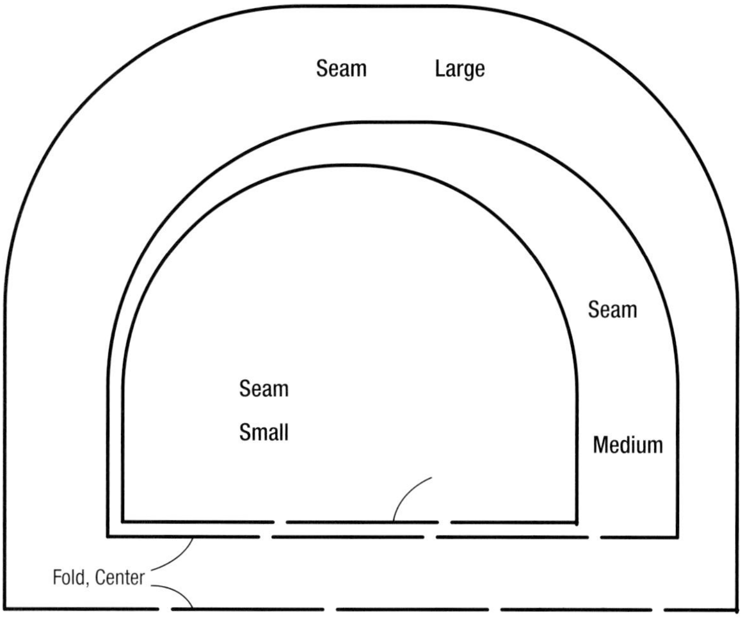

Seam Large

Seam

Seam

Small

Medium

Fold, Center

#5 Shell-shaped, Quilted, Zippered Pouch on page 14

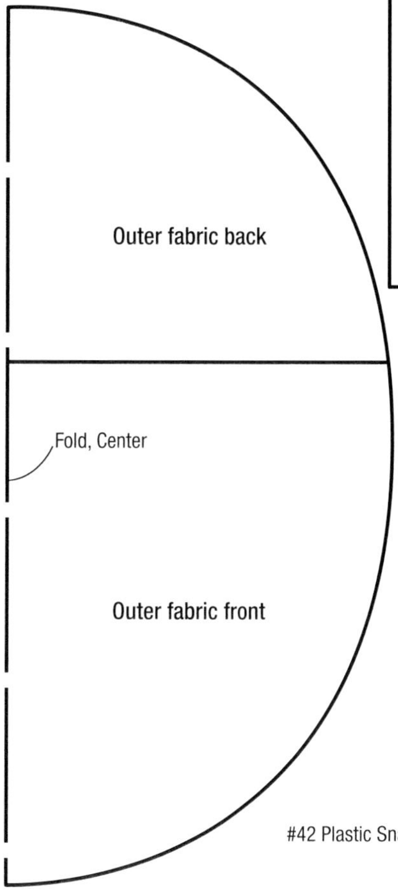

Outer fabric back

Fold, Center

Outer fabric front

#42 Plastic Snap Pouch on page 66

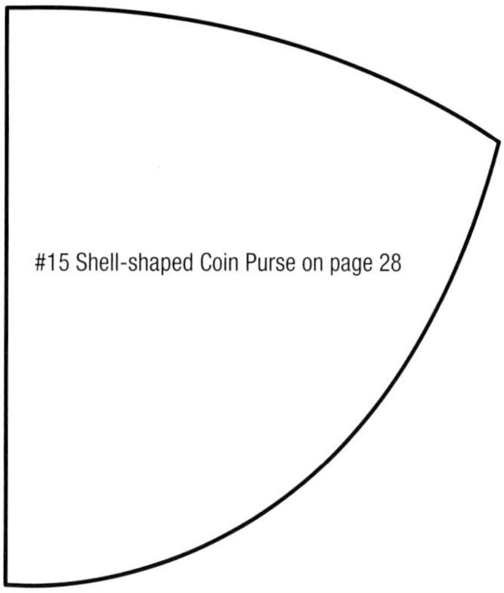

#15 Shell-shaped Coin Purse on page 28

8 Slim Pen Case with Gusset

6.5 x 18 cm (2⅝" x 7⅛")
Design: Sakura Yamamoto

Materials
Outer fabric (including tabs): 30 x 15 cm (11⅞" x 5⅞") / Bottom gusset (including side gussets): 35 x 10 cm (13¾" x 4") / Lining fabric: 30 x 20 cm (11⅞" x 7⅞") / Extra thin fusible batting: 20 x 20 cm (7⅞" x 7⅞") / One zipper: 20 cm (7⅞")

Key points
- It is not necessary to fuse on batting if you use thick fabric.
- When you sew the gusset to the outer fabric, align with the center of the bottom seam. Sew each side seam first and then sew the bottom.

Instructions
1 Assemble the quilt top. After fusing with extra thin fusible batting, quilt as desired.
2 Put the lining and the outer fabric together with the right sides facing each other. Place a zipper between them and sew them together.
3 Sew the gusset to the outer fabric with the right sides together.
4 Do the same for the lining fabric's gusset and leave an opening for turning the gusset.
5 Turn the fabric right side out. Close the opening used for turning. Close mouth of the gusset as well.
6 Attach a tab to both end of the zipper tape.

Outer fabric: one piece

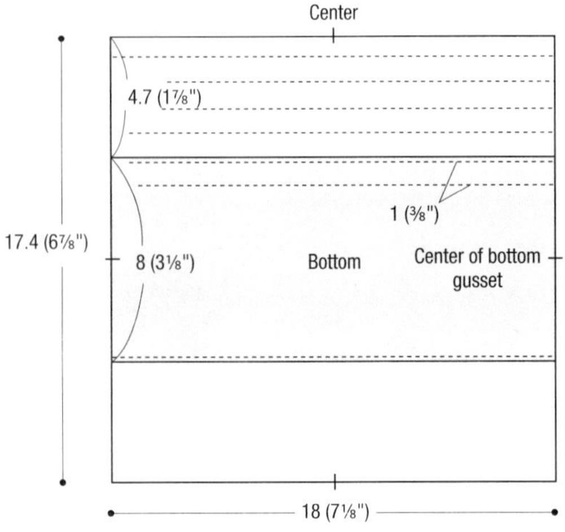

* Prepare lining as indicated above.

Tab: two pieces

Gusset: two pieces

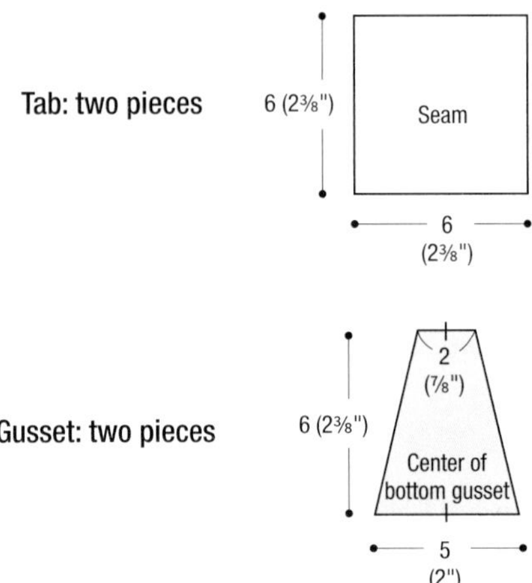

* Prepare lining as indicated above.

Instructions

①

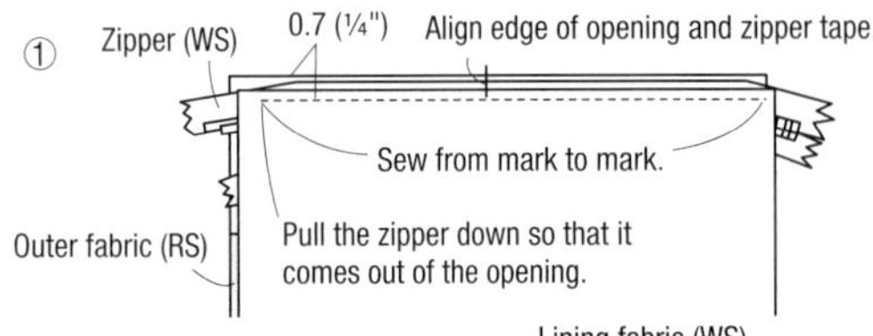

Place the lining fabric on the outer fabric with the right sides together. Place a zipper between the fabrics and sew together from mark to mark. Do the same for the other zipper tape.

②

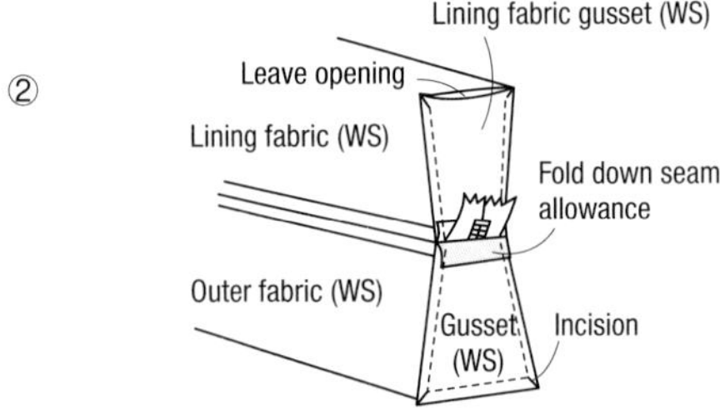

Align the body of the pouch and gusset with the right sides together. Sew side seam, then bottom. Sew lining at the same time. Leave opening for turning.

③

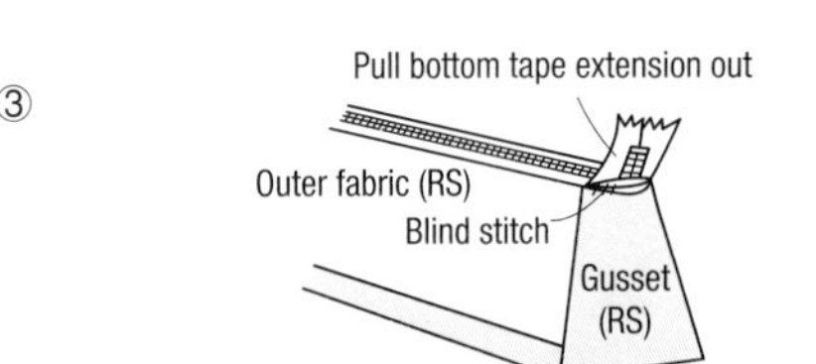

Turn the fabrics right side out. Fold the seam allowance of the opening inward and blind stitch the opening to close. Align the opening of the gusset with the lining fabric and blind stitch to close.

How to Attach a Tab

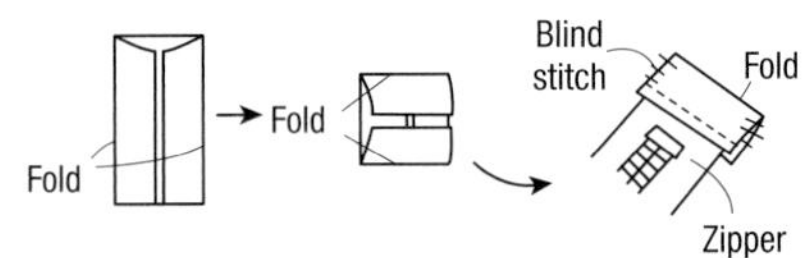

Fold vertically, then fold horizontally.

Wrap zipper tape extension with a tab and bind the edge

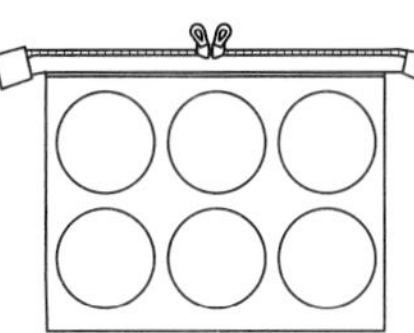

18 x 19.5 cm (7⅛" x 7¾")

Design: Sachiko Ishikawa

9 Appliqué Flat Pouch

Materials

Appliqué fabric 6 pieces: each 10 x 10 cm (4" x 4") / Outer fabric, Fusible batting: each 45 x 20 cm (17¾" x 7⅞") / Lining fabric (including a pocket): 70 x 20 cm (27½" x 7⅞") / 2.5 cm (1") wide bias tape: 50 cm (19¾") / One double slider zipper: 20 cm (7⅞") / Leather (decoration): 5 x 5 cm (2" x 2") / #8 needlework thread

Key points

- Refer to instructions on page 11 for installing zipper.
- Use needlework thread to outline quilting.

Instructions

1 Sew appliqué on quilt top and assemble.
2 Fuse batting on quilt top and quilt as desired.
3 Make a pocket and sew on the lining.
4 Put the lining fabric over the outer fabric (right sides together) and sew side seams and center seam.
5 Turn the fabric right side out, bind piping along the opening of the pouch.
6 Install a zipper on the right side of the outer fabric.
7 Attach a decoration on both ends of the zipper.

Outer fabric: one piece

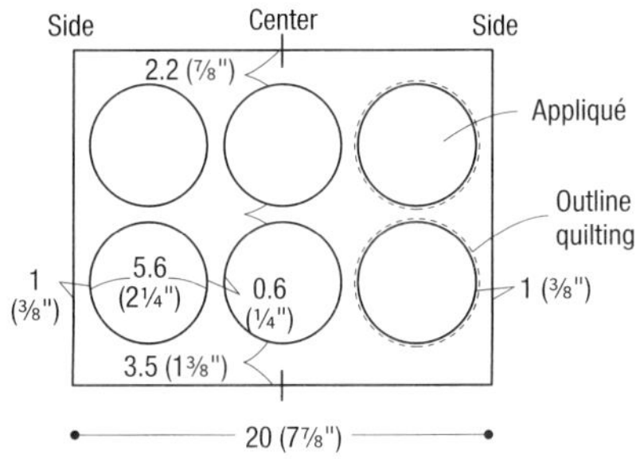

Side
Center
Side
2.2 (⅞")
Appliqué
Outline quilting
1 (⅜")
5.6 (2¼")
0.6 (¼")
1 (⅜")
3.5 (1⅜")
20 (7⅞")

Back of outer fabric: one piece

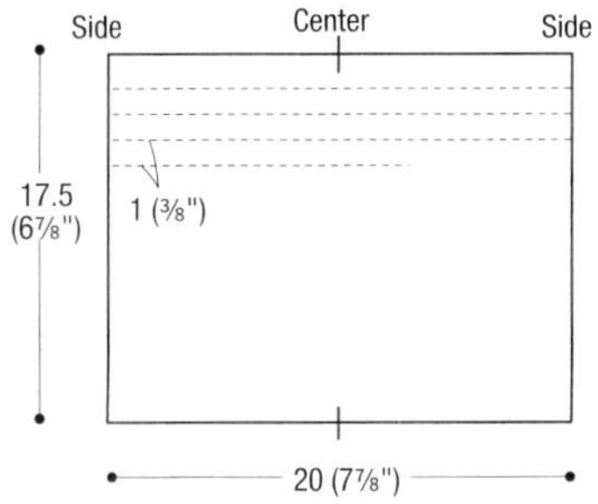

Side
Center
Side
17.5 (6⅞")
1 (⅜")
20 (7⅞")

Lining fabric: two pieces

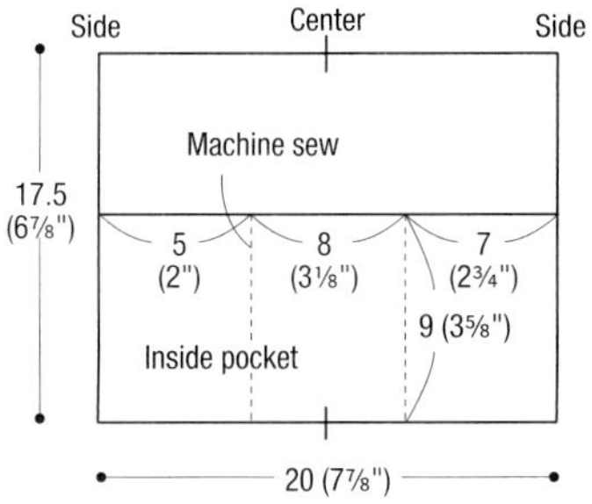

Side
Center
Side
Machine sew
17.5 (6⅞")
5 (2")
8 (3⅛")
7 (2¾")
9 (3⅝")
Inside pocket
20 (7⅞")

* A pocket is attached on one side

Pocket: one piece

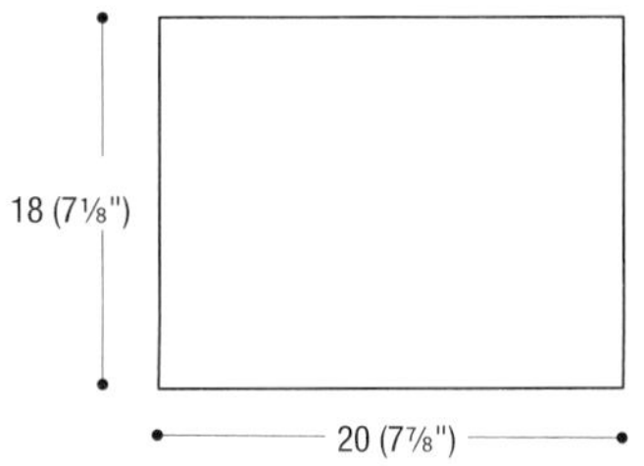

18 (7⅛")
20 (7⅞")

How to Make a Pocket

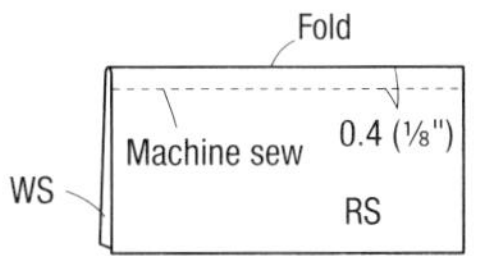

Fold
Machine sew
0.4 (⅛")
WS
RS

Machine sew the raw edge with right sides out.

How to Sew a Running Stitch

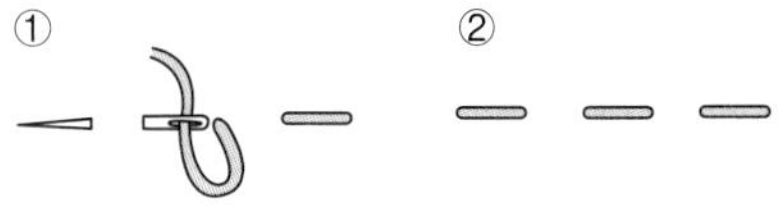

①
②

Instructions

①

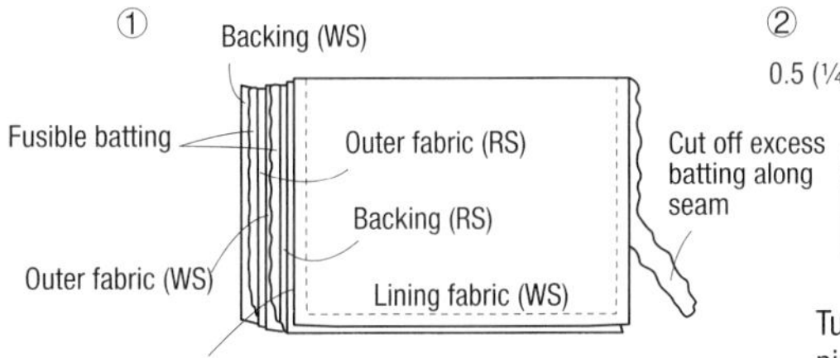

Backing (WS)
Fusible batting
Outer fabric (RS)
Backing (RS)
Outer fabric (WS)
Lining fabric (WS)
Lining fabric (RS)
Cut off excess batting along seam

Put the lining fabric over the outer fabric (right sides together) and sew side seams and center seam.

②

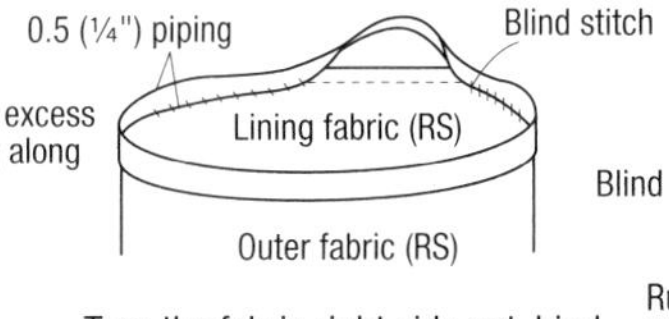

0.5 (¼") piping
Blind stitch
Lining fabric (RS)
Outer fabric (RS)

Turn the fabric right side out, bind piping along opening of the pouch.

③

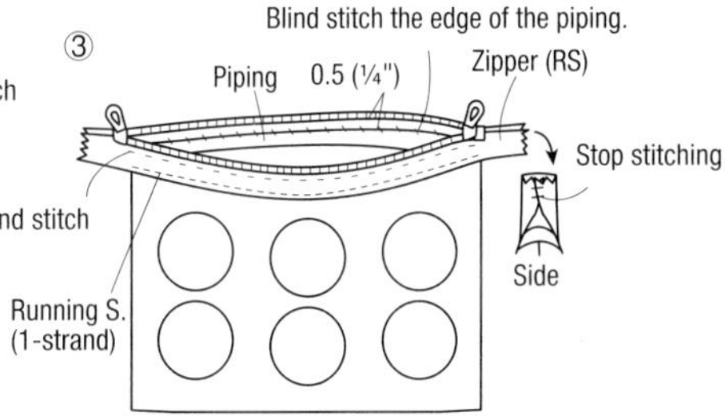

Blind stitch the edge of the piping.
Piping
0.5 (¼")
Zipper (RS)
Stop stitching
Blind stitch
Side
Running S. (1-strand)

Align both edges of the piping and the zipper tape and install a zipper. Fold both top and bottom tape extensions with the wrong sides together.

④

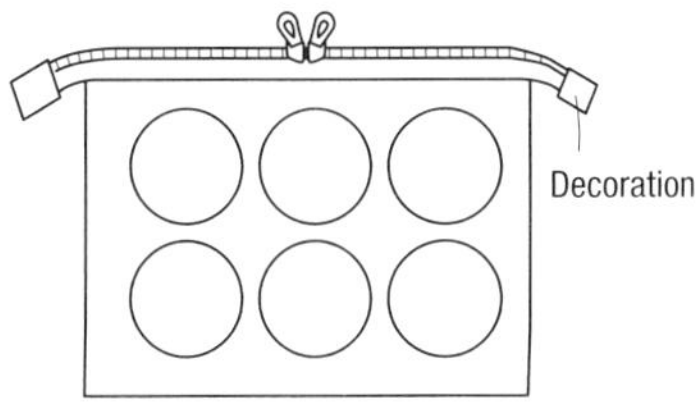

Decoration

Wrap both ends of the zipper tape with a decoration.

Leather (decoration): two pieces

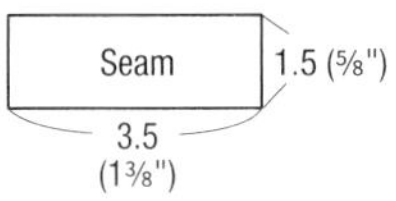

Seam
1.5 (⅝")
3.5 (1⅜")

How to Attach a Decoration

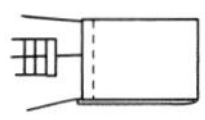

Wrap the end of the zipper tape then bind.

10 Flat Wool Pouch

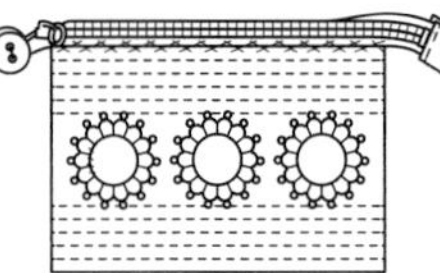

17 x 25.5 cm (6¾" x 10")
Design: Sachiko Ishikawa

Materials
Outer fabric, Fusible batting: each 65 x 25 cm (25⅝" x 9⅞") / Lining fabric (including a pocket): 60 x 50 cm (23⅝" x 19¾") / Felt for appliqué: 25 x 10 cm (9⅞" x 4") / 2.5 cm (1") wide bias tape: 60 cm (23⅝") / Self-covered button fabric: 3 different types each 10 x 10 cm (4" x 4") / Three 4 cm (1⅝") diameter buttons / One zipper: 30 cm (11⅞") / Two 2 cm (⅞") diameter button / 3 cm (1¼") wide leather tape: 5 cm (2") / Approx. 75 pieces of 0.4 cm (⅛") diameter wooden beads / #8 needlework thread

Key points
- Add seam allowance: mouth of pouch 0.5 cm (¼"), sides 0.7 cm (¼").

Instructions
1 Fuse batting to the outer fabric then quilt as desired.
2 Appliqué on the outer fabric and assemble front and back of the outer fabric.
3 Make a pocket and sew it on the lining fabric.
4 Fold both the outer and lining fabric in half separately, with the right sides together. Then put the lining fabric on the outer fabric. Sew both sides and bottom edge.
5 Turn the fabric right side out, bind piping along mouth.
6 Install zipper. The zipper tape is exposed along the edge of the outer fabric.
7 Attach a button on the top zipper tape extension and leather tape on the bottom zipper tape extension. Make self-covered buttons and sew them, as well as wooden beads, on the front of the pouch.

Front outer fabric: one piece / **Back outer fabric: one piece**

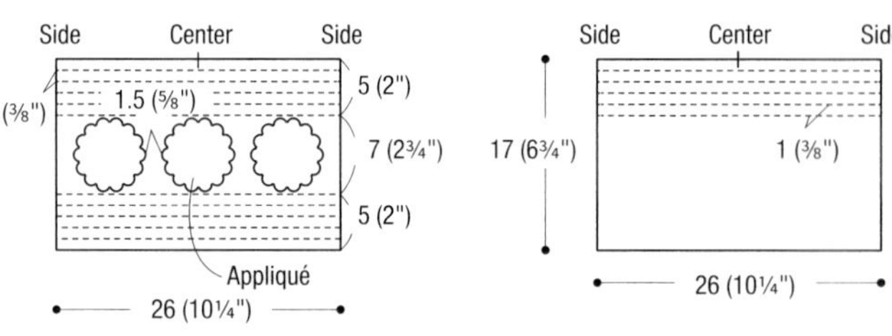

Front lining fabric: one piece / **Back lining fabric: one piece**

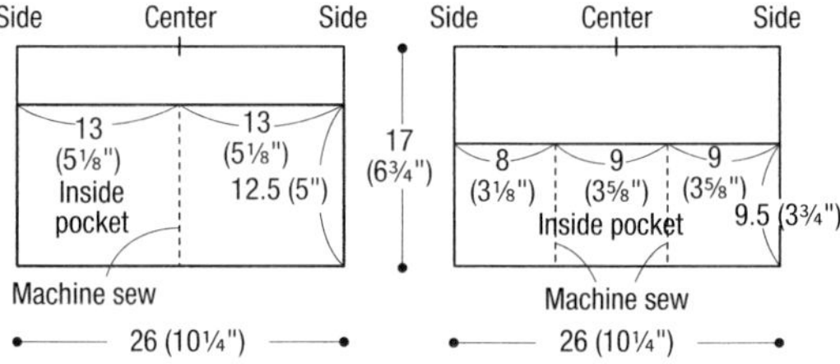

Appliqué: three pieces

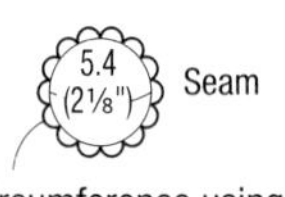

Cut circumference using scalloped pinking shears.

How to Sew on Appliqué

Put a needle at the center then pull thread.

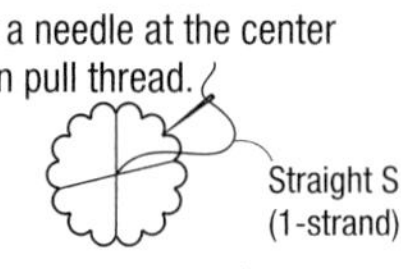

Temporarily secure appliqué on the pouch using craft glue. Stitch.

Front inside pocket: one piece

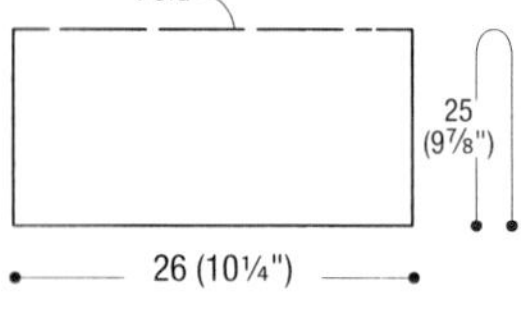

Back inside pocket: one piece

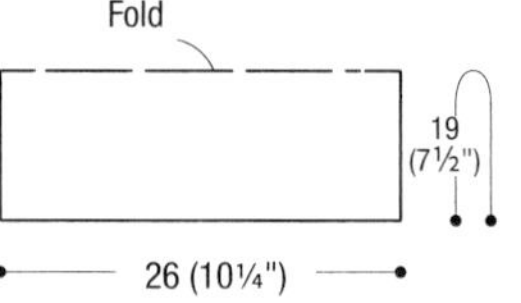

Self-covered button: three pieces

How to Make Self-covered Buttons

How to Straight Stitch

Wrap a button with fabric and running stitch the edge of the fabric. Pull the thread to gather the fabric.

How to Make a Pocket

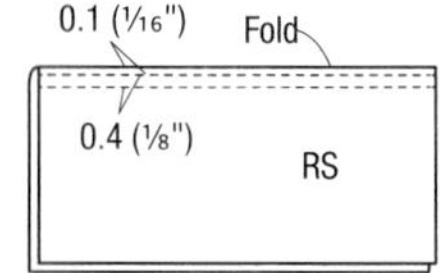

Fold the fabric in half, with right sides out, machine sew along folded edge.

How to Assemble Front Outer Fabric

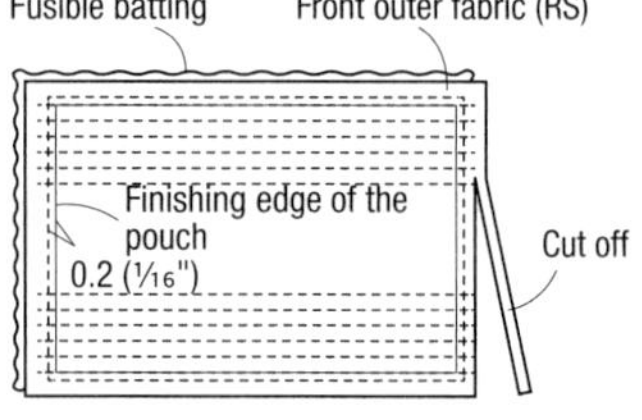

Cut front outer fabric slightly larger than its measurement. Machine sew 0.2 cm (¹⁄₁₆") from finished edge to prevent fraying. After adding seam allowance, cut off excess fabric.

Instructions

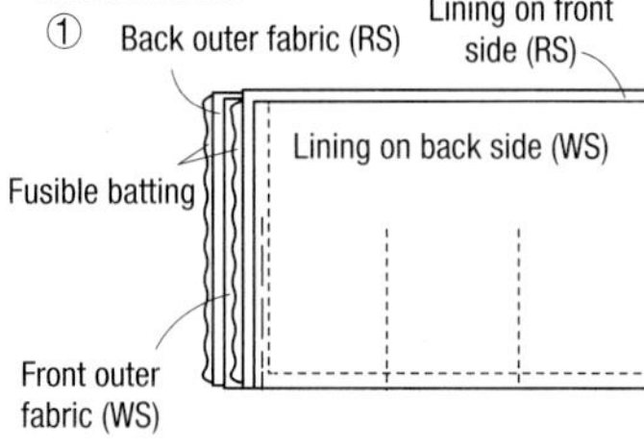

Fold both the outer and lining fabric in half separately, with the right sides together. Overlay the lining fabric on the outer fabric. Sew both sides and the bottom.

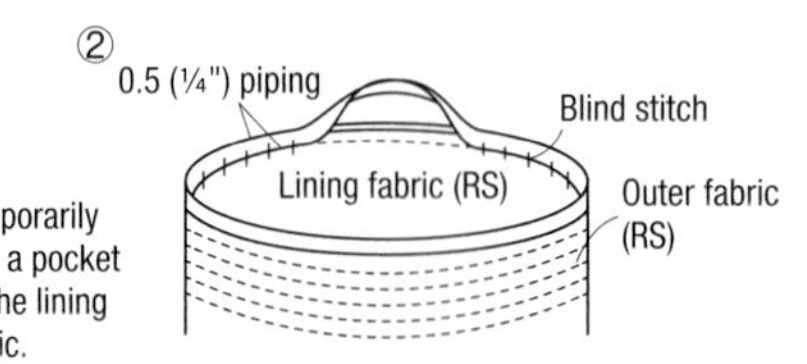

Turn the fabric right side out, bind piping along the mouth of the pouch.

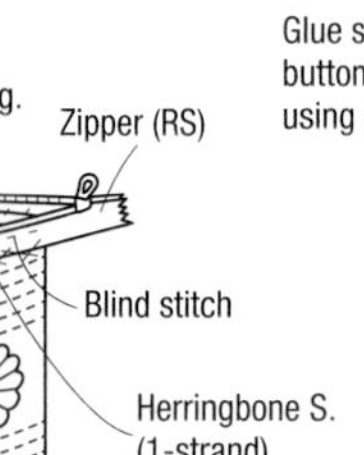

Align the edge of the piping and the edge of the zipper tape. Install zipper manually. Fold down top zipper tape extension and whip stitch the edges.

④
Buttons
Machine sew
Fold
3 (1¼")
2 (⅞")
Glue self-covered buttons on the pouch using craft glue.
Leather tape
Wooden beads
Blind stitch

Glue a button on each side of the folded top zipper tape extension of the zipper. Cover bottom zipper tape extension with leather tape and bind. Glue wooden beads and covered buttons on front of the pouch.

12 Hat-shaped Pouch Made from Six Fabric Scraps

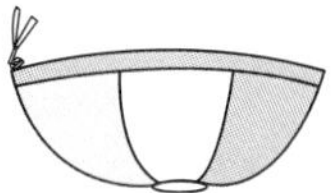

5.5 x 12 cm (2⅛" x 4¾")
Design: Naomi Sato

Materials
Outer fabric: 6 pieces each 10 x 10 cm (4 x 4") / Lining fabric: 35 x 10 cm (13¾" x 4") / Extra thin fusible batting: 25 x 10 cm (9⅞" x 4") / 3.5 cm (1⅜") wide bias tape: 25 cm (9⅞") / One zipper: 20 cm (7⅞") / One 1.1 cm (⅜") diameter button / 0.5 cm (¼") wide ribbon: 10 cm (4")

Key points
- Add 0.5 cm (¼") seam allowance.
- When you cut the batting, add a seam allowance only to the mouth of the pouch. You can use adhesive interfacing instead. If you use interfacing, add a seam allowance to all sides.
- Use a Flatknit®-type zipper and cut off excess zipper tape after installing.

Instructions
1 Fuse extra thin batting on all 6 pieces of the outer fabric. Join them together. Do the same for the lining fabric.
2 Fuse extra thin batting on the bias tape and sew both ends together making a loop. Fold lengthwise in half.
3 With the right side facing down, align the bias tape along the edge of the outer fabric. Sew.
4 With the right side facing down, align the zipper tape along the bias tape and sew on the zipper.
5 Blind stitch the lining fabric inside the outer fabric.
6 Sew a button at the bottom of the pouch. Attach a ribbon on the zipper slider.

Outer fabric: six pieces

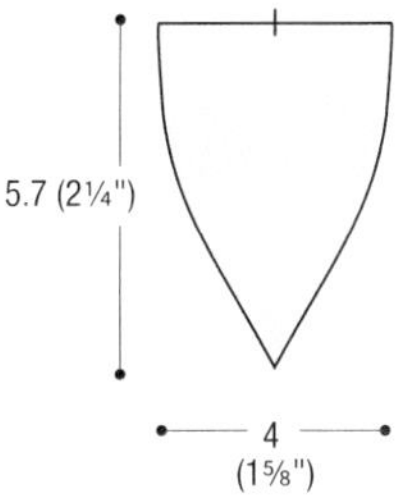

5.7 (2¼")
4 (1⅝")

* Prepare lining as indicated above.

Bias tape: one piece

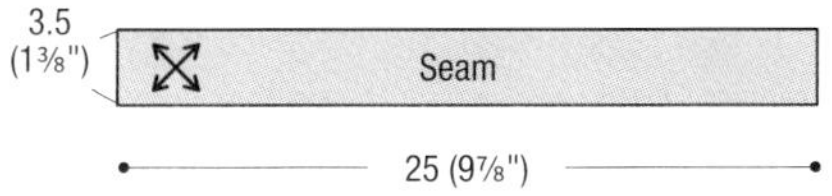

3.5 (1⅜")
Seam
25 (9⅞")

How to Make Bias Tape

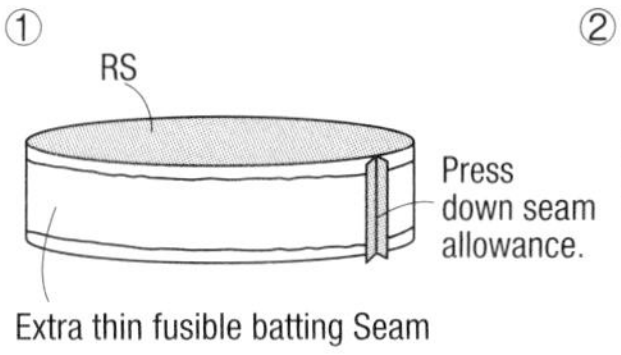

① RS
Press down seam allowance.
Extra thin fusible batting Seam
Make a loop

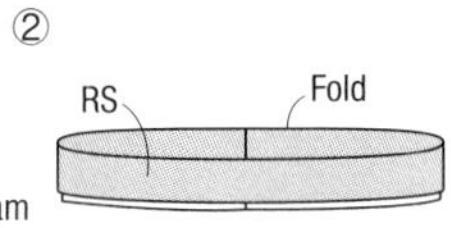

② RS
Fold
Fold lengthwise in half.

How to Assemble Outer and Lining Fabrics

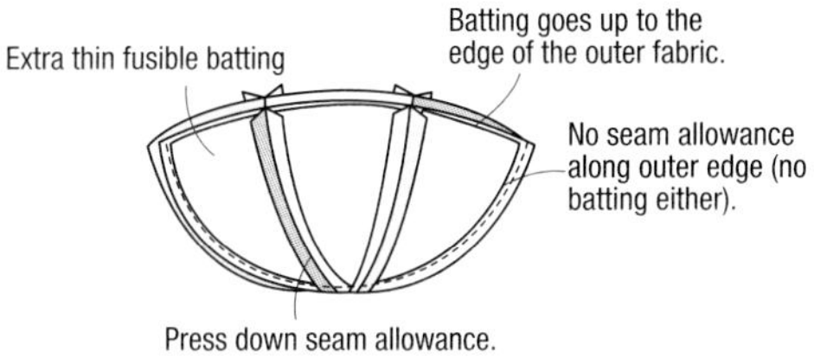

Extra thin fusible batting
Batting goes up to the edge of the outer fabric.
No seam allowance along outer edge (no batting either).
Press down seam allowance.

After fusing the extra thin batting, join 6 pieces of the fabric with right sides facing together.

Instructions

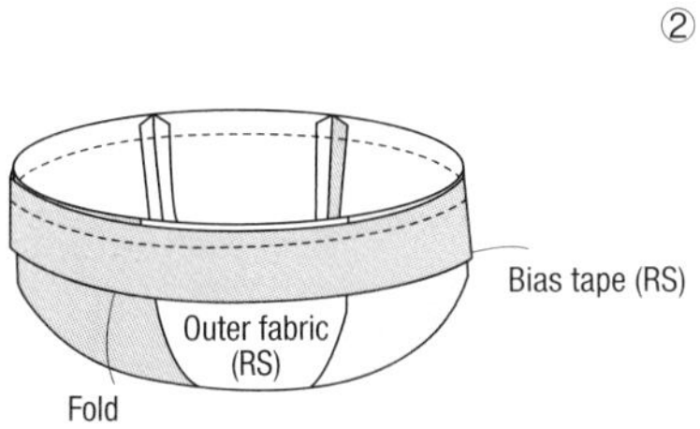

①
Bias tape (RS)
Outer fabric (RS)
Fold

With the right side facing down, align the bias tape along the edge of the outer fabric. Sew.

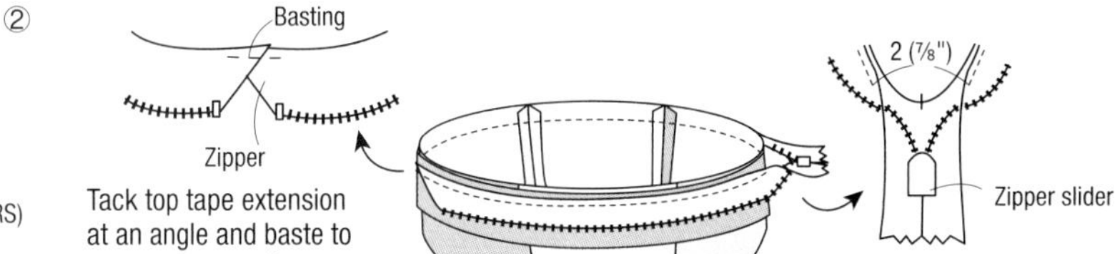

②
Basting
Zipper
Tack top tape extension at an angle and baste to secure temporarily.
2 (⅞")
Zipper slider

Align the zipper tape along the bias tape and sew on the zipper over the stitch that binds the bias tape.

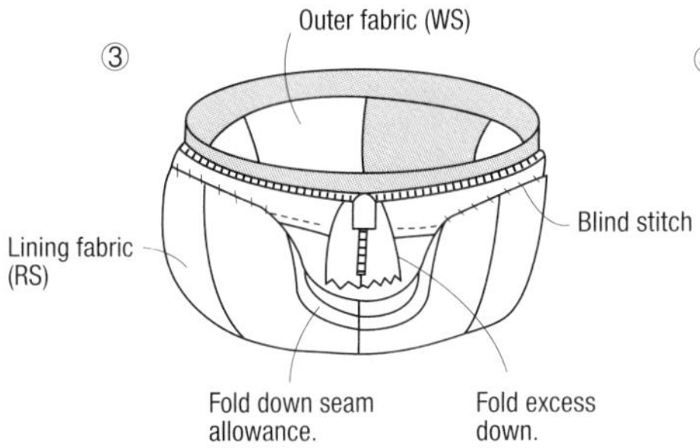

③
Outer fabric (WS)
Lining fabric (RS)
Blind stitch
Fold down seam allowance.
Fold excess down.

Fold down seam allowance on the lining fabric. With the wrong sides facing together, align the lining with the outer fabric. And, blind stitch the lining onto the zipper tape.

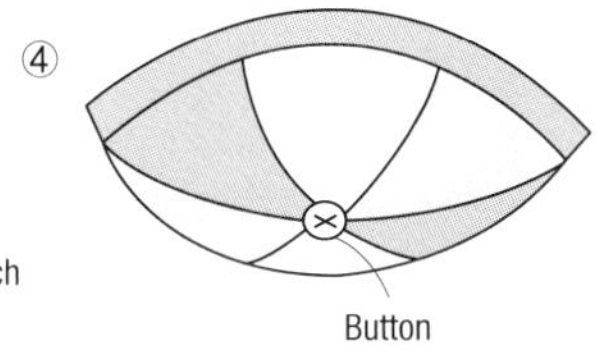

④
Button

Attach a button at the bottom putting the needle through to the lining fabric.

How to Attach a Ribbon on the Zipper Slider Pull

①
Zipper slider
Ribbon: 7 cm (2¾")

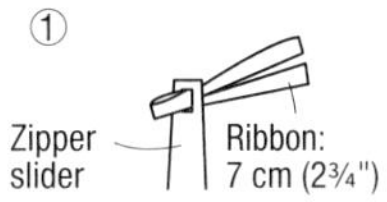

Put the folded end of the ribbon through the hole on the zipper slider pull.

②
Fold

Put the loose end of the ribbon through the folded end and tighten.

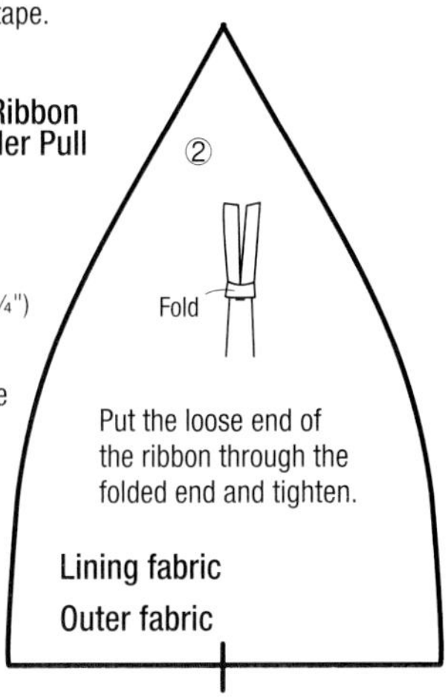

Full size pattern

Lining fabric
Outer fabric

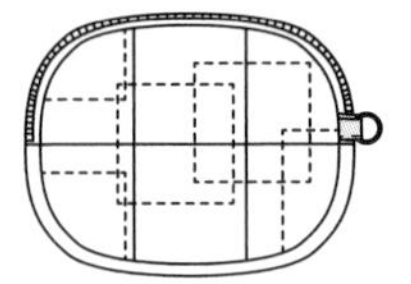

8.5 x 11 cm (3⅜" x 4⅜")
Design: Shigeyo Nakayama

13 Oval-shaped Mini Pouch

Materials

Outer fabric: 6 pieces each 15 x 10 cm (5⅞" x 4") / Gusset: 20 x 5 cm (7⅞" x 2⅜") / Loop: 5 x 5 cm (2" x 2") / Batting, Backing: each 30 x 20 cm (11⅞" x 7⅞") / One zipper: 15 cm (6") / One O-ring: inner diameter 1 cm (⅜")

Key points

- Use variegated thread to create interesting effects on your quilting.
- Attach a strap to the O-ring if you desire.

Instructions

1 Assemble the outer fabric by piecing. The outer fabric of the zipper gusset uses plain fabric.
2 Fuse batting on the wrong side of each outer fabric. Lay outer fabric flat on the backing fabric, then baste. Quilt as desired.
3 Make a zipper gusset.
4 Make a loop of fabric, then temporarily secure to the outer fabric.
5 With the right sides together, put the zipper gusset on the outer fabric. Sew along the circumference.
6 Cover the seam of the backing fabric, on the zipper gusset, with zipper tape. Sew.

Outer fabric: two pieces

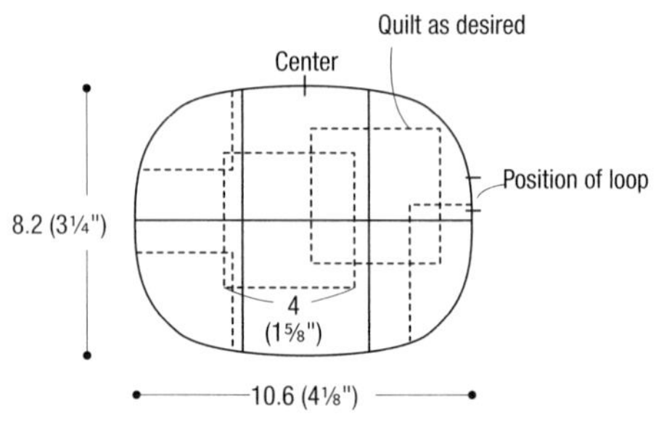

Loop: one piece

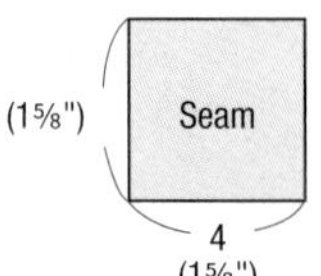

How to Make a Fabric Loop

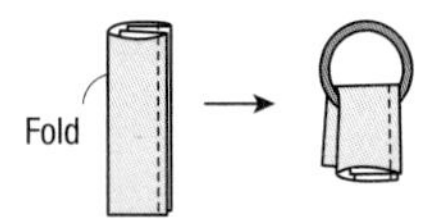

Fold the fabric while aligning the right and left edged at the center. Fold again along the center. Pass a ring through.

Gusset: one piece

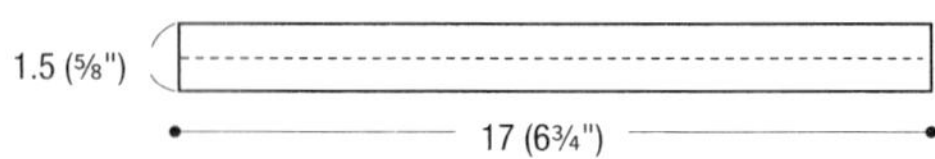

How to Make a Zippered-gusset

①

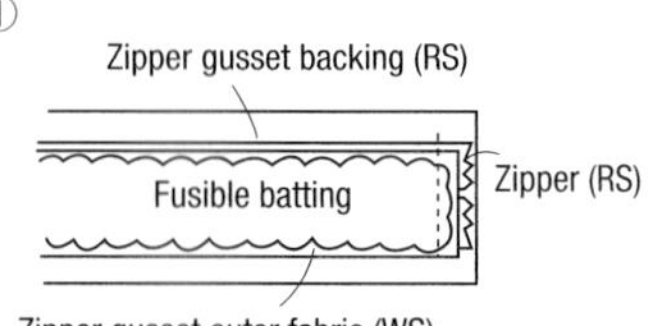

Fuse batting on the wrong side of the zipper gusset outer fabric. With the right sides together, put a zipper on the backing fabric and put the zipper gusset over that - right side down. Sew the sides together to make a loop. Note: make seam allowance of the backing fabric slightly wider than normal.

②

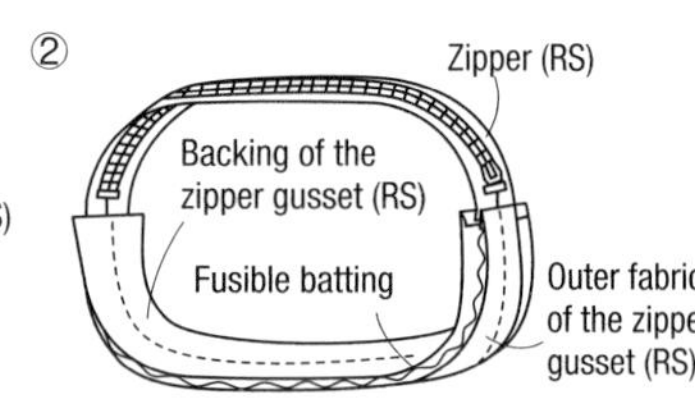

Turn the fabric right side out. Quilt along center of the zipper gusset.

Full size pattern

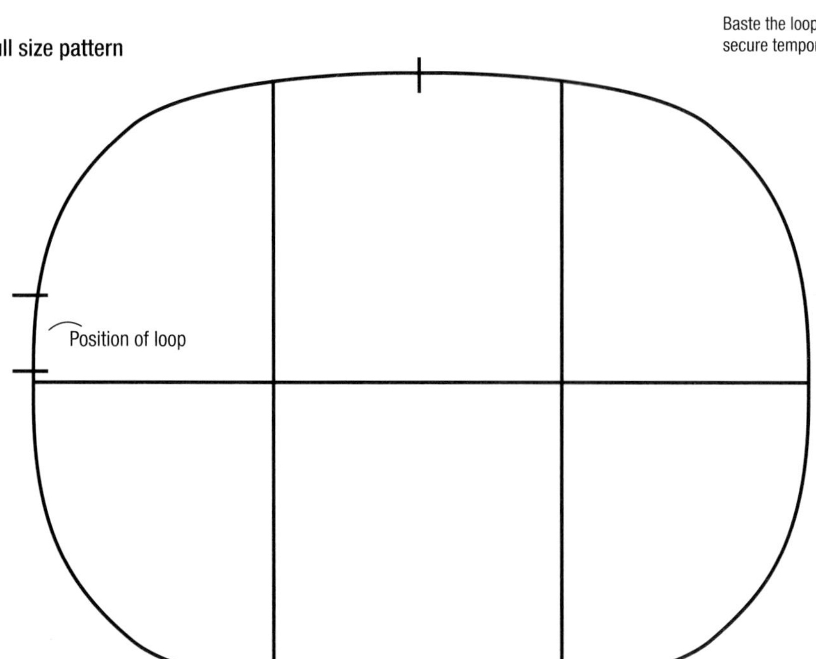

Instructions

①

With the right sides together, align the outer fabric and the zipper gusset. Insert the loop between them and sew circumference.

②

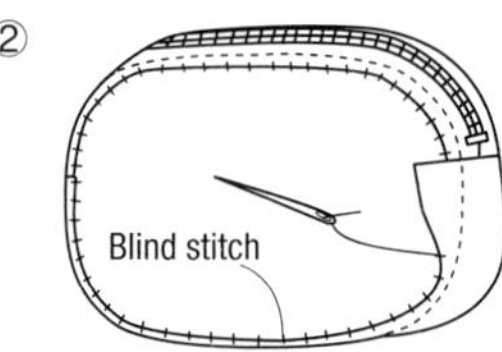

Cut off excess seam allowance on the outer fabric. Cover seam with backing fabric and zipper tape to bind.

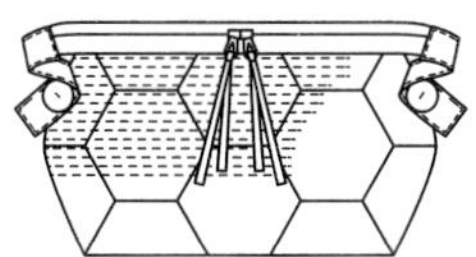

15 x 25 cm (5⅞" x 9⅞")

Design: Chizuko Kojima

- Full size patterns are on page 95.

18 Colorful Hexagon Patchwork Pouch

Materials

Various fabric pieces for paper piecing and self-covered button / Lining fabric, Fusible batting: each 60 x 60 cm (23⅝" x 23⅝") / Fabric for zipper tape decoration: 20 x 10 cm (7⅞" x 4") / Double slider invisible zipper: one piece, 30 cm (11⅞") / Two 2.3 cm (⅞") diameter buttons / 0.7 cm (¼") wide ribbon: 50 cm (19¾")

Key points

- After joining the outer and lining fabric, make an incision at the seam allowance in the corners.
- You can use bias cut fabric for a zipper decoration instead of a ribbon.

Instructions

1 Assemble outer fabric using by piecing.
2 Fuse batting to the wrong side of the outer fabric, then quilt as desired.
3 With the right sides together, fold the lining fabric in half. Sew the bottom edge leaving an opening for turning.
4 Place lining fabric on outer, right sides together, and join. Turn right side out using the opening. Then close the opening.
5 Join the edges by matching up the corresponding marks on the diagram.
6 Attach a piece of fabric on both zipper tape extensions.
7 Install a zipper along the mouth of the pouch.
8 Make self-covered buttons and sew on the cover of the zipper tape extension. Attach a ribbon to both zipper sliders.

Outer fabric: one piece

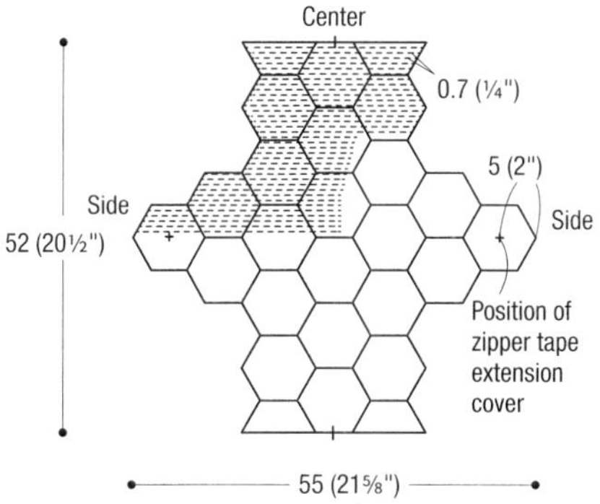

Center
0.7 (¼")
5 (2")
Side
Side
52 (20½")
Position of zipper tape extension cover
55 (21⅝")

Lining fabric: two pieces

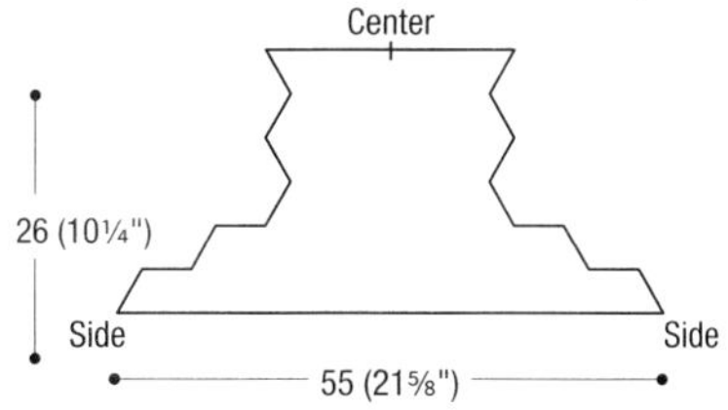

Center
26 (10¼")
Side
Side
55 (21⅝")

Fabric to cover button: two pieces

4.5 (1¾")
Seam

Zipper tape extension cover: two pieces

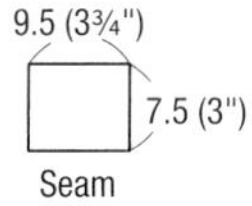

9.5 (3¾")
7.5 (3")
Seam

How to Make a Self-covered Button

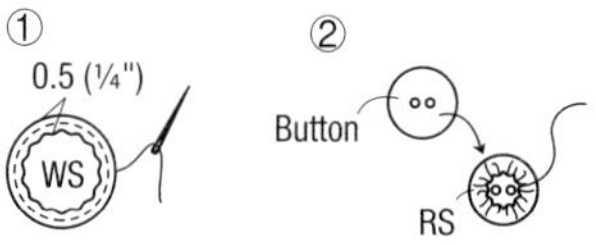

① 0.5 (¼") WS
Fold down the edge of the fabric and running stitch the circumference.

② Button RS
Cover button with fabric and pull the thread to gather the fabric.

Instructions

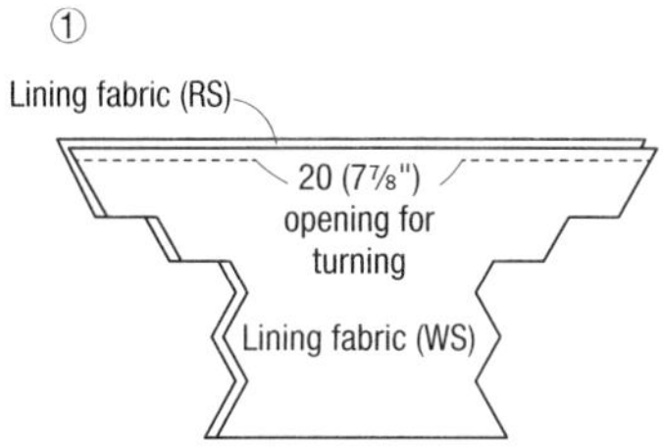

① Lining fabric (RS) 20 (7⅞") opening for turning Lining fabric (WS)
With the right sides together, fold the lining fabric in half. Sew the bottom edge leaving an opening for turning.

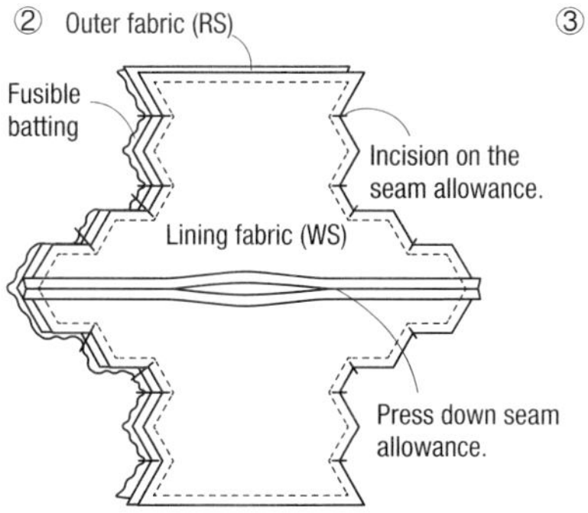

② Outer fabric (RS) Fusible batting Incision on the seam allowance. Lining fabric (WS) Press down seam allowance.
With the right sides together, join the outer and lining fabric.

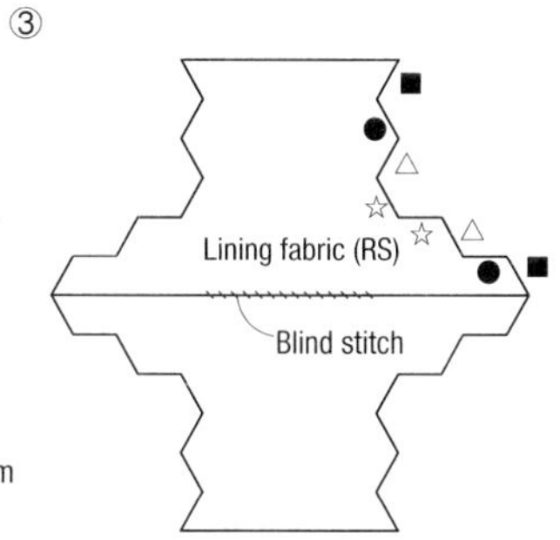

③ Lining fabric (RS) Blind stitch
Turn the fabric right side out, then close the opening.

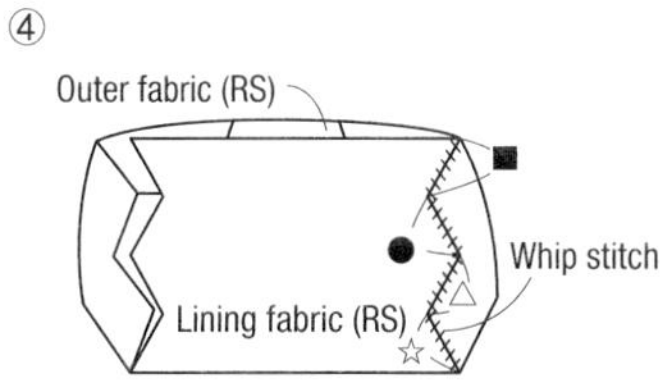

④ Outer fabric (RS) Whip stitch Lining fabric (RS)
With the right sides together, join the outer edges of the hexagon by matching up corresponding marks.

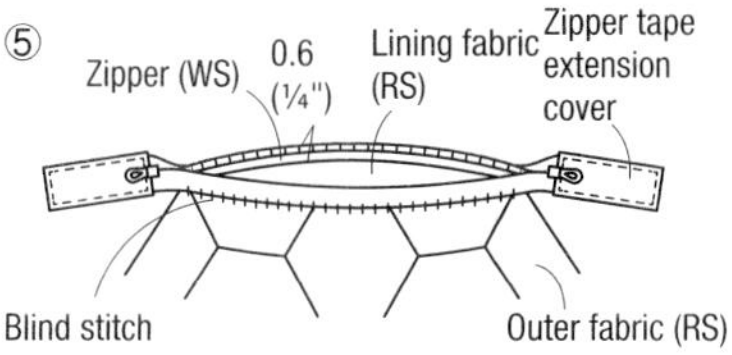

⑤ Zipper (WS) 0.6 (¼") Lining fabric (RS) Zipper tape extension cover Blind stitch Outer fabric (RS)
Cover both ends of the zipper tape with fabric. Pull the ends outside and sew onto body of the pouch.

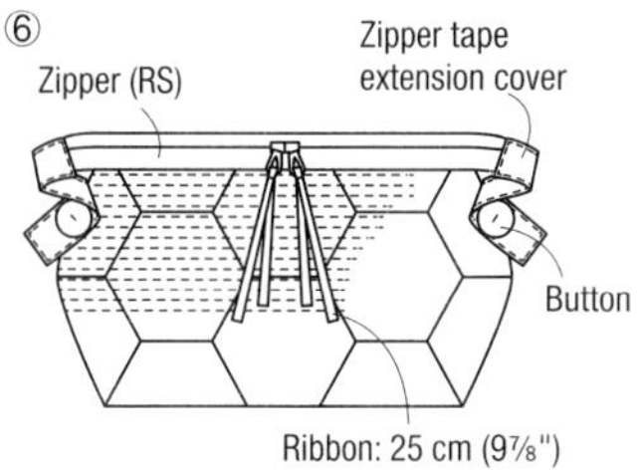

⑥ Zipper (RS) Zipper tape extension cover Button Ribbon: 25 cm (9⅞")
Sew on the zipper tape extension cover onto the pouch with a button. Put a ribbon through the zipper sliders and tie off.

Instructions

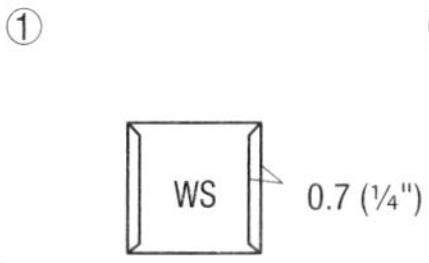

① WS 0.7 (¼")
Fold both edges

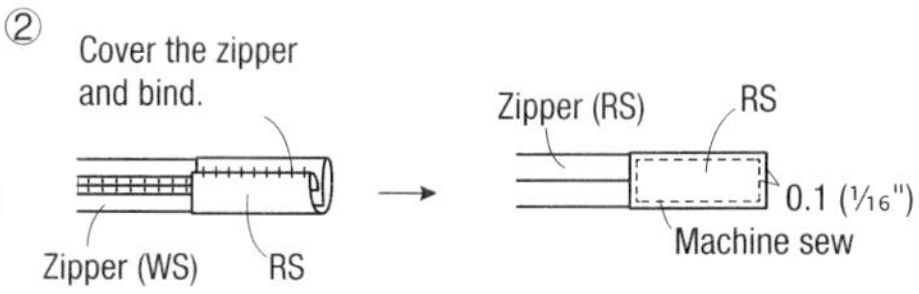

② Cover the zipper and bind. Zipper (WS) RS → Zipper (RS) RS 0.1 (1/16") Machine sew
Cover both ends of the zipper tape with fabric and bind.

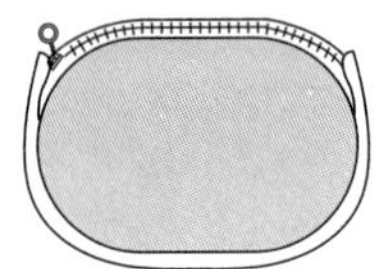

6.5 x 10 cm (2⅝" x 4")
Design: Noriko Hosoo

• Full size patterns are on page 95.

14 Whip-stitched Easy-to-Make Coin Purse with a Key Case

Materials

Front of the case, Pockets: each 15 x 10 cm (4⅞" x 4") / Back of the case (including a loop, a self-covered button, pocket's lining), / Lining of the case (including gusset's lining): each 25 x 15 cm (9⅞" x 5⅞") / Gusset: 25 x 5 cm (9⅞" x 2") / Fusible batting: 40 x 15 cm (15¾" x 5⅞") / One 1.5 cm (⅝") diameter button / One 1 cm (⅜") diameter magnetic snap / One zipper: 12 cm (4¾")

Key points

- When joining the case and the gusset, whip stitch the right sides of both fabrics to join.

Instructions

1 Join the outer and lining fabric of each component: front, back, pocket, and gusset.
2 Make a fabric loop and a self-covered button.
3 Join the gusset to the front and back of the case.
4 Install a zipper.
5 Attach fabric loop and magnetic snap socket on back of the case.
6 Install magnetic snap stud on the pocket. Join the pocket to the back of the case by whip stitching along the edge of the gusset.

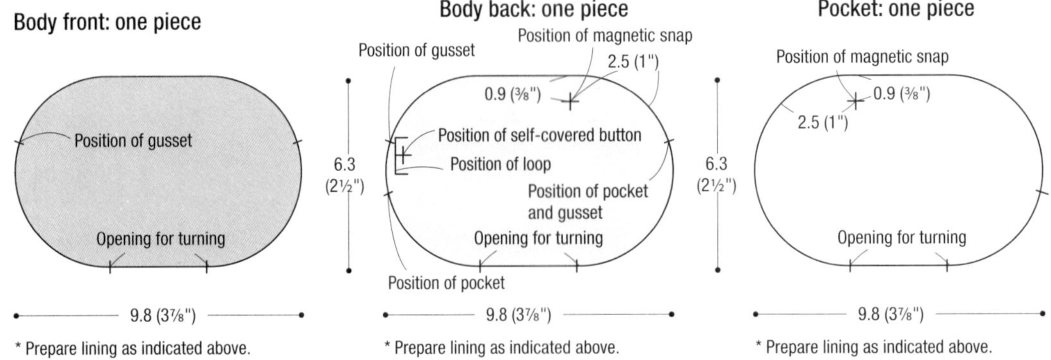

* Prepare lining as indicated above.

* Prepare lining as indicated above.

* Prepare lining as indicated above.

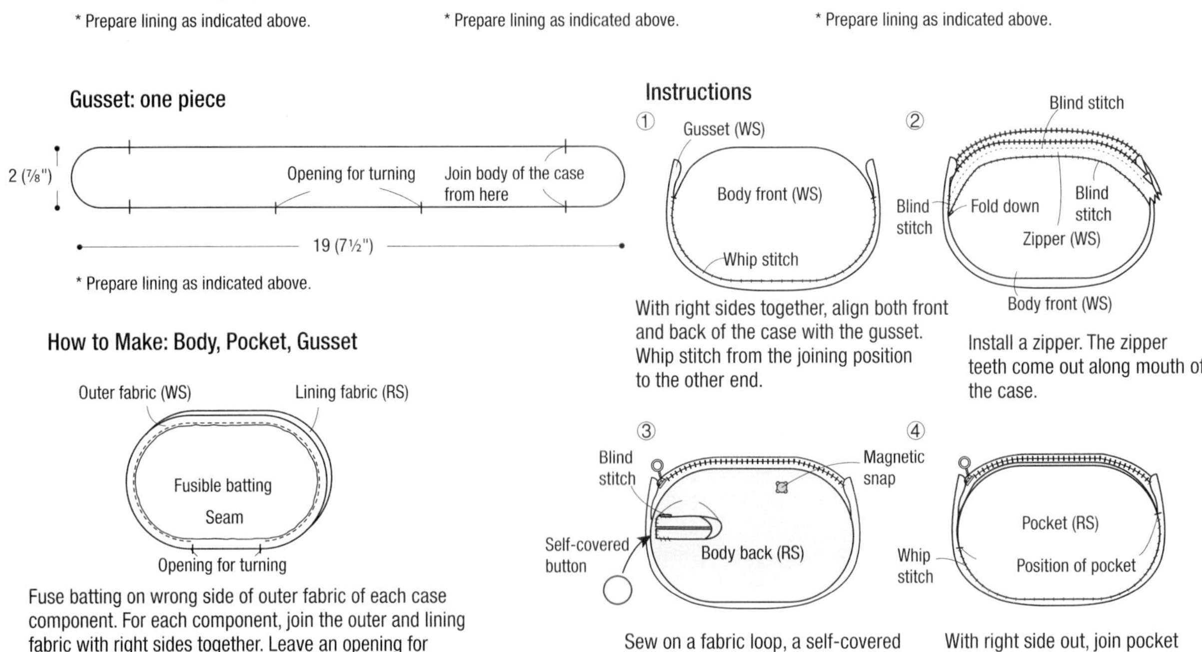

* Prepare lining as indicated above.

Fuse batting on wrong side of outer fabric of each case component. For each component, join the outer and lining fabric with right sides together. Leave an opening for turning. Turn the fabric right side out, then blind stitch the opening to close.

① With right sides together, align both front and back of the case with the gusset. Whip stitch from the joining position to the other end.

② Install a zipper. The zipper teeth come out along mouth of the case.

③ Sew on a fabric loop, a self-covered button, and magnetic snap socket.

④ With right side out, join pocket to the back of the case.

Fabric loop: one piece

2.5 (1")
Seam
10 (4")

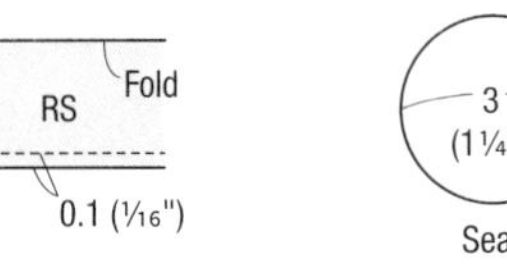

Double fold then sew.

How to Make Self-covered Button

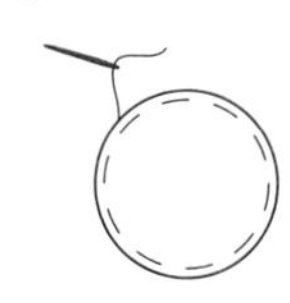

Running stitch the circumference

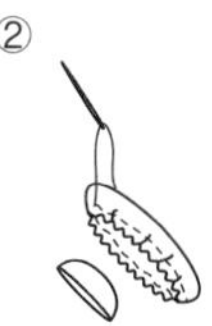

Cover button with fabric and pull the thread to gather the fabric.

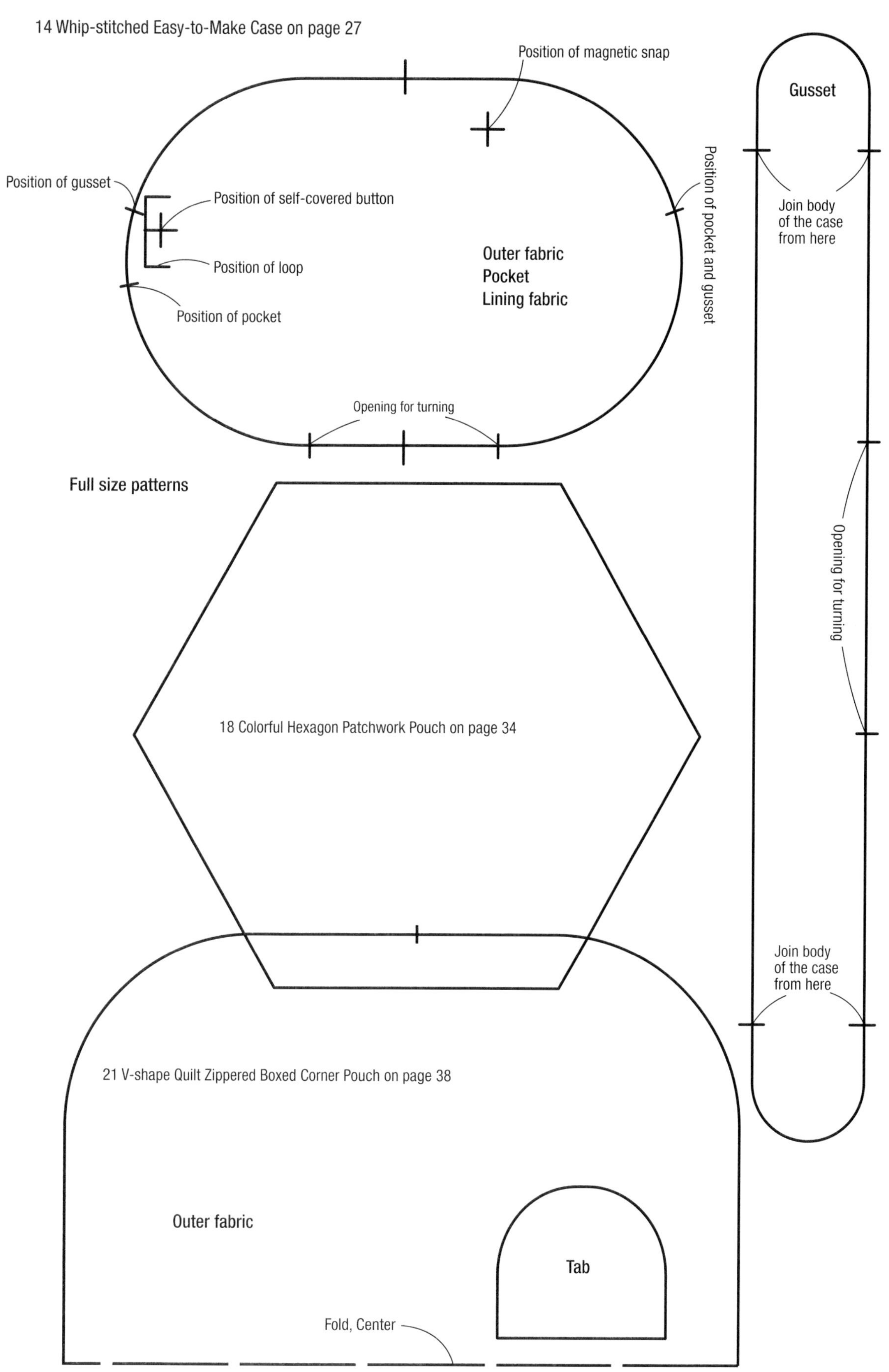
14 Whip-stitched Easy-to-Make Case on page 27
Position of magnetic snap
Gusset
Position of gusset
Position of self-covered button
Position of pocket and gusset
Join body of the case from here
Outer fabric
Pocket
Lining fabric
Position of loop
Position of pocket
Opening for turning
Full size patterns
Opening for turning
18 Colorful Hexagon Patchwork Pouch on page 34
Join body of the case from here
21 V-shape Quilt Zippered Boxed Corner Pouch on page 38
Outer fabric
Tab
Fold, Center

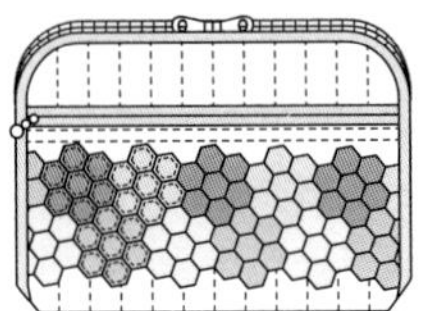

31.5 x 21.5 cm (12⅜" x 8½")
Design: Sachiko Ishikawa
• Full size patterns are on page 97.

19 Hexagonal Flower Pouch

Materials
Various fabrics for appliqué / Pouch Fabric A: 35 x 20 cm (13¾" x 7⅞") / Pouch Fabric B: 35 x 10 cm (13¾" x 4") / Pouch Fabric C (incl. piping at bottom): 70 x 60 cm (27½" x 23⅝") / Back pocket: 35 x 20 cm (13¾" x 7⅞") / Lining fabric (including inside pocket): 75 x 55 cm (29½" x 21⅝") / Backing, Batting: 70 x 40 cm (27½" x 15¾") / One double slider zipper: 36 cm (14¼") / One zipper: 30 cm (11⅞") / False bottom: 30 x 5 cm (11⅞" x 2")

Key points
- For a beautiful finish use English Paper Piece method (see p. 37) for the appliqué.
- After attaching appliqué on Fabric B, cut off Fabric B where the appliqué overlaps if you wish to make it easier to quilt.
- It will look good if you quilt according to the pattern printed on your fabric.

Instructions
1 Assemble outer fabric for Fabric B and C. The outer of the bottom gusset for Fabric A is plain fabric.
2 For Fabric A, B, and C, fuse backing and quilt the top using double-sided fusible batting. Quilt as desired.
3 Sew piping along the bottom edge of Fabric A and top edge of Fabric B. Install a zipper to assemble Fabric A and B for the front of the pouch.
4 Sew piping along the top edge of the back pocket fabric.
5 Join the front of the pouch, the bottom gusset, and the back of the pouch. Assemble back pocket at the same time.
6 Make an inside pocket then sew it on the lining fabric.
7 Fold the lining fabric along the folding line indicated on the diagram with the right side out. Machine sew to join the lining fabric with the outer fabric.
8 Sew piping along the circumference.
9 Install a zipper along the mouth of the pouch. Whip stitch to join both side seams, from the end of the zipper down to the bottom.
10 Join bottom gusset to the side seam of the pouch. After joining, bind bias tape along joined seam.
11 Insert a false bottom

Fabric A: one piece
Side / Center / Side
5 (2") / 2.4 (1") Fabric A / 0.7 (¼") wide piping / Front pocket top edge / 30 (11⅞")

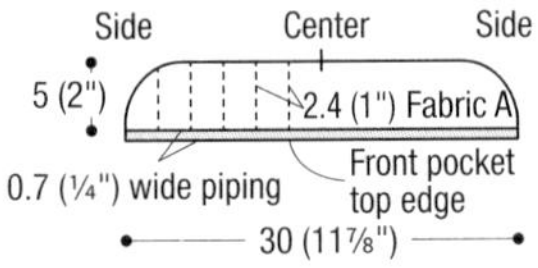

Fabric B: one piece
Front pocket lower edge / Fabric B / 0.7 (¼") wide piping / Side / Center / Side
0.2 (1⁄16") / 1.5 (⅝") / 14.5 (5¾") / Appliqué / 3.5 (1⅜") / 11 (4⅜") / Quilt to match the quilt design on Fabric A
0.3 (⅛") / 1.3 (½") / 1.5 (⅝") / 2.4 (1") / Outline quilting / 30 (11⅞")

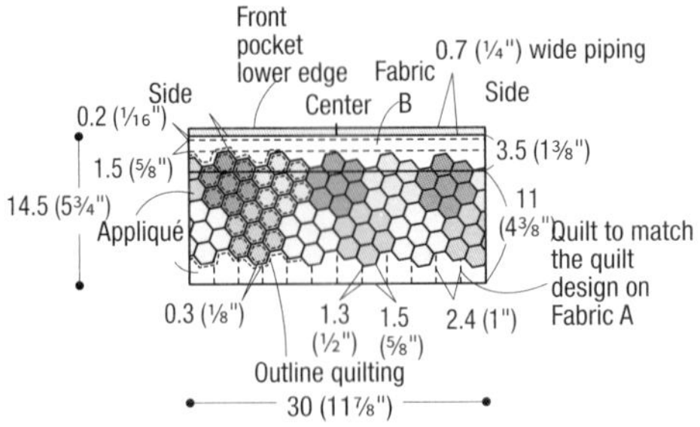

Fabric C: one piece
30 (11⅞") / Side / Center / Side
2.4 (1") / 16 (6⅜") / Fabric C / Fabric A / 5 (2") / 21 (8¼") / Outline quilting

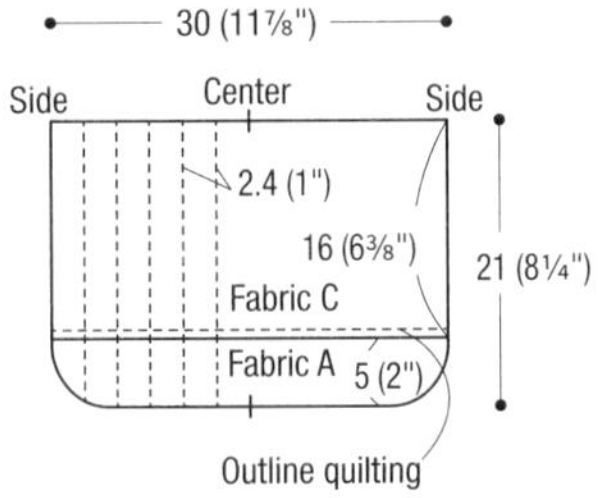

Bottom gusset: one piece
1.5 (⅝") / Center / 1 (⅜") / 1 (⅜") / 3.5 (1⅜") / 28 (11")

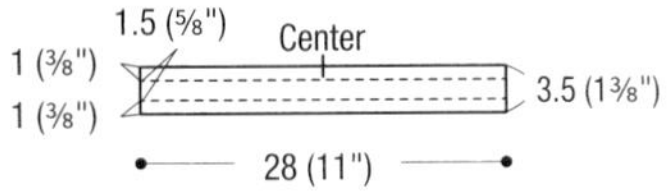

False bottom: one piece
3.5 (1⅜") / 26 (10¼")

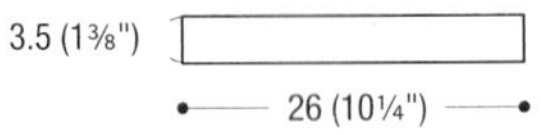

Pocket: one piece
Side / Side / 0.7 (¼") wide piping / 16 (3⅜") / Tulle fabric / Center / 30 (11⅞")

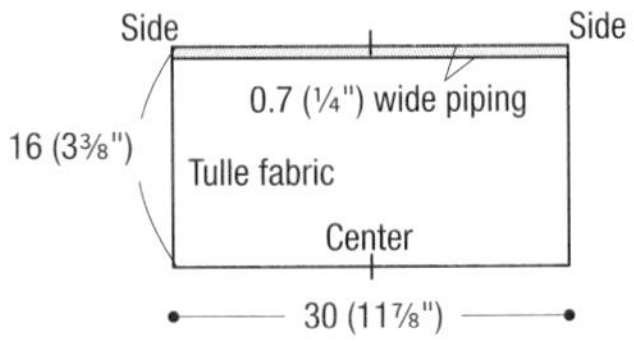

Lining fabric: one piece
Side / Center / Side
Seam / 21.7 (8½") / Folding line / 68.5 (27")
Inside pocket / 16 (6⅜") / 0.2 (1⁄16") / 14 (5½") / Opening / 6 (2⅜") / 33 (13")

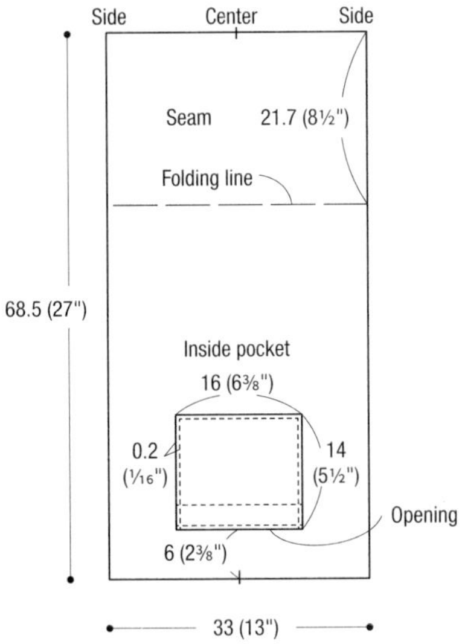

Inside pocket: one piece
28 (11") / Fold / 16 (6⅜")

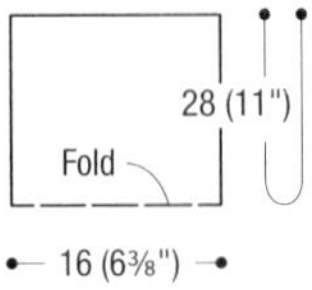

How to Make the Inside Pocket

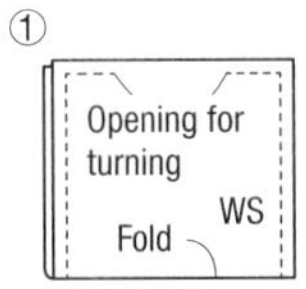

① Opening for turning / Fold / WS
With the right sides together, fold the fabric in half then sew the sides. Leave an opening for turning.

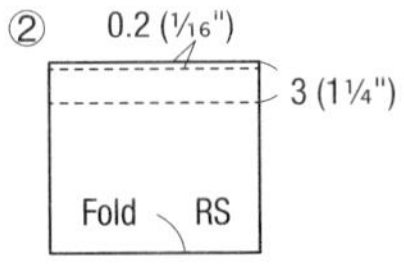

② 0.2 (1⁄16") / 3 (1¼") / Fold / RS
Turn the fabric right side out, machine sew the opening to close.

Instructions

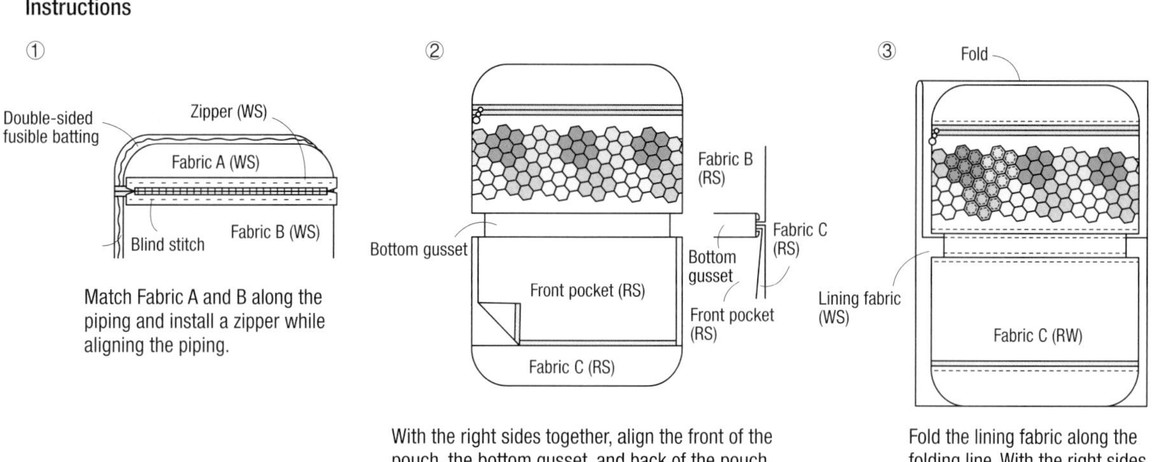

① Match Fabric A and B along the piping and install a zipper while aligning the piping.

② With the right sides together, align the front of the pouch, the bottom gusset, and back of the pouch. Insert the edge of the back pocket between the bottom gusset and the back of the pouch. Sew to join the bottom gusset. Fold seam allowance down to the bottom gusset.

③ Fold the lining fabric along the folding line. With the right sides out, put the outer fabric on the lining fabric. Machine sew.

④

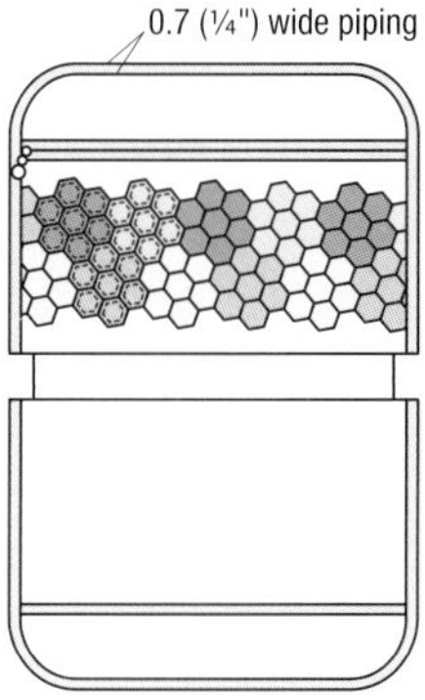

0.7 (¼") wide piping

Trim edges of the outer fabric and bind piping along the edge.

⑤

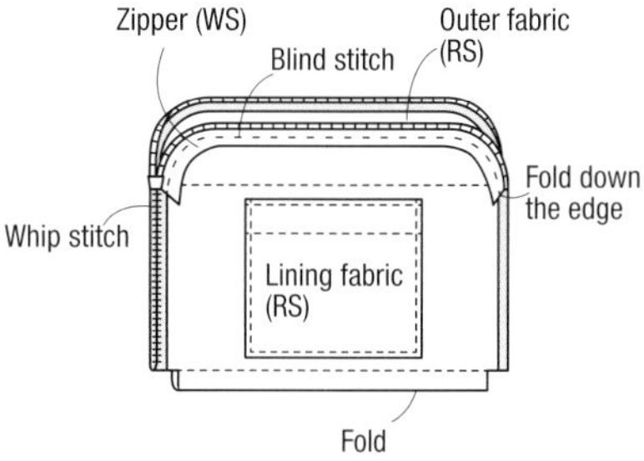

Zipper (WS)

Blind stitch

Outer fabric (RS)

Whip stitch

Fold down the edge

Lining fabric (RS)

Fold

Align the edge of the piping and the zipper teeth. Match the center of the zipper to the center of the edge, then install the zipper. Whip stitch to join side edges, from the end of the zipper down to the bottom.

⑥

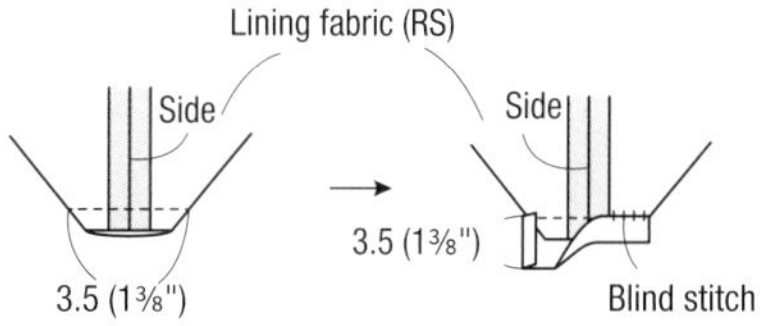

Lining fabric (RS)

Side

Side

3.5 (1⅜")

3.5 (1⅜")

Blind stitch

Join the end of the side seam to the edge of the bottom gusset. Sew the joining seam with bias tape.

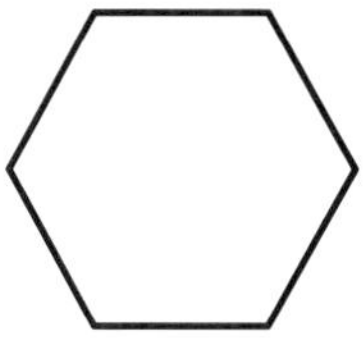

Full size patterns

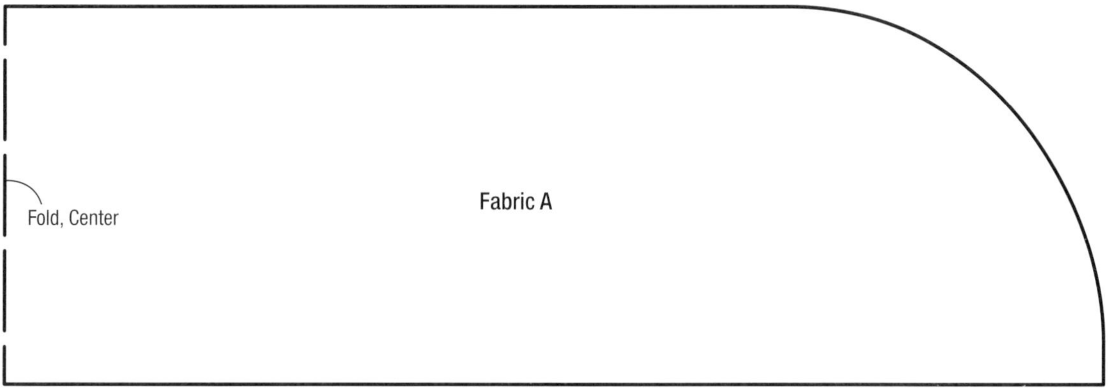

Fold, Center

Fabric A

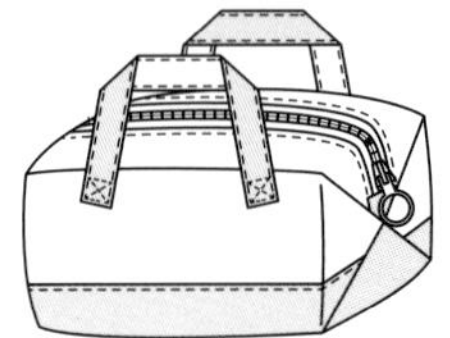

11 x 20 cm (4⅜" x 7⅞")
Design: Yasuko Hara

20 Easy-to-Make Duffel Bag Shaped Pouch

Materials
Outer fabric (including backing of handles): 50 x 30 cm (19¾" x 11⅞") / Lining fabric (including bottom, handles, tabs): 80 x 50 cm (31½" x 19¾") / Fusible batting: 40 x 50 cm (15¾" x 19¾") / Two freestyle zippers: 35 cm (13¾") / Adhesive interfacing as needed

Key points
- Put adhesive interfacing on the wrong side of the handle's outer fabric.
- This particular pouch uses a freestyle zipper that combines two different colored pieces of zipper tape. When you use the same color, just use 70 cm (27½").
- Add 1 cm (⅜") seam allowance.

Instructions
1 Assemble the outer fabric of the pouch. Fuse batting on the wrong side of the outer fabric.
2 With the right sides together, put the lining fabric over the outer fabric. Place zipper tape, right side down, along the top and bottom edge.
3 Make handles and attach them to the outer fabric.
4 Make tabs and insert one on each side of the pouch. Then sew each side seam.
5 Sew bias tape along the side seams.

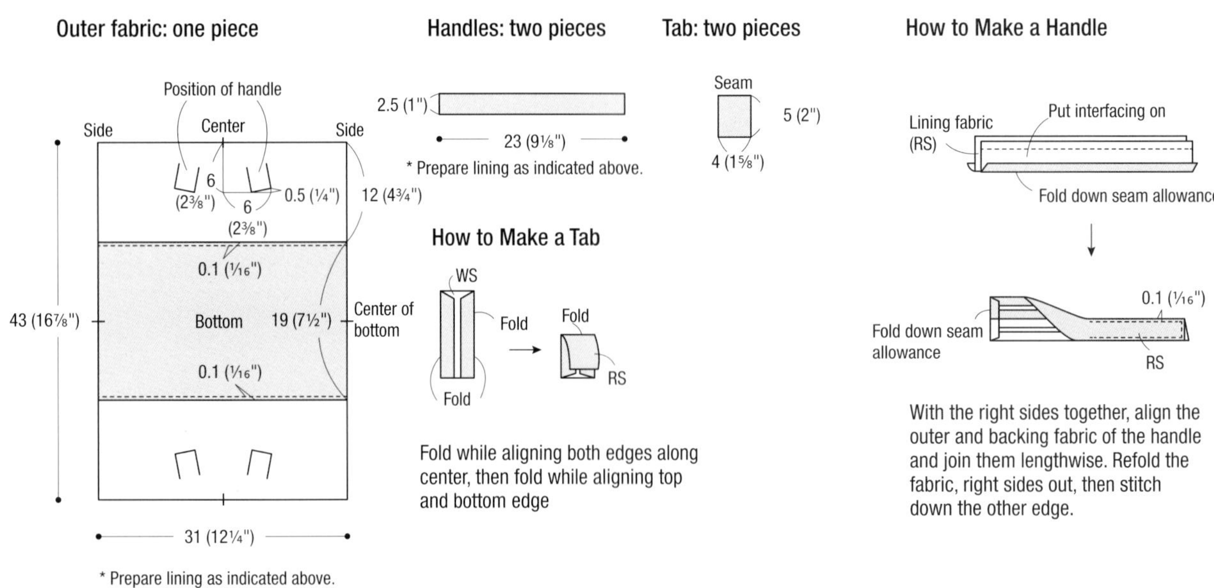

Instructions

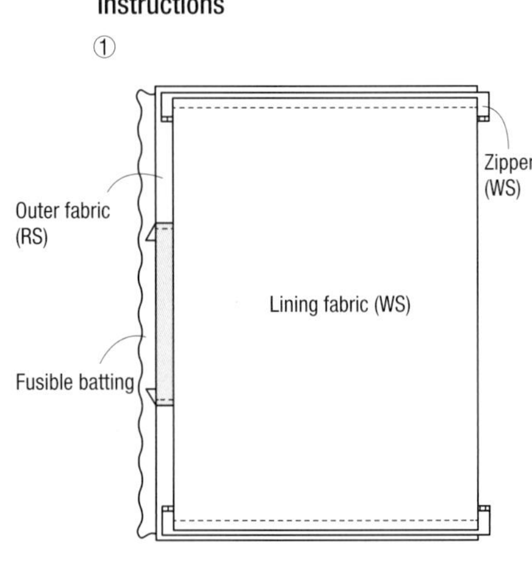

With the right sides together, put the lining fabric over the outer fabric. Place zipper tape, facing right side down, along the top and bottom edge. Sew.

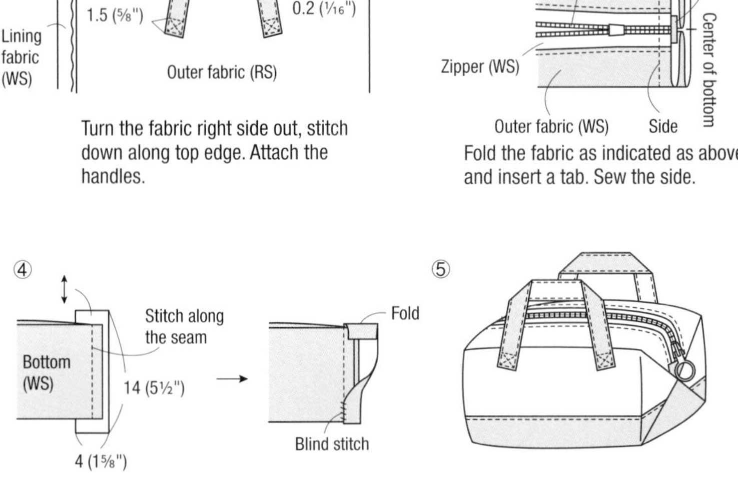

② Turn the fabric right side out, stitch down along top edge. Attach the handles.

③ Fold the fabric as indicated as above and insert a tab. Sew the side.

④ Bind bias tape along the side seams.

⑤ Turn the pouch right side out through the mouth of the pouch. Adjust the shape.

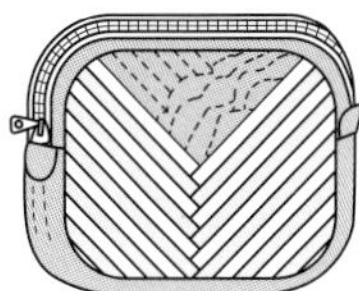

13 x 16 cm (5⅛" x 6⅜")
Design: Noriko Hosoo
• Full size patterns are on page 95.

21 V-shape Quilt Zippered Boxed Corner Pouch

Materials

Various fabric for pressed quilt and tabs / Zipper gusset (incl. bottom gusset), / Double-sided fusible batting: each 35 x 20 cm (13¾" x 7⅞") / Fusible batting: 40 x 20 cm (15¾" x 7⅞") / Baking fabric (incl. zipper gusset backing): 70 x 40 cm (27½" x 15¾") / One zipper: 25 cm (9⅞")

Key points

- Since the zipper gusset is slightly longer, join the body of the pouch to the zippered-gusset by aligning the marked positions and gathering the fabric of the body of the pouch along the curved corners.

Instructions

1 Put the pressed quilt directly on a fusible batting and assemble the front and back panels of the pouch.
2 Layer the backing fabric, double-sided fusible batting, and outer fabric of the bottom gusset. Fuse them together. Quilt as desired.
3 Make a zipper gusset.
4 Make tabs.
5 With the right sides together, lay the zipper gusset and the bottom gusset flat. Insert a tab between them. Then sew together.
6 Join the front and back panels of the pouch to the gussets. Sew bias tape along the joined seam.

Body panel front: one piece

Quilt as you trace the fabric pattern.
8 (3⅛")
8 (3⅛")
1 (⅜")
Center of bottom
14.8 (5⅞")

Body panel back: one piece

Pressed quilt
11.9 (4¾")
1 (⅜")
14.8 (5⅞")

* Add 0.7 cm (¼") seam allowance.
* Prepare backing as indicated above.

Zipper gusset: two pieces

2 (⅞")
25 (9⅞")

* Add 1 cm (⅜") seam allowance.

How to Pressed Quilt

① Fabric-1 (RS)
2.5 (1")
Fabric-2 (WS)
Fusible batting

② Fabric-1 (RS)
Fabric-2 (RS)
Fabric-3 (WS)

Place a triangle piece (Fabric-1) at the center of the top edge. With the right side down, lay the next piece (Fabric-2) flat over Fabric-1, being sure to align the edges. Join the edges. Turn Fabric-2 right side up.

Lay Fabric-3 flat, with the right side down, over Fabric-1, while being sure to align the edges. Join Fabric-3 to Fabrics-1 and -2. Continue joining pieces until the batting is covered. Fuse batting to the pressed quilt top.

Bottom gusset: one piece

1 (⅜")
5 (2")
Position of tab
1.5 (⅝")
1.5 (⅝")
1 (⅜")
26 (10¼")

* Add 1 cm (⅜") seam allowance.

How to Make a Zippered-gusset

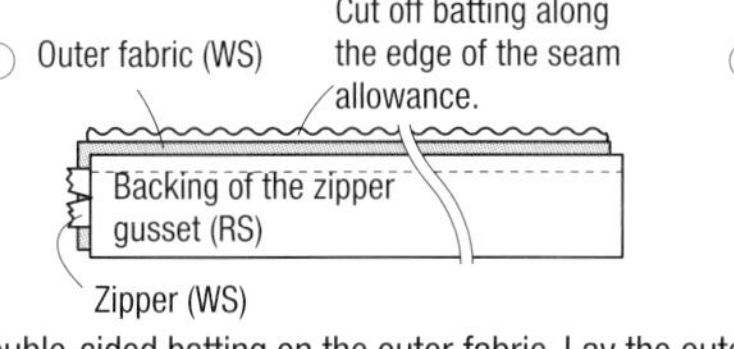

Fuse double-sided batting on the outer fabric. Lay the outer fabric flat, right side up. Lay zipper tape down flat, right side down, then put the backing fabric of the zippered-gusset over the outer fabric. Sew along the top edge.

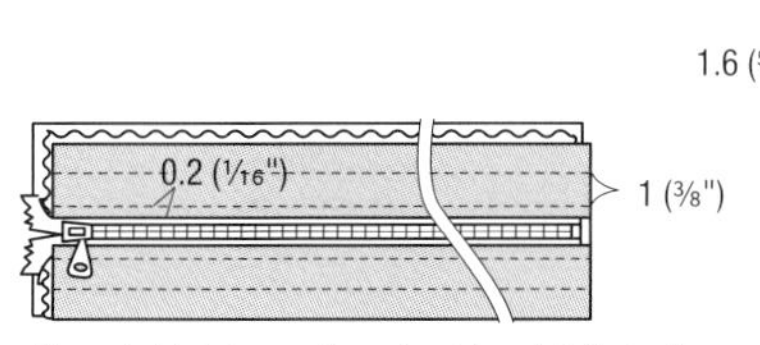

Turn right side up, fuse backing fabric to the outer fabric using the double-sided fusible batting previously fused on the wrong side of the outer fabric. Quilt as desired.

Tab: four pieces

1.6 (⅝")
3 (1¼")

How to Make a Tab

WS
RS
Fusible batting
Opening for turning

Fuse the cut batting without adding a seam allowance on one of the pieces. With the right sides together, join the two pieces and turn them right side out.

① **Instructions**

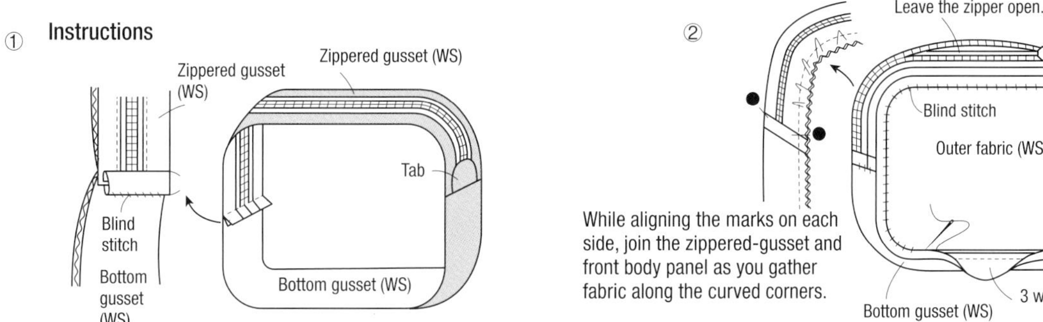

While aligning the marks on each side, join the zippered-gusset and front body panel as you gather fabric along the curved corners.

Sew bias tape along the seam.

With the right sides together, lay the bottom and the zipper gusset flat. Insert one of the tabs between. Sew them together so the bottom and the zipper gusset makes a loop.

Lay backing fabric on the front body panel. With the right sides together, join the backing to the gussets assembled in the previous step. Bind bias tape along the seam. Do the same for the back body panel.

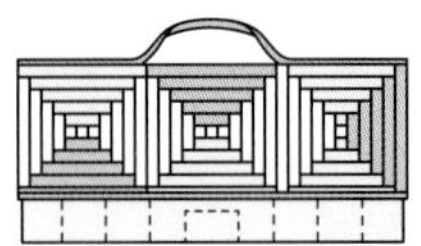

11 x 24 cm (4⅜" x 9½")
Design: Masayo Otsuka

22 Modern Log Cabin Quilted Pouch

Materials

Various pieces of fabric for piecing, Magnetic snaps / Outer fabric: 30 x 30 cm (11⅞" x 11⅞") / Fusible batting, Backing fabric: each 30 x 50 cm (11⅞" x 19¾") / 1.5 cm (⅝") diameter magnetic snap: one set / 0.5 cm (¼") wide leather tape: 50 cm (19¾")

Key points

- Cut off batting along the stitch line.
- Sew on leather tape for the handle. Make it loose enough to comfortably grip the handle.

Instructions

1 Assemble the outer fabric by piecing.
2 Apply fusible batting to the wrong side of the outer fabric. With the right sides together, lay the outer flat over the backing fabric. Then, sew the edges all the way around. Leave an opening for turning.
3 Turn the fabric right side out, sew the opening to close.
4 With the right sides together, fold the outer fabric along the folding line indicated in the diagram. Stitch along the folded edge.
5 With the right side out, refold the outer fabric while aligning the two bottom centers as indicated on the diagram. That way there will be two compartments inside. Then, whip stitch each side edge for both compartments.
6 Make a set of self-covered magnetic snaps and attach them to the pouch.
7 Attach leather tape along the edge of the flap for the handle.

Outer fabric: one piece

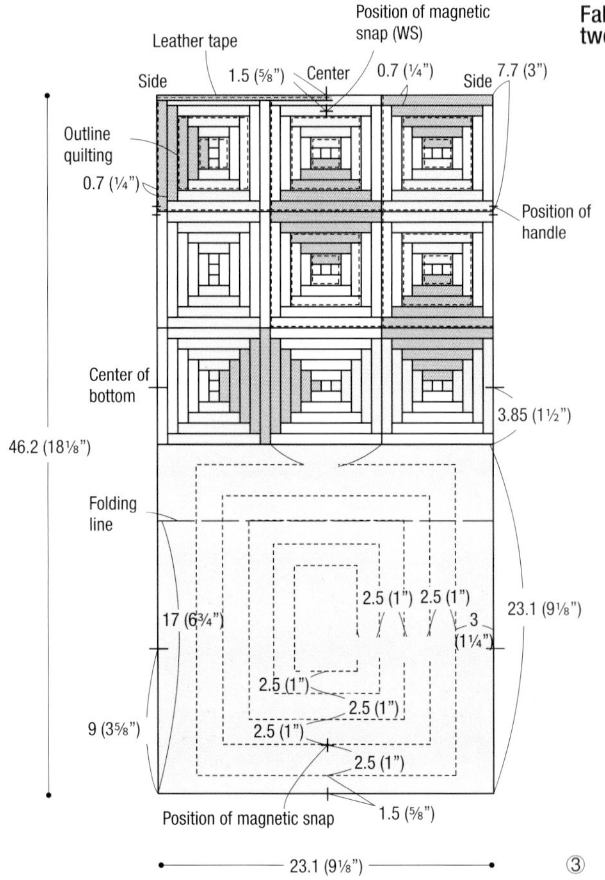

Leather tape
Position of magnetic snap (WS)
Side
1.5 (⅝")
Center
0.7 (¼")
Side
7.7 (3")
Outline quilting
0.7 (¼")
Position of handle
Center of bottom
3.85 (1½")
46.2 (18⅛")
Folding line
2.5 (1") 2.5 (1")
3 (1¼")
23.1 (9⅛")
17 (6¾")
2.5 (1")
2.5 (1")
9 (3⅝")
2.5 (1")
2.5 (1")
Position of magnetic snap
1.5 (⅝")
23.1 (9⅛")

Fabric for self-covered magnetic snap: two pieces

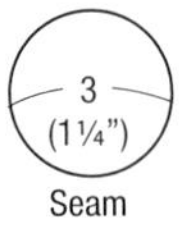

3 (1¼")
Seam

Instructions

①
Fusible batting
Outer fabric (RS)
Backing fabric (WS)
Opening for turning

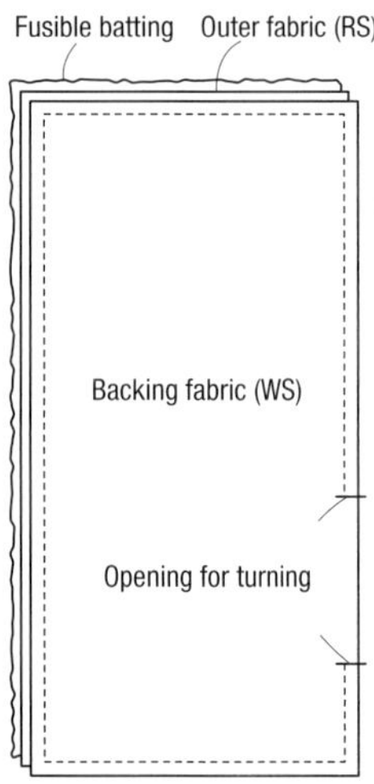

Fuse batting to wrong side of the outer fabric. With the right sides together, lay the backing flat over the outer fabric. Then, sew the edge all around leaving an opening for turning. Turn the fabric right side out, blind stitch the opening to close. Quilt as desired.

②
Folding line
0.2 (1⁄16")
6 (2⅜")
6 (2⅜")
Machine sew
17 (6¾")
6 (2⅜")
Outer fabric (WS)

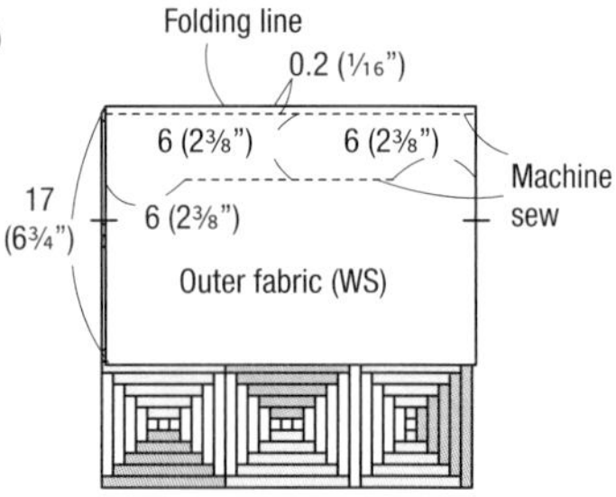

Fold the outer fabric along the folding line indicated on the diagram with the right sides together. Then, machine sew along the folded edge.

③
Magnetic snap
Flap (WS)
Whip stitch
Pouch front (RS)
9 (3⅝")
Center of bottom, Fold

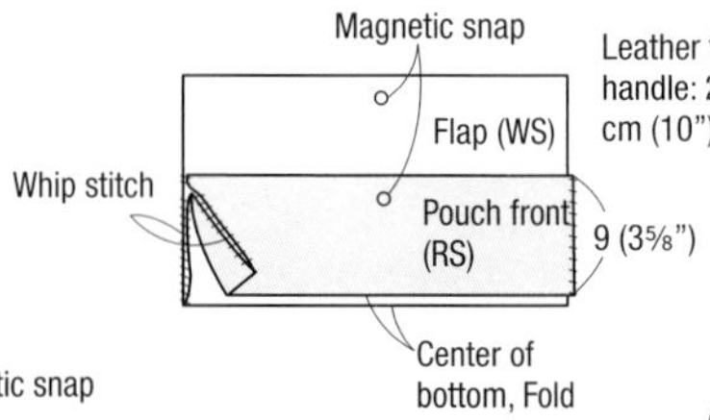

With right side out, fold the outer fabric while aligning the two bottom centers as indicated in the diagram. Then, join both side edges of the compartments. Attach a set of magnetic snaps.

④ 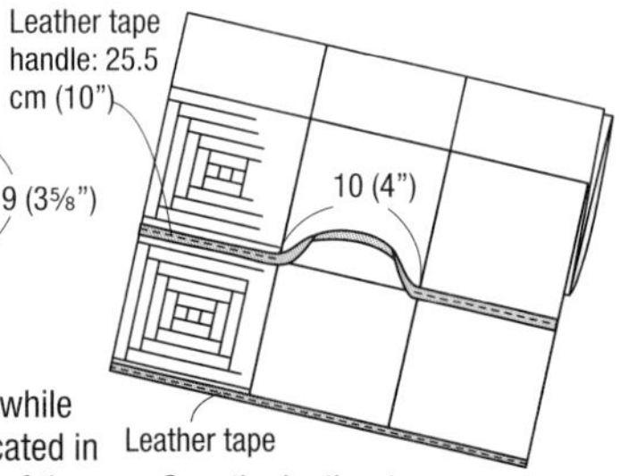
Leather tape handle: 25.5 cm (10")
10 (4")
Leather tape

Sew the leather tape where the edge of the flap and the handle meet

How to Make Self-covered Magnetic Snaps

①
Washer ring
Fabric (RS)
Prong

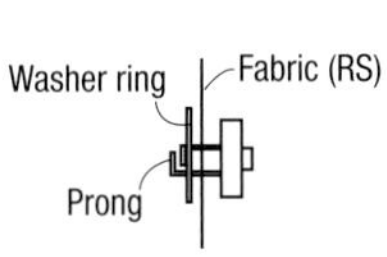

Insert the prongs of the socket into the fabric. Slip a washer ring over the prongs. Fold down the prongs.

②

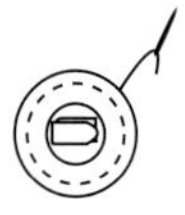

Cover the base of the stud with the fabric. Running stitch the circumference. Pull the thread to gather the fabric.

③ 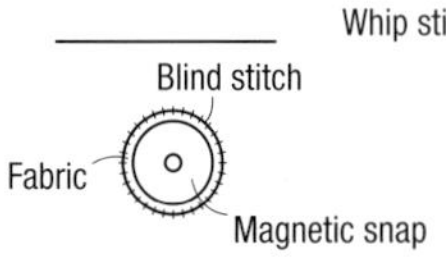
Blind stitch
Fabric
Magnetic snap

Blind stitch the fabric part onto the pouch.

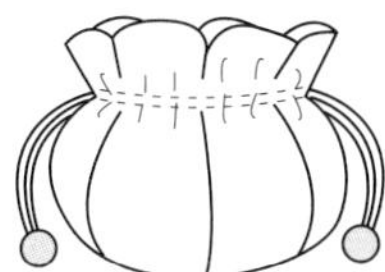

23 Flower Drawstring Pouch

9 x 11 cm (3⅝" x 4⅜")
Design: Noriko Hosoo
• Full size patterns are on page 127.

Materials
Bottom fabric (including piecing fabric): 60 x 15 cm (23⅝" x 5⅞") / Two types of fabric for piecing (including string decorations): 35 x 15 cm (13¾" x 5⅞") / Lining fabric: 35 x 35 cm (13¾" x 13¾") / 0.5 cm (¼") wide ribbon: 120 cm (47¼") / Fusible batting (as necessary)

Key points
- Be creative with the decoration attached to the drawstring.
- Add 1 cm (⅜") seam allowance.
- Make a small incision at the corner of the lining fabric's seam allowance.

Instructions
1 Assemble the outer fabric by piecing.
2 Lay the outer fabric flat over the lining with the right sides together. Then sew along the outer edges.
3 Turn the fabric right side out, sew on the bottom fabric.
4 Stitch the fabric to make a drawstring case.
5 Thread a string through the casing and attach decorations to both ends of the string.

Outer fabric: one piece | Lining fabric: one piece | Bottom: one piece | String decoration: eight pieces

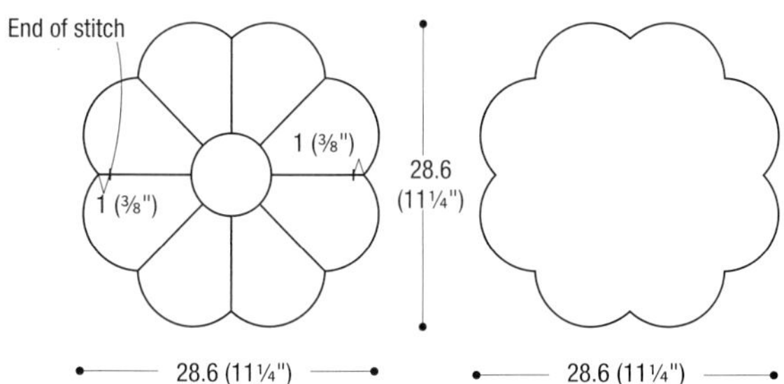

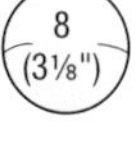

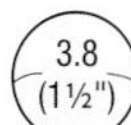

Instructions

①

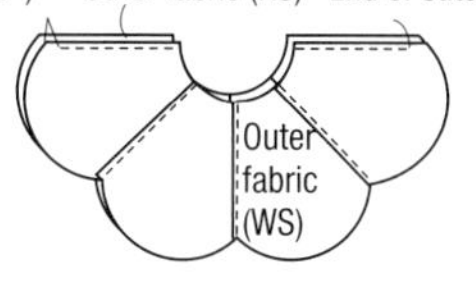

Assemble the outer fabric by piecing. Leave a 1 cm (⅜") gap between the tip of the edge and the end of the stitch.

②

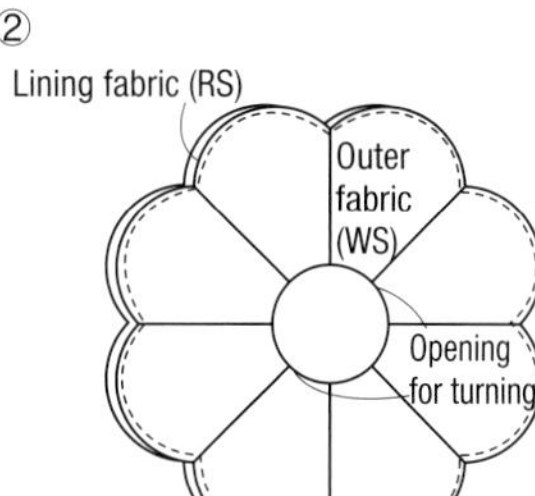

Lay the outer fabric flat over the lining with the right sides together. Sew along the outer edges and turn the fabric right side out using the opening.

③

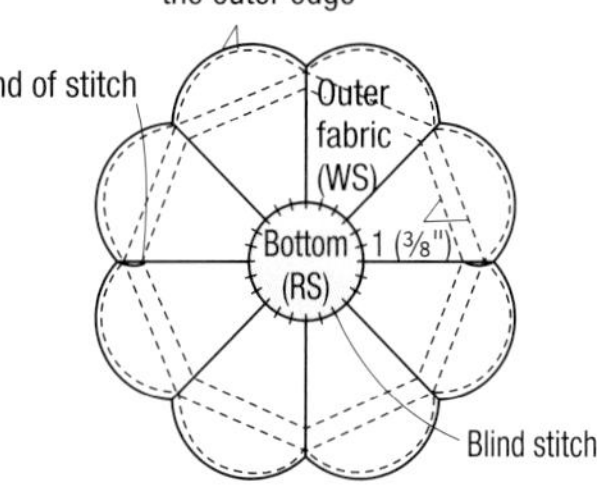

Join the bottom fabric using a blind stitch. Stitch along the outer edge of the pouch. Sew the drawstring casing.

How to Make Drawstring Decorations

①

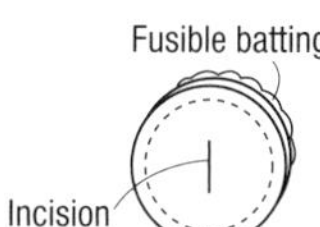

Join two pieces with the right sides together. On one side, fuse batting that has been cut without a seam allowance. Make a small incision at the center. Make four pieces.

②

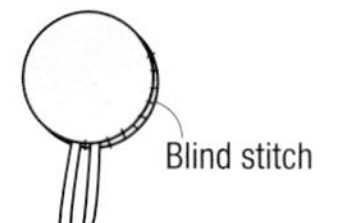

Place a ribbon in between two of the pieces. Blind stitch around circumference.

How to Thread a Ribbon

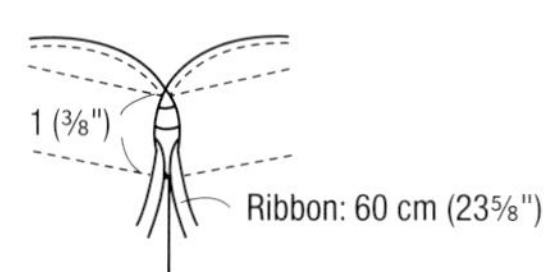

Thread a ribbon through from the opening on the left side.

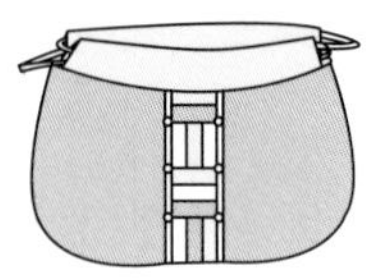

16 x 23 cm (6⅜" x 9⅛")
Design: Sachiko Ohara

24 Flat Drawstring Pouch

Materials
Various fabrics for piecing / Outer fabric, Lining fabric: each 55 x 20 cm (21⅝" x 7⅞") / Drawstring casing: 20 x 15 cm (7⅞" x 5⅞") / 1 cm (⅜") wide ribbon: 100 cm (39⅜") / 0.9 cm (⅜") diameter button: 12 pieces

Key points
- When joining the patchwork fabric to the body, bind both side edges of the patchwork fabric with a thin strip that has the same color combination as the patchwork and body.

Instructions
1 Assemble the outer fabric by piecing.
2 Sew the bottom and side edges of the outer fabric with the right sides together.
3 Do the same for the lining fabric.
4 Make the drawstring casings, then sew them along the top edge of the outer fabric with the right sides together.
5 Insert the lining into outer fabric. Blind stitch on a drawstring casing.
6 Thread a ribbon to the drawstring casing.

Outer fabric: two pieces

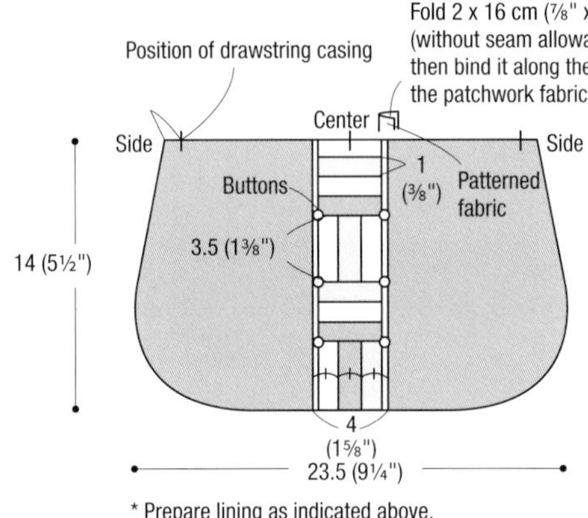

* Prepare lining as indicated above.

Drawstring casing: two pieces

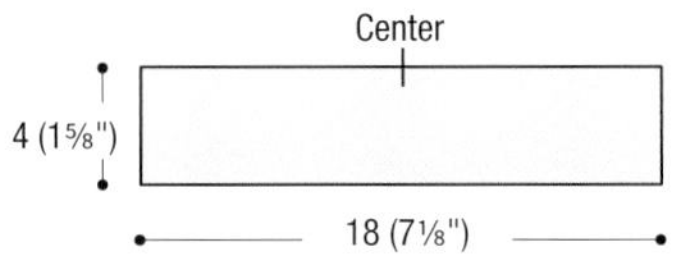

How to Make a Drawstring Casing

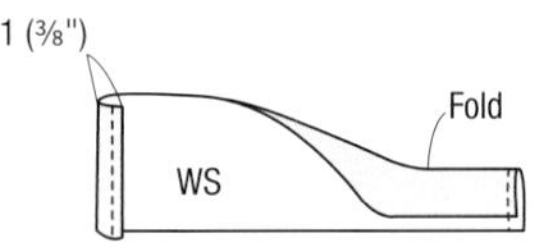

Fold both side edges and sew.
Then fold in half horizontally.

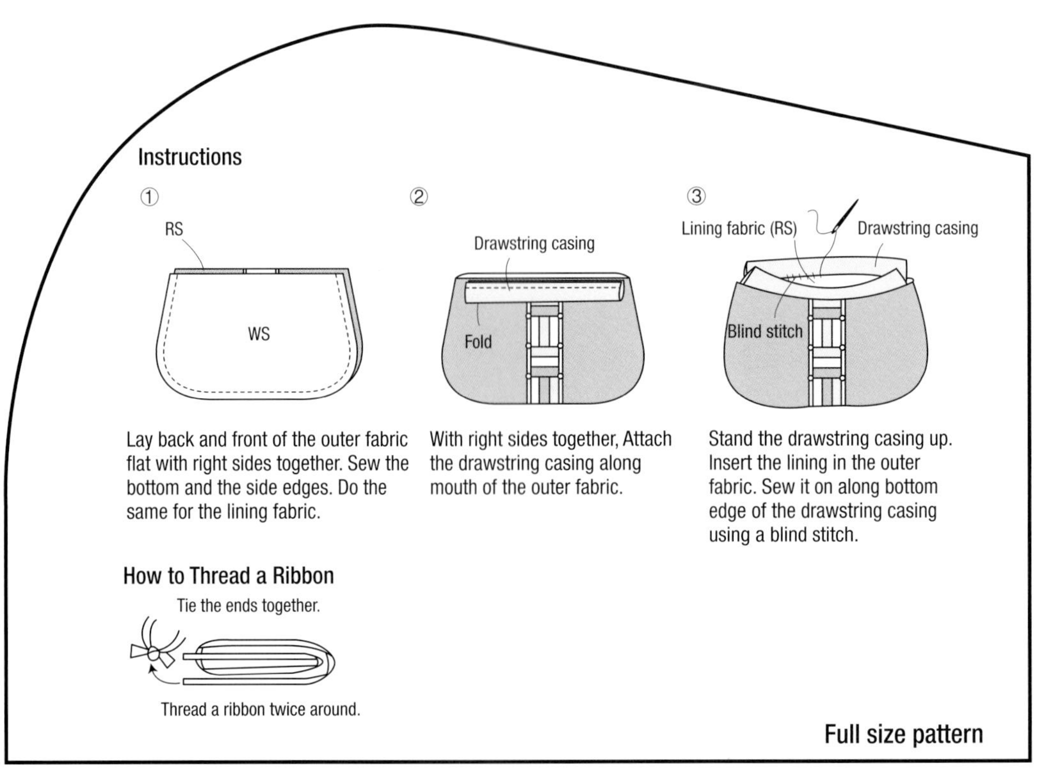

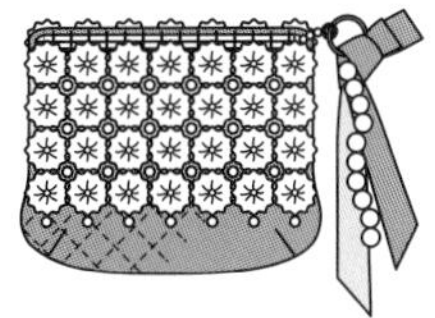

14.5 x 19 cm (5¾" x 7½")
Design: Sachiko Ishikawa

25 Girly Pouch with Yo-yos and Wooden Beads

Materials

Various fabric for making yo-yos / Fabric-A (including ribbon backing): 65 x 15 cm (25⅝" x 5⅞") / Fabric-B (including ribbon, piping): 55 x 55 cm (21⅝" x 21⅝") / Backing fabric: 50 x 35 cm (19¾" x 13¾") / Double-sided fusible batting: 55 x 20 cm (21⅝" x 7⅞") / One zipper: 20 cm (7⅞") / Key ring with inner diameter 2.5 cm (1"): one / O-ring with inner diameter 0.5 cm (¼"): one / 0.8 cm (⅜") diameter wooden beads: thirty-six white pieces, fourteen red pieces / 1 cm (⅜") wide lace trim as necessary

Key points

- Tie a ribbon as desired and embellish with lace trim. In this particular work, the ribbon is bias cut to make the stripe pattern appear diagonal.

Instructions

1 Assemble fabric-A and -B by piecing to make the front and back of the outer fabric.
2 Layer the backing, double-sided fusible batting, and the front of the outer fabric and fuse the layers together. Next, quilt as desired. Do the same for back of the outer fabric.
3 Sew the darts on both the front and back of the outer fabric. Press down the seam toward the center.
4 With right sides together, join the front and back of the outer fabric by sewing the bottom and the side edges. Wrap the seams with bias tape and sew on.
5 Attach piping along mouth of the outer fabric. Install a zipper.
6 Make yo-yos and join them into a quilt.
7 Glue the connected yo-yos onto the outer fabric using craft glue. Sew on wooden beads.
8 Make a ribbon. Thread it through the key ring then tie a knot.

Outer fabric: two pieces

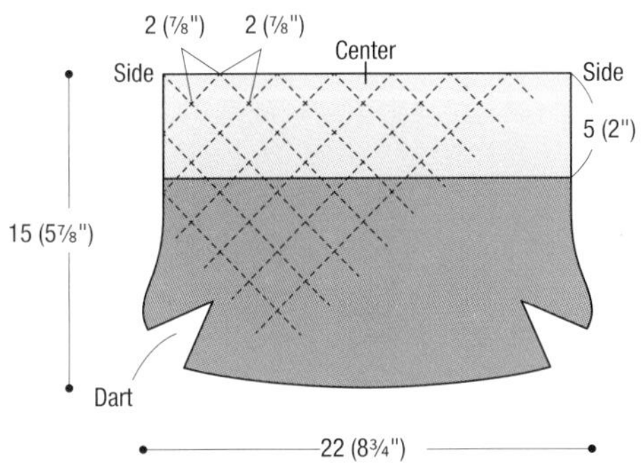

Outer and backing of ribbon: one piece each

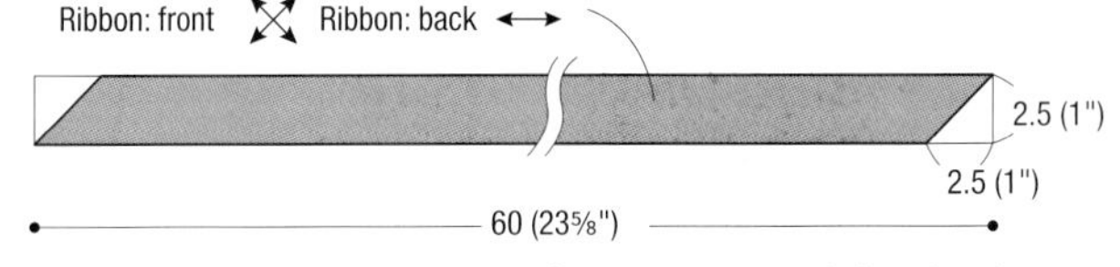

* Cut one piece symmetrically to the other.

Yo-yo quilt: 56 pieces

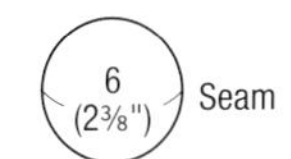

How to Connect Yo-yos

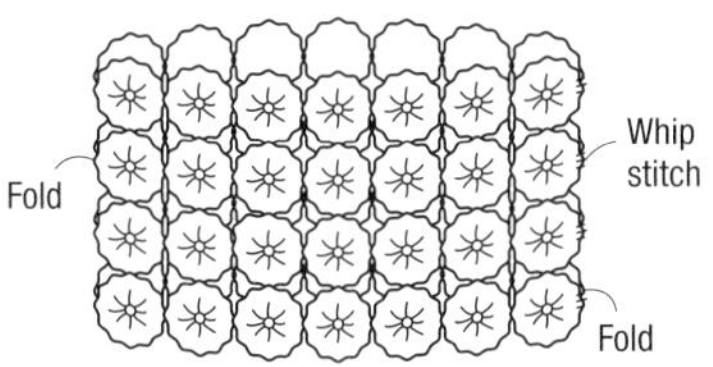

Line up yo-yos into a quilt, 7 pieces long and 4 pieces wide. Connect. Join the beginnings and ends of the rows with right sides out.

Instructions

①

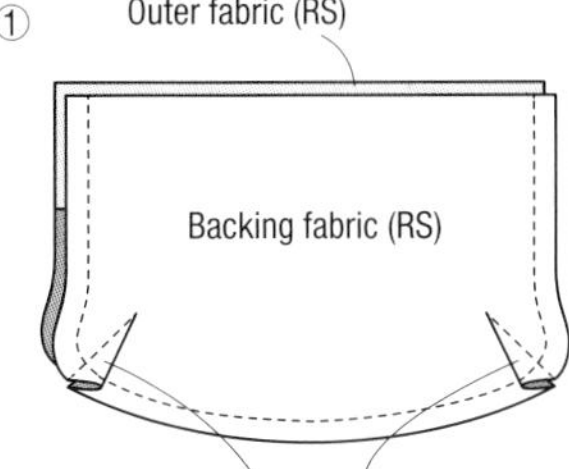

Sew the darts. With right sides together, join the front and back of the outer fabric together.

②

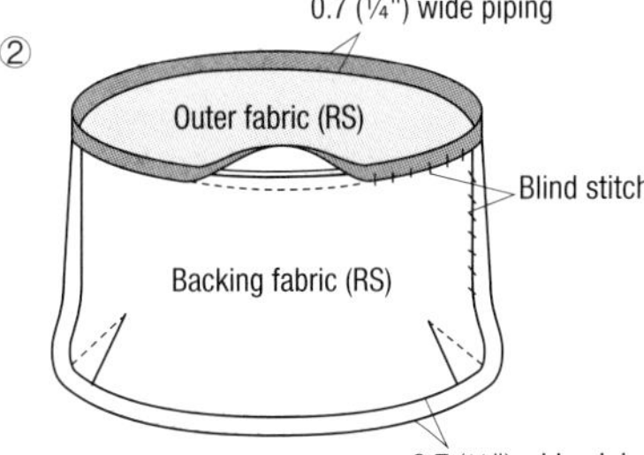

Bind bias tape along the seams.
Bind piping along mouth of the outer fabric.

③

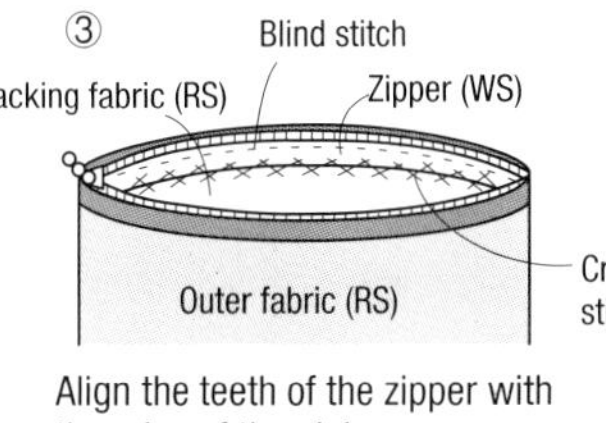

Align the teeth of the zipper with the edge of the piping.
Install the zipper.

④

Slide the connected yo-yo quilt over the outer fabric, then glue on using craft glue. Sew on wooden beads. Attach the O-ring and the key ring to the zipper slider, then tie a ribbon on the key ring.

How to Make and Attach a Ribbon

①

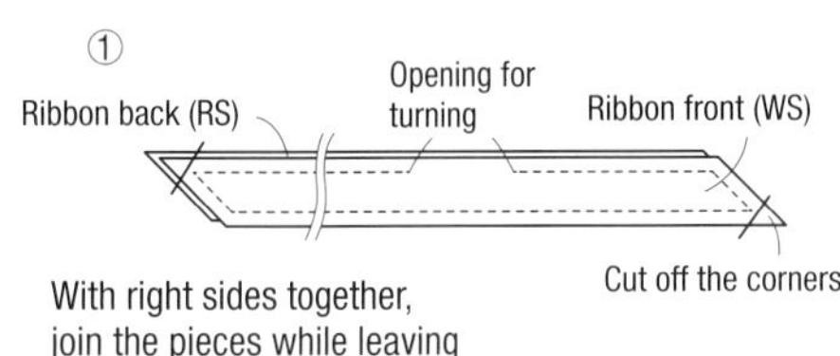

With right sides together, join the pieces while leaving an opening for turning.

②

Turn the fabric right side out, stitch the opening to close.

③

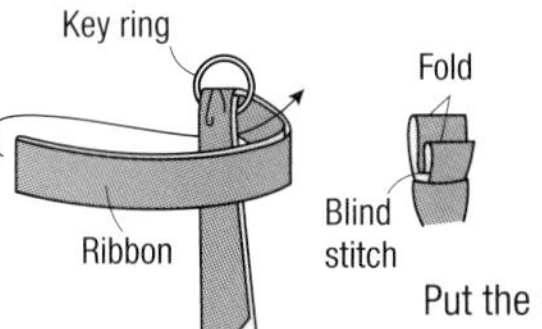

Put the ribbon through the key ring, then tie a knot and bind the folded end onto the knot.

16 x 22 cm (6⅜" x 8¾")
Design: Masayo Otsuka

26 Sturdy and Soft Tablet Case

Materials

Various fabrics for piecing / Outer fabric: 30 x 30 cm (11⅞" x 11⅞") / Backing fabric, Batting: each 30 x 45 cm (11⅞" x 17¾") / 2.6 cm (1") diameter button: two pieces / 0.4 cm (⅛") wide ribbon: 50 cm (19¾")

Key points

- Join a belt-like piece of fabric as desired.
- Instead of stitching a proper bar-tack you can wrap thread around the needle many times and pull the thread through.

Instructions

1 Assemble outer fabric by piecing.
2 Lay the backing fabric over the outer fabric flat with right sides together. Put the layers on batting and sew along the edges while leaving an opening for turning.
3 Turn the fabric right side out and quilt as desired.
4 With the right sides together, fold the fabric along the folding line indicated on the diagram. Join the overlapping side edges.
5 Turn the fabric right side out. Bar-tack the side seams.
6 Attach the button and the ribbon.

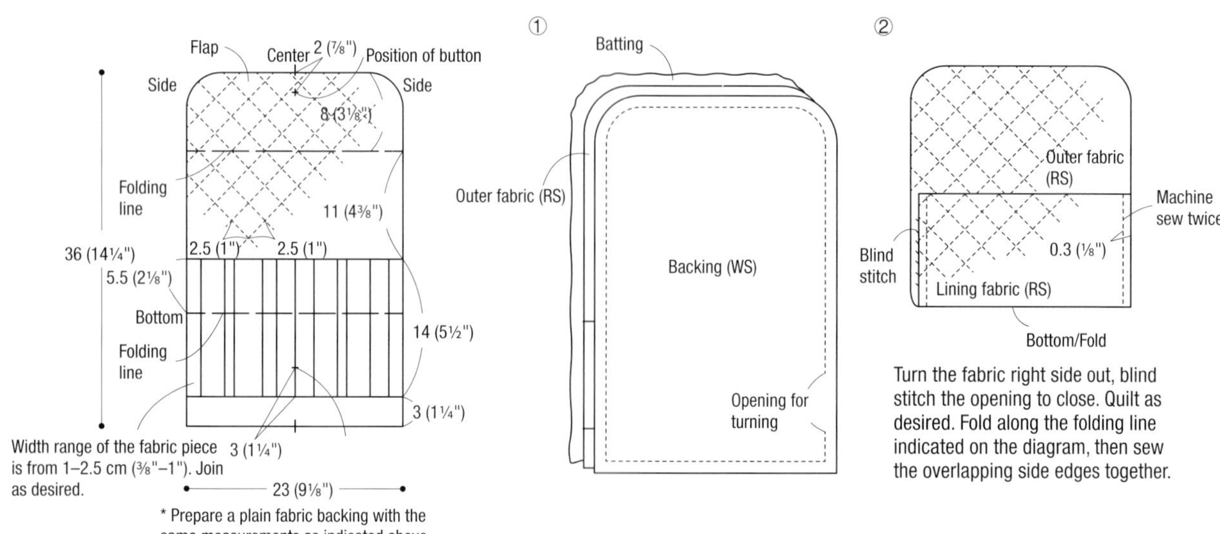

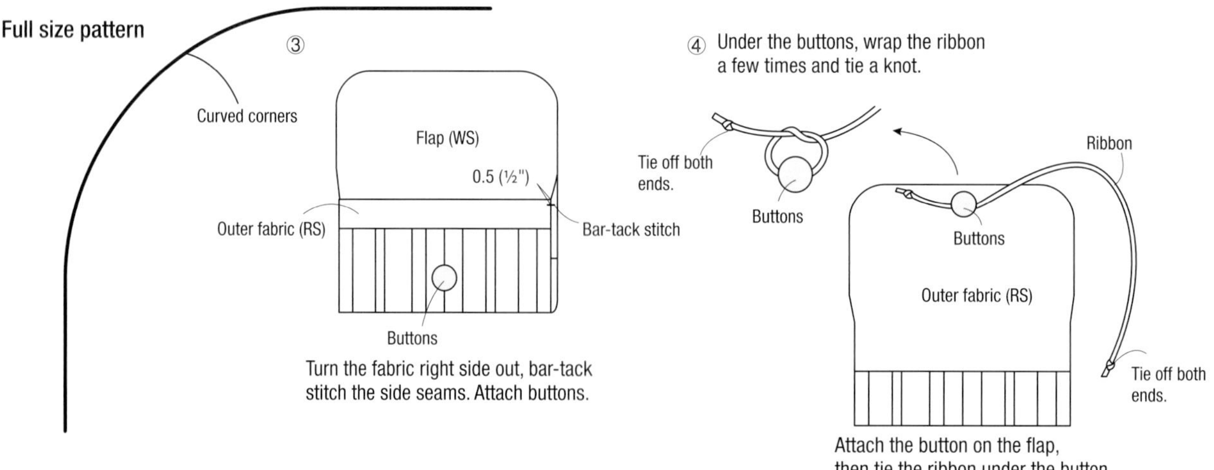

How to Bar-tack Stitch

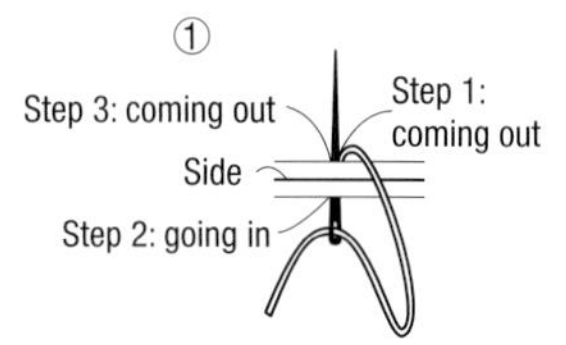

Put the needle in from the back, come out the front.

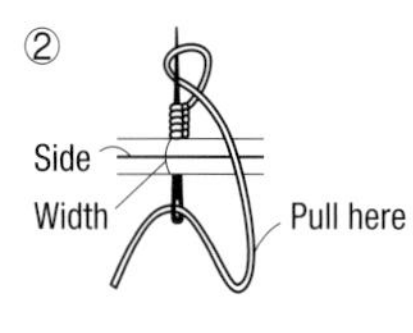

Wrap the trailing thread around the needle and pull through. Repeat

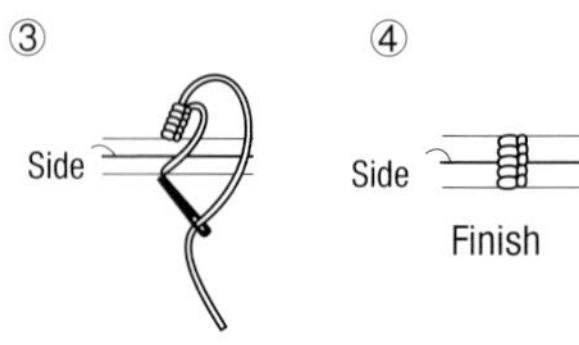

While holding the thread down, push the needle through. Pull the thread down and push the needle through to the same position. Tie off.

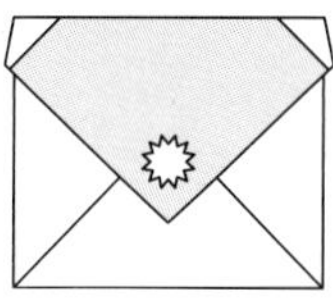

11 x 13.5 cm (4⅜" x 5⅜")
Design: Mutsuko Tanino

27 Love Letter Pouch

Materials
Fabric-A: 15 x 15 cm (5⅞" x 5⅞") / Fabric-B: 30 x 25 cm (11⅞" x 9⅞") / Lining fabric, Fusible batting: 25 x 25 cm (9⅞" x 9⅞") / 1.5 cm (⅝") diameter magnetic snaps: one set / 2 cm (⅞") diameter button: one piece

Key points
- Fuse batting, without any seam allowance, on wrong side of the outer fabric.

Instructions
1 Assemble the outer fabric by piecing fabric-A and -B.
2 Fuse batting on wrong side of the outer fabric, then outline quilt.
3 Lay the lining fabric flat over the outer fabric with the right sides together. Then, sew the top edge and the left edge.
4 Sew the outer and lining fabric separately with right sides together (see step 3 below).
5 Turn the fabric right side out. Sew the opening to close.
6 Blind stitch along the edges of the flap, then attach magnetic snaps.
7 Attach decoration to the flap.

Outer fabric: one piece

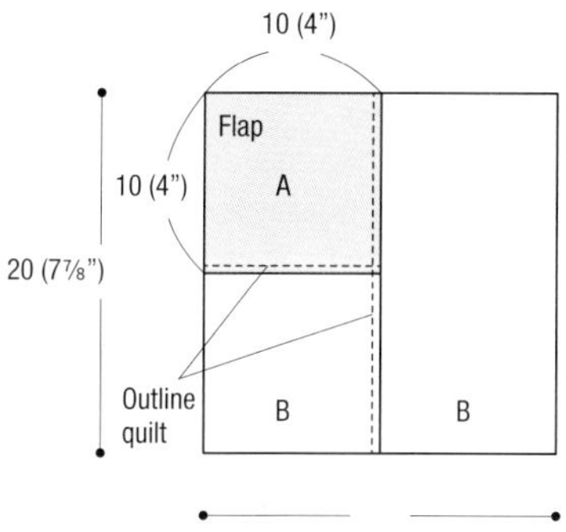

* Prepare lining as indicated above.

Instructions

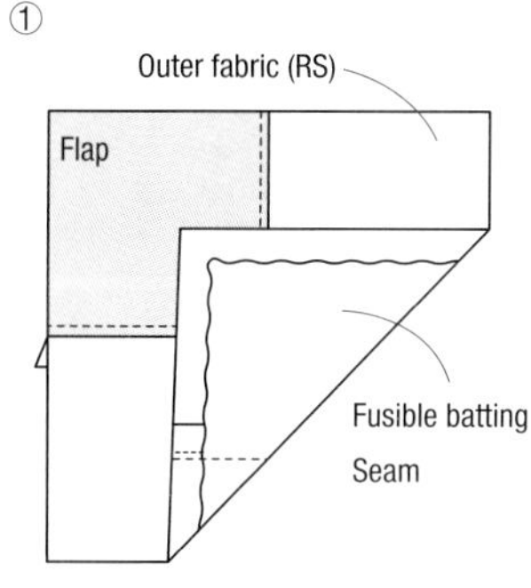

Fuse batting on wrong side of the outer fabric, then outline quilt.

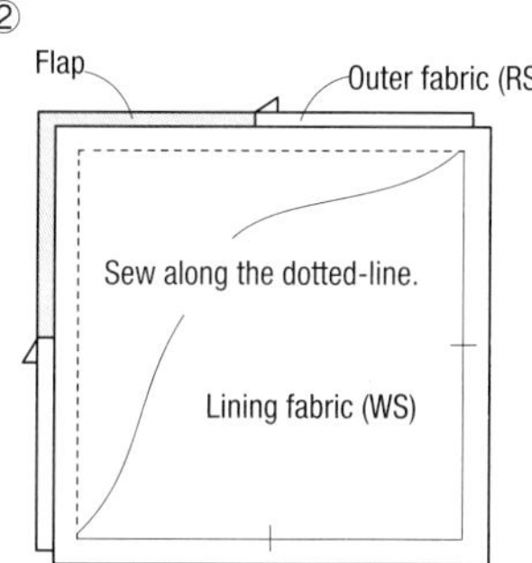

Lay the lining fabric flat over the outer fabric with the right sides together. Then, sew the two edges above the flap.

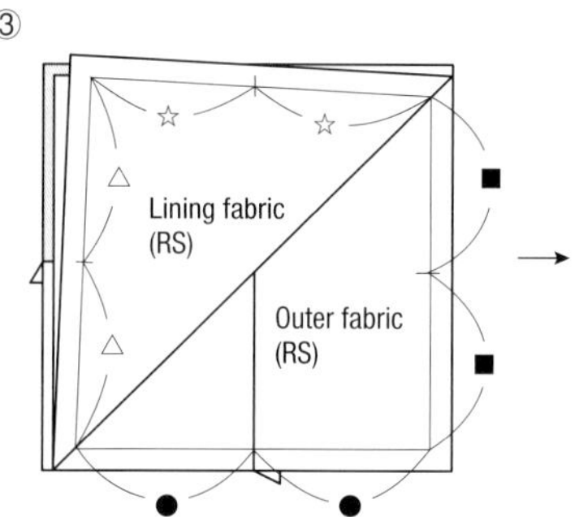

Matching up the same marks (△ and △, ☆ and ☆) sew the edges, with right sides together, on the lining fabric. Leave an opening for turning. Do the same for the outer fabric without leaving an opening.

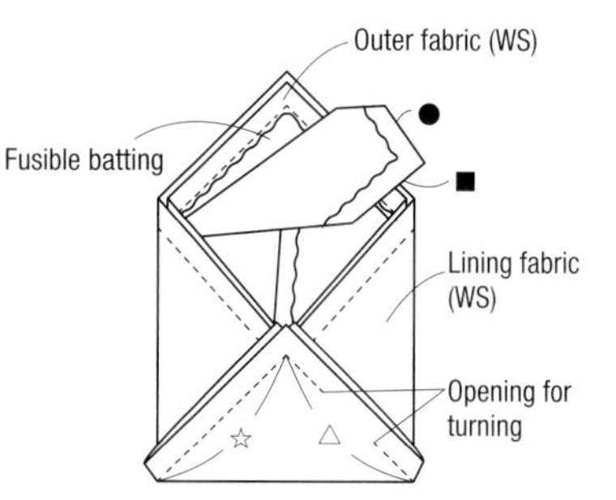

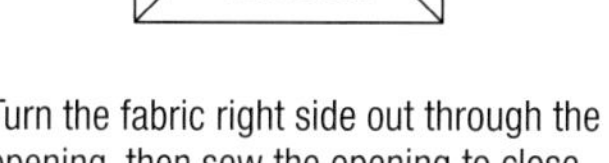

Turn the fabric right side out through the opening, then sew the opening to close.

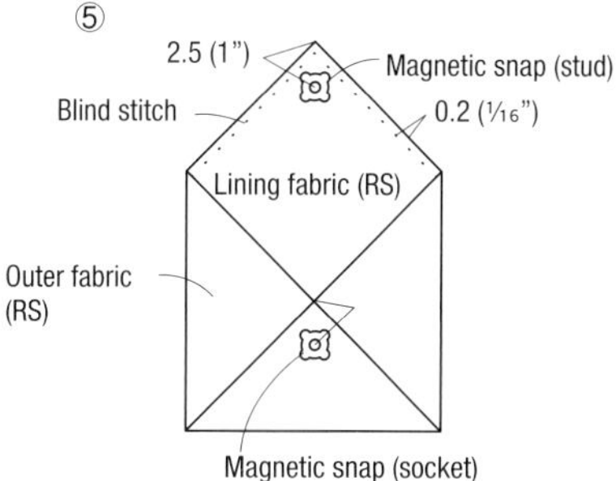

Turn the fabric right side out and blind stitch along the edge of the flap. Attach magnetic snap.

⑥

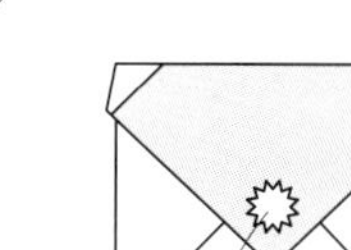

Attach a button to embellish.

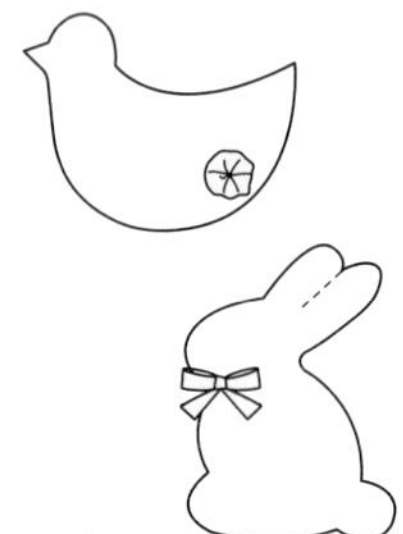

28, 29 Rabbit Pouch and Bird Pouch

The Rabbit: 20 x 15 cm (7⅞" x 5⅞")
The Bird: 14 x 20 cm (5½" x 7⅞")
Design: Ryoko Matsumoto
• Full size patterns are on page 107.

Materials
The Rabbit
Outer fabric front: 20 x 25 cm (7⅞" x 9⅞") / Outer fabric back-A: 15 x 25 cm (5⅞" x 9⅞") / Outer fabric back-B: 10 x 20 cm (4" x 7⅞") / Lining fabric: 40 x 25 cm (15¾" x 9⅞") / 1.5 cm (⅝") diameter button: two pieces / 0.3 cm (⅛") wide leather cord: 25 cm (9⅞") / 2.5 cm (1") wide ribbon: 30 cm (9⅞")

The Bird
Outer fabric front: 25 x 20c cm (9⅞" x 7⅞") / Outer fabric back-A, Outer fabric back-B: each 25 x 15 cm (9⅞" x 5⅞") / Lining fabric: 50 x 25 cm (19¾" x 9⅞") / 1.5 cm (⅝") diameter button: two pieces / 0.3 cm (⅛") wide leather cord: 25 cm (9⅞") / 2.5 cm (1") wide ribbon: 20 cm (7⅞")

Key points
• Apply interfacing when you use knitted fabric.

Instructions (For both rabbit pouch and bird pouch)

1 Temporarily secure leather cord to outer fabric back-A. Sew the lining fabric with right sides together.
2 Join outer fabric back-B and the lining with the right sides together. Turn the fabric right side out, stitch along the straight edge.
3 With right side out, lay the lining fabric flat on the outer fabric front. With the right side facing down, place outer fabric back-A and -B over the outer fabric front. Then sew along outer edge. Zigzag stitch seam allowance all the way around.
4 Turn the fabric right side out and attach a ribbon if you are making the rabbit pouch, or attach a ribbon yo-yo if you are making the bird pouch.
5 Make a loop out of the leather cord and attach buttons on back of the pouch.

The Rabbit – Outer fabric front: one piece

21 (8¼")
Position or ribbon
15.5 (6⅛")

* Prepare lining as indicated above. Cut lining fabric symmetric to the outer fabric.

The Rabbit – Outer fabric front: one piece

21 (8¼")
Position of leather cord
Position of button
11.1 (4½")

* Prepare lining as indicated above. Cut the lining fabric symmetric to the outer fabric.

The Rabbit – Outer fabric back-B: one piece

17.2 (6¾")
5.6 (2¼")

How to Make Outer Fabric Back-A

Outer fabric back-A (WS)
Lining fabric (WS)
Cord
Lining fabric (WS)
Length: 5 cm (2")
Cord: two piecespieces
Outer fabric back-A (WS)

Temporarily secure the cord on outer fabric back-A. Sew straight edges together with the right sides together.

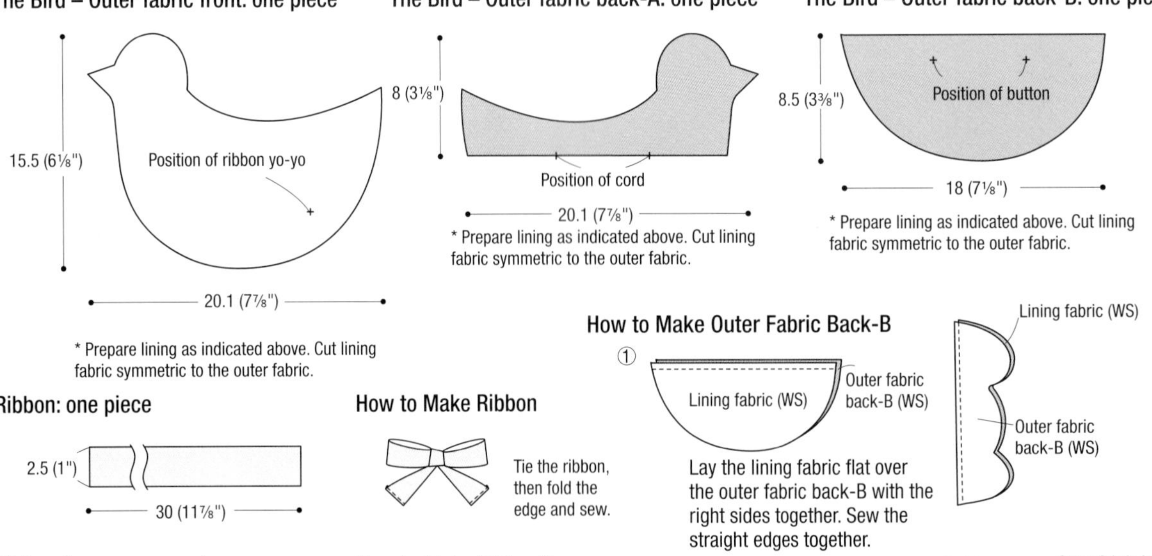

2.5 (1")
16 (6⅜")

①
RS
Join the ends of the ribbon to make a loop. Running stitch along the circumference.

②
Pull the thread to gather the fabric.

② Stitch 0.5 cm (¼") inside the edge
0.5 (¼")
Outer fabric back-B (WS)
Turn the fabric right side out and stitch along the straight line.

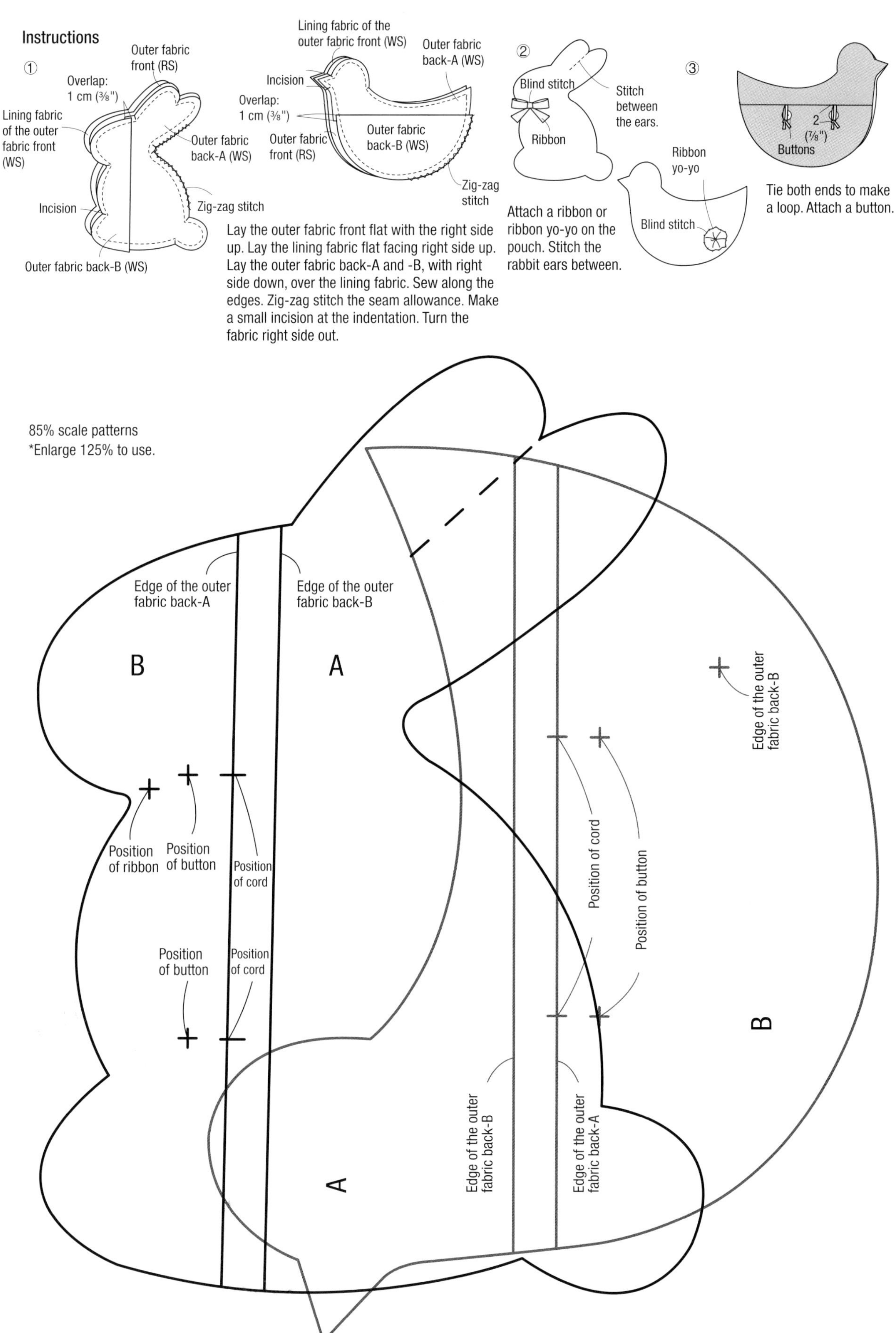
Instructions
①
Outer fabric front (RS)
Overlap: 1 cm (3⁄8")
Lining fabric of the outer fabric front (WS)
Outer fabric back-A (WS)
Zig-zag stitch
Incision
Outer fabric back-B (WS)
Lining fabric of the outer fabric front (WS)
Outer fabric back-A (WS)
Incision
Overlap: 1 cm (3⁄8")
Outer fabric front (RS)
Outer fabric back-B (WS)
Zig-zag stitch
Lay the outer fabric front flat with the right side up. Lay the lining fabric flat facing right side up. Lay the outer fabric back-A and -B, with right side down, over the lining fabric. Sew along the edges. Zig-zag stitch the seam allowance. Make a small incision at the indentation. Turn the fabric right side out.
②
Blind stitch
Stitch between the ears.
Ribbon
Ribbon yo-yo
Blind stitch
Attach a ribbon or ribbon yo-yo on the pouch. Stitch the rabbit ears between.
③
2
(7⁄8")
Buttons
Tie both ends to make a loop. Attach a button.
85% scale patterns
*Enlarge 125% to use.
Edge of the outer fabric back-A
Edge of the outer fabric back-B
B
A
Position of ribbon
Position of button
Position of cord
Position of button
Position of cord
A
Edge of the outer fabric back-B
Edge of the outer fabric back-A
Position of cord
Position of button
Edge of the outer fabric back-B
B

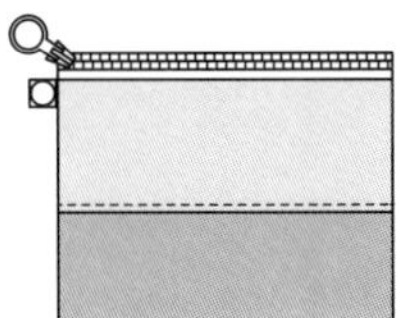

12.5 x 16.5 cm (5" x 6½")
Design: Yasuko Hara

30 Pouch with Pocket Tissue Case

Materials

Fabric-A: 20 x 25 cm (7⅞" x 9⅞") / Fabric-B: 20 x 40 cm (7⅞" x 15¾") / Lining fabric (including inside pocket): 40 x 30 cm (15¾" x 11⅞") / Extra thin fusible batting: 25 x 30 cm (7⅞" x 11⅞") / One zipper: 16 cm (6⅜") / 1.5 cm (⅝") diameter button: two pieces / 1.5 cm (⅝") wide leather tape: 5 cm (2")

Key points

- Fuse extra thin batting after folding the fabric to make a pocket on the front side for holding tissue.
- Add 0.7 cm (¼") seam allowance along zipper opening, 1 cm (⅜") for other edges.

Instructions

1 Piece fabric-A and -B together to make the outer fabric. Fold the outer fabric to make a pocket for holding tissue. Then fuse extra thin batting.
2 Make an inside pocket, then sew on the lining fabric.
3 Lay the lining fabric flat over the outer fabric with the right sides together. Insert the zipper between them.
4 With right sides together, fold the outer fabric and the lining fabric separately. Insert a tab and sew each of the side edges.
5 Turn the fabric right side out, sew the opening to close.
6 Attach a button on each side of the tab.

Outer fabric: one piece (after piecing outer fabric-A and -B)

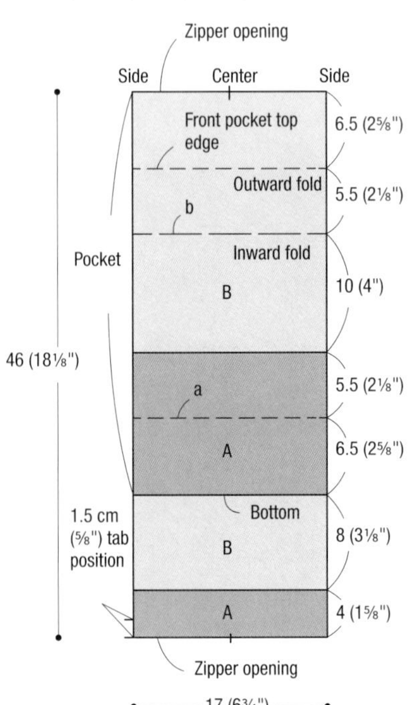

Inside pocket: one piece

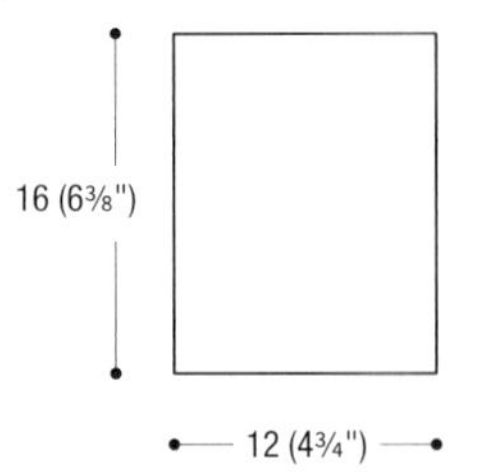

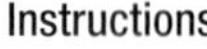

How to Make a Pocket

①

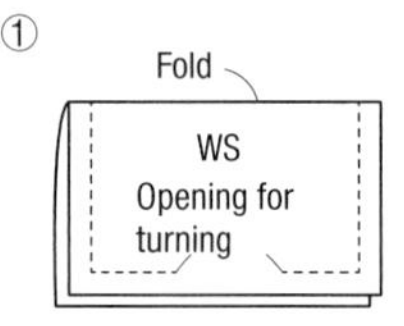

Fold in half with the right sides together. Sew the edges while leaving an opening for turning, then turn the fabric right side out.

②

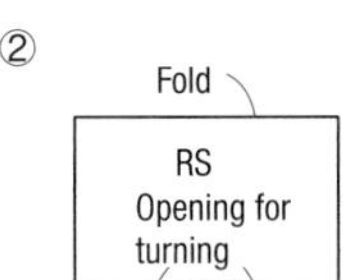

Turn the fabric right side out and tuck seam allowance along the opening inside.

Instructions

①

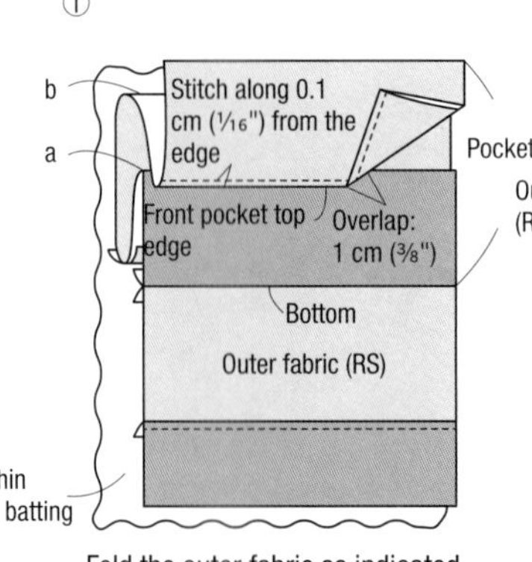

Fold the outer fabric as indicated on the diagram, then fuse extra thin batting on the wrong side.

②

Lay the lining fabric flat over the outer fabric with the outer sides together. Insert zipper and sew along the dotted line as indicated in the diagram. Do the same for the other side.

Lining fabric: one piece

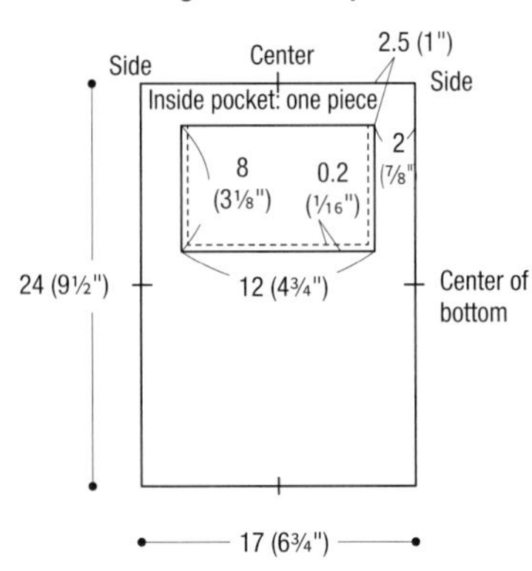

③

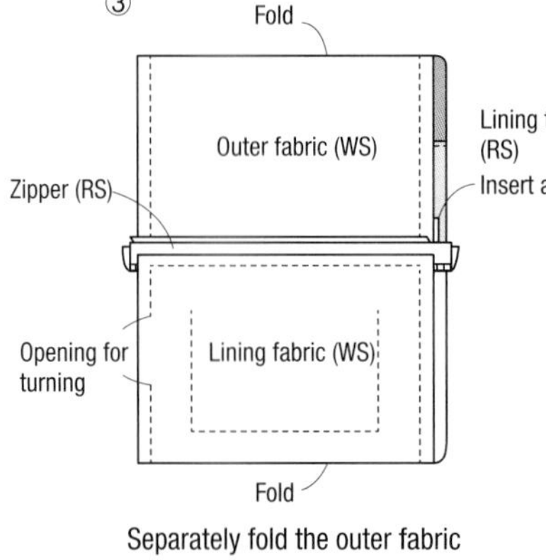

Separately fold the outer fabric and the lining fabric in half with the right sides together. Sew sides while aligning the fabric along zipper opening. Leave an opening for turning the lining fabric.

④

Turn the fabric right side out using the opening. Tuck seam allowance along the opening inside, then sew to close.

How to Make a Tab

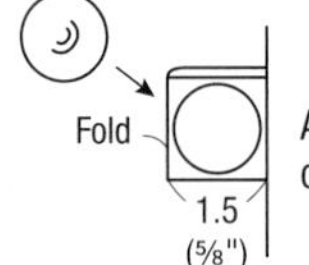

Attach a button on both sides.

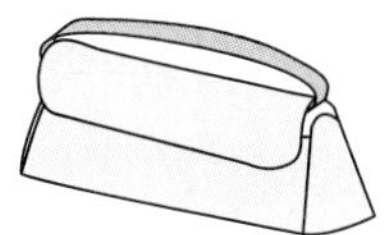

8 x 20 cm (3⅛" x 7⅞")
Design: Noriko Hosoo
• Full size patterns are on page 113.

33 Sewing Case Bag

Materials
Outer fabric (including flap and gusset): 50 x 25 cm (19¾" x 9⅞") / Backing fabric (including backing of flap and pocket-B): 50 x 30 cm (19¾" x 11⅞") / Fusible batting: 45 x 25 cm (17¾" x 9⅞") / Pocket-A (including backing of gusset): 40 x 15 cm (15¾" x 5⅞") / One zipper: 20 cm (7⅞") / 1.5 cm (⅝") wide ribbon: 30 cm (9⅞") / 1 cm (⅜") diameter sew-on magnetic snaps: two sets / #25 needlework thread

Key points
• When whip stitching the outer fabric to the gusset, stitch right sides of both fabrics together.

Instructions
1 Fuse batting on wrong side of the outer fabric. Then quilt as desired.
2 Make the flap and the gussets.
3 Make pocket-A and -B, then sew them onto the backing of the outer fabric.
4 Lay the backing fabric flat over the outer fabric with the right sides together. Sew the zipper opening and both side edges.
5 Turn the fabric right side out, sew on the flap.
6 Whip stitch the gussets onto the outer fabric.
7 Sew pocket-B on the outer fabric and install the zipper.
8 Attach magnetic snaps and the ribbon for the handle.

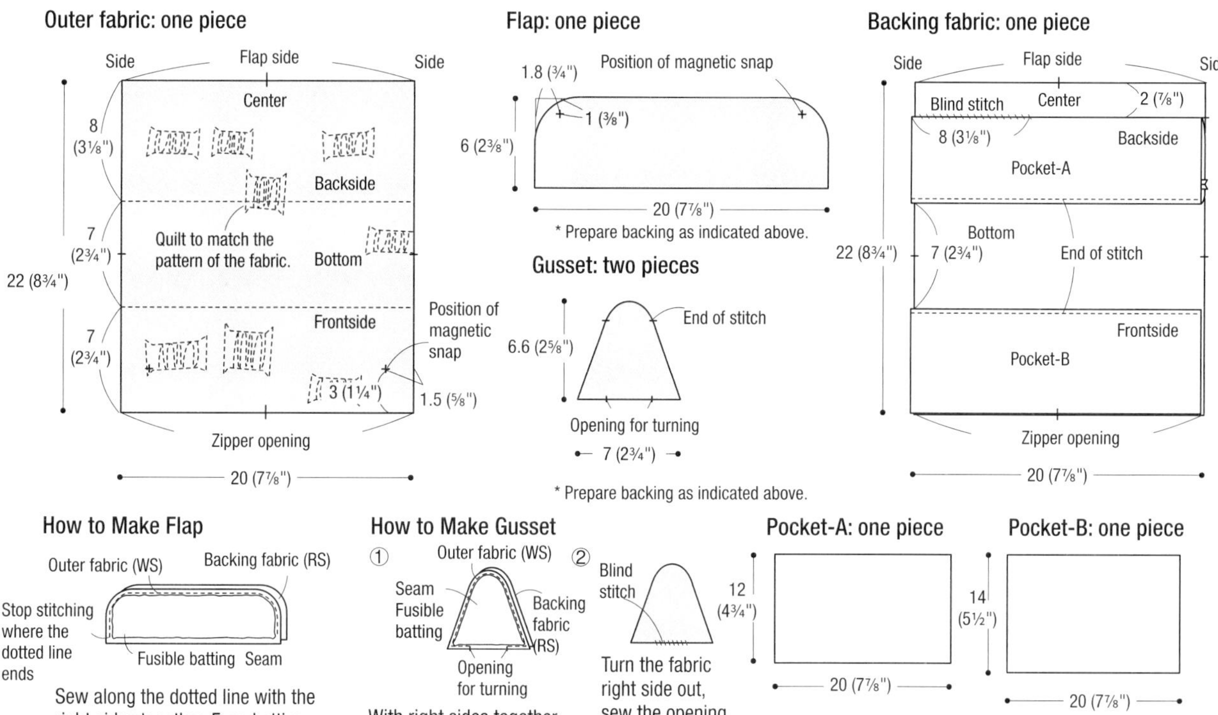

How to Make Pocket-A and -B

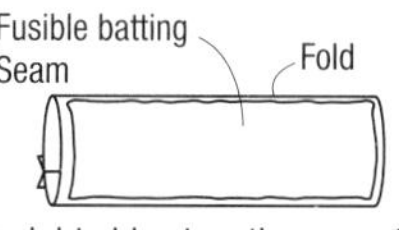

With right sides together, sew the top and bottom edges together. Turn the fabric right side out. Fuse batting on one side of the pocket-A.

Instructions

①

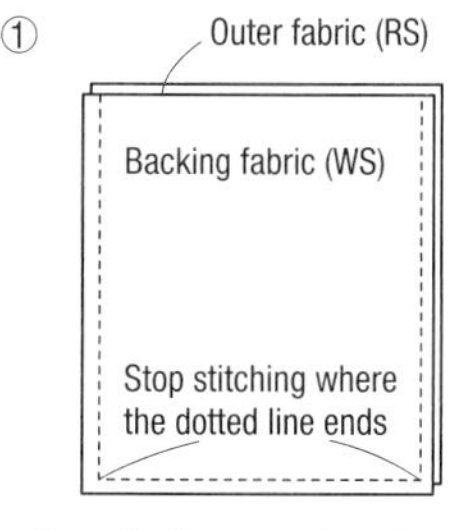

Sew the bottom edge along the dotted line. Do not stitch down opening of pocket-B. Sew both side edges.

②

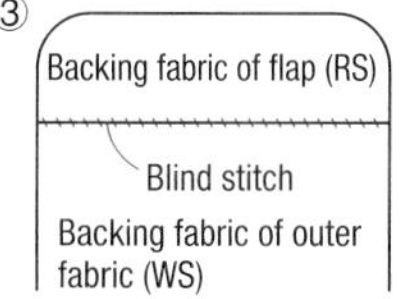

With right sides together, lay the flap flat over the outer fabric along the edge. Sew the flap to the outer fabric.

③

Backing fabric of flap (RS)
Blind stitch
Backing fabric of outer fabric (WS)

Press down the seam on the backing fabric of the flap. Blind stitch onto the backing fabric of the outer fabric.

④

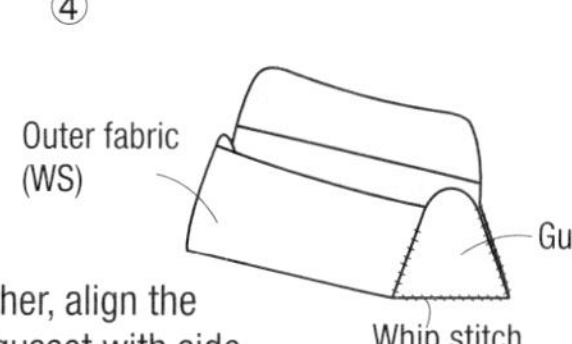

With right sides together, align the bottom edges of the gusset with side edges of the outer fabric. Whip stitch all around the edges.

⑤

Blind stitch
Zipper (WS)
Tack edge under
Pocket-B (WS)
Outer fabric (WS)
Running S. (#25 thread, 2-stand)

Align the zipper along the backing fabric of the outer fabric and pocket-B. Install zipper so that the teeth protrude from the mouth of the case.

⑥ Tack under and blind stitch.

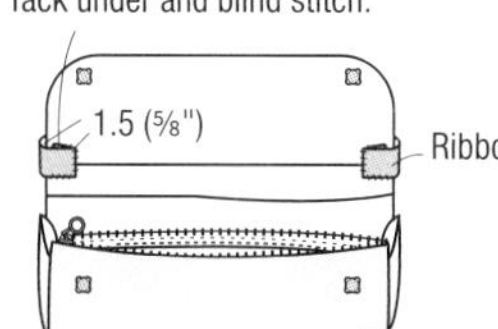

Attach magnetic snaps and ribbon for the handle.

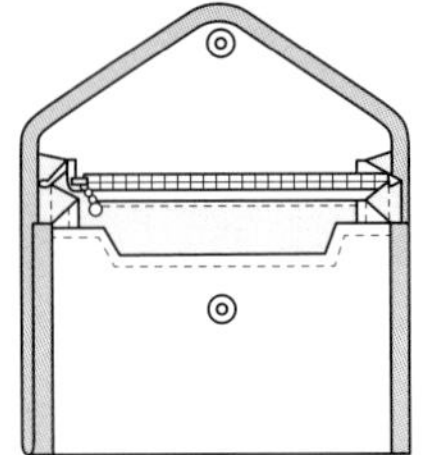

13.5 x 22.5 cm (5⅜" x 8⅞")
Design: Yuko Nishijima
• Full size patterns are on page 111.

32 Fashionable Envelope-shaped Case

Materials

Outer fabric (including pocket): 75 x 25 cm (29½" x 9⅞") / Backing fabric (including gusset, inside pocket): 100 x 40 cm (39⅜" x 15¾") / Fusible batting: 40 x 25 cm (15¾" x 9⅞") / Fusible interfacing: 50 x 30 cm (19¾" x 11⅞") / 4 cm (1⅝") wide bias tape: 100 cm (39⅜") / One zipper: 20 cm (7⅞") / 1.3 cm (½") diameter plastic snap: one set

Key points

• Apply interfacing on half of the fabric for the gusset and the pocket.
• See p. 67 for installing plastic snap.

Instructions

1 Make the back panel pocket. Secure it temporarily on the back panel of the case.
2 With the right sides together, lay back panel of the case flat over the front panel of the case. Sew bottom edge.
3 Fuse batting on the fabric sewn together in step 2. Lay the backing fabric flat over facing right side down. Sew the top edge; turn the backing fabric right side out and stitch along the top edge.
4 Sew partitions of the inside pocket.
5 Make the body of both the zippered pocket and the gussets. Join the zippered pocket to the gussets.
6 With the right sides out, sew the side edges of the outer fabric and the gusset. Sew piping along the seams all around.
7 Attach plastic snap.

Outer fabric front: one piece

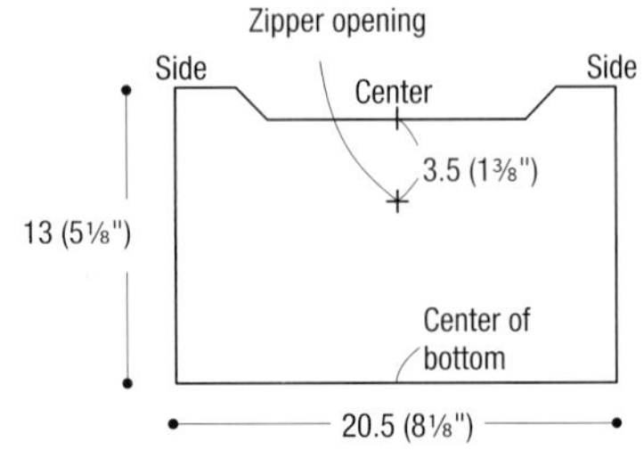

Zipper opening
Side
Center
Side
3.5 (1⅜")
13 (5⅛")
Center of bottom
20.5 (8⅛")

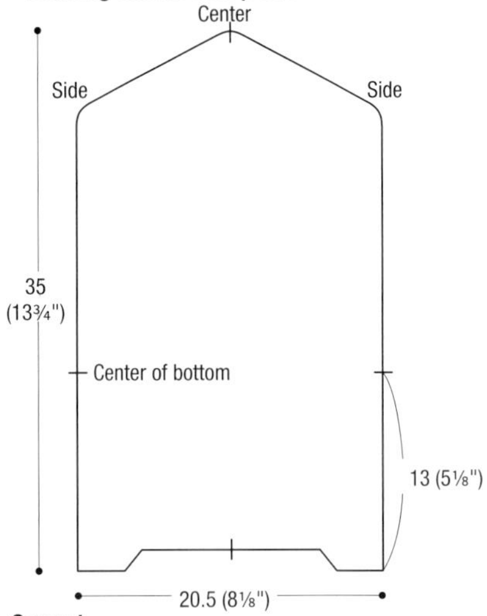

Back panel pocket: one piece

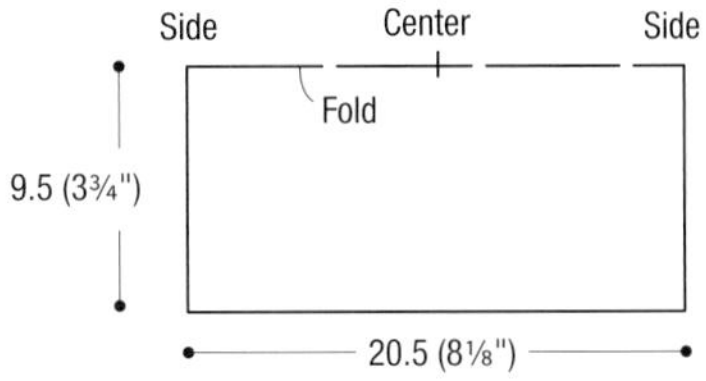

Side
Center
Side
Fold
9.5 (3¾")
20.5 (8⅛")

* Fusible interfacing: 20.5 x 9.5 cm (8⅛" x 3¾")

Inside Pocket: one piece

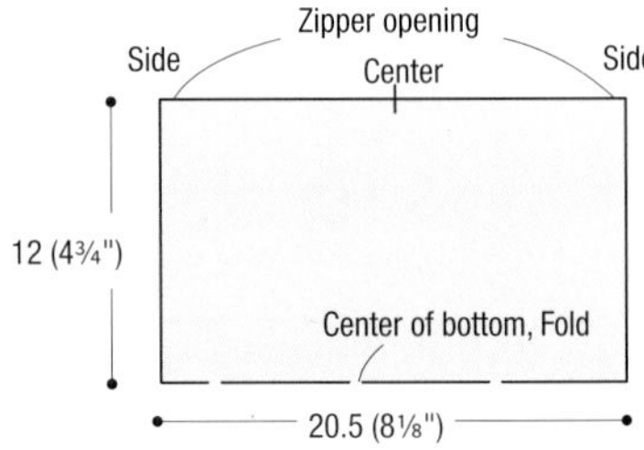

Zipper opening
Side
Center
Side
12 (4¾")
Center of bottom, Fold
20.5 (8⅛")

Outer fabric back: one piece

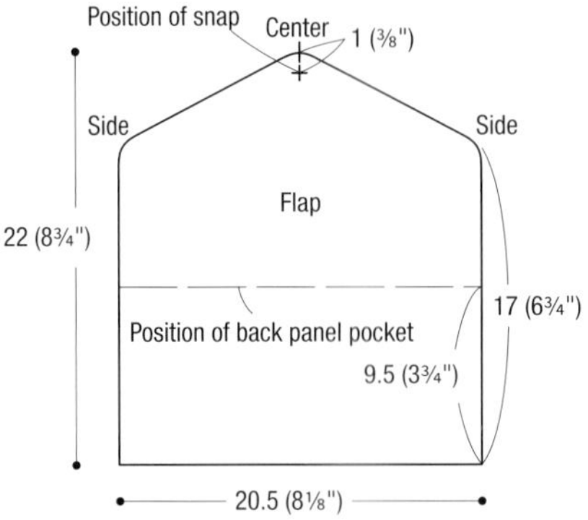

Position of snap
Center
1 (⅜")
Side
Side
Flap
22 (8¾")
17 (6¾")
Position of back panel pocket
9.5 (3¾")
20.5 (8⅛")

Gusset: two pieces

Position of inside pocket
Center
Fold
12 (4¾")
Tack
Divide equally into 4 parts
10.5 (4⅛")

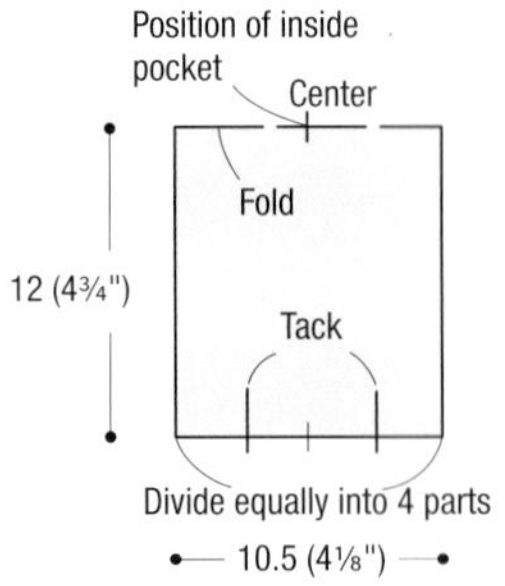

* Fusible interfacing: 10.5 x 12 cm (4⅛" x 4¾")

Backing fabric: one piece

Center
Side
Side
35 (13¾")
Center of bottom
13 (5⅛")
20.5 (8⅛")

How to Make Gusset

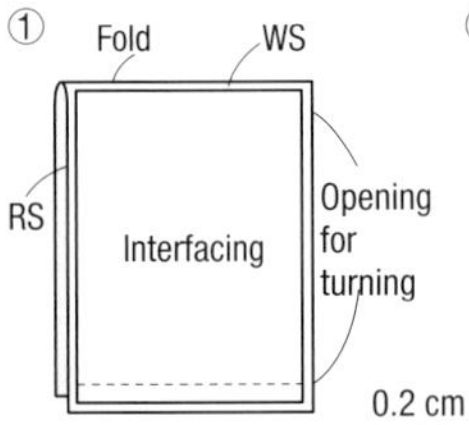

①
Fold
WS
RS
Interfacing
Opening for turning

With right sides together, fold the fabric in half. Apply interfacing on one side. Sew the bottom edge.

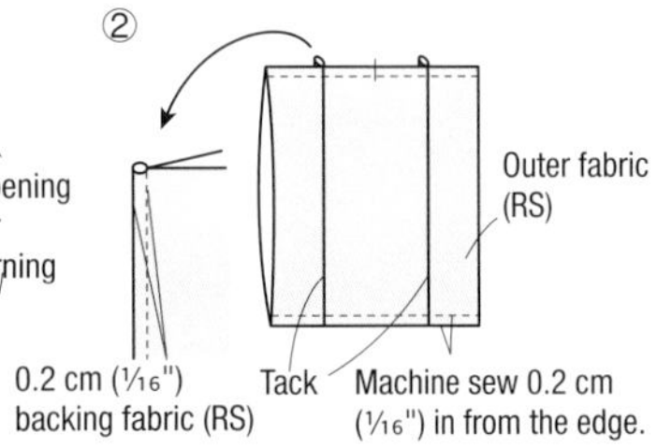

②
Outer fabric (RS)
0.2 cm (1⁄16") backing fabric (RS)
Tack
Machine sew 0.2 cm (1⁄16") in from the edge.

Turn the fabric right side out, sew the top and bottom edge. Tack the fabric as indicated in the diagram. Sew down the tack using a sewing machine.

How to Make Inside Pocket

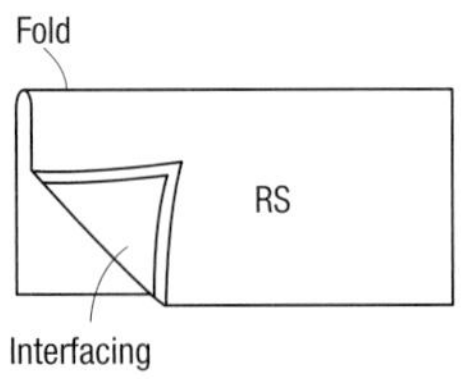

Fold
RS
Interfacing

Apply interfacing to half of the fabric, then fold the fabric with right side out.

How to Make Zippered Pocket

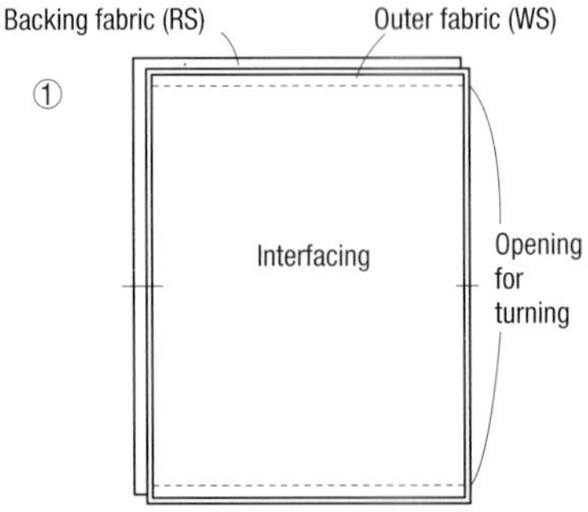

①
Backing fabric (RS)
Outer fabric (WS)
Interfacing
Opening for turning

With right sides together, lay the backing fabric over the outer fabric. Sew the top and the bottom edge.

②
Double-sided tape
Zipper (WS)
Backing fabric (RS)
Zipper (WS)
Machine sew
Outer fabric (WS)

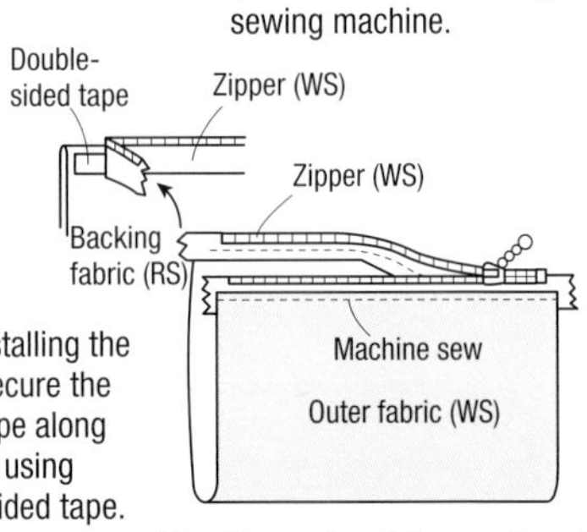

When installing the zipper, secure the zipper tape along the edge using double-sided tape.

Align the center of the mouth and the zipper. Adjust the zipper tape so that the teeth protrude and stitch.

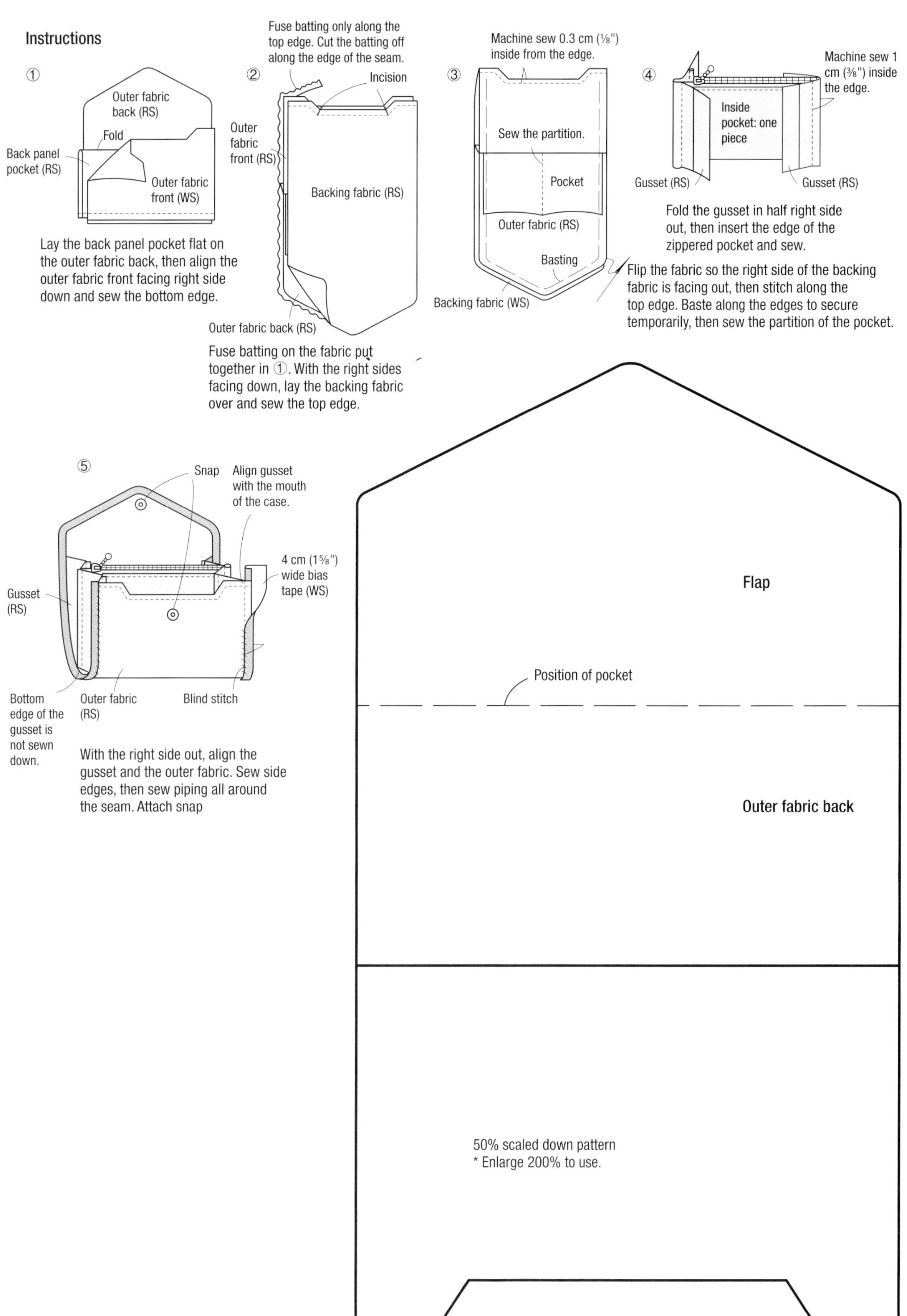
Instructions
①
Outer fabric back (RS)
Fold
Back panel pocket (RS)
Outer fabric front (WS)
Lay the back panel pocket flat on the outer fabric back, then align the outer fabric front facing right side down and sew the bottom edge.
②
Fuse batting only along the top edge. Cut the batting off along the edge of the seam.
Incision
Outer fabric front (RS)
Backing fabric (RS)
Outer fabric back (RS)
Fuse batting on the fabric put together in ①. With the right sides facing down, lay the backing fabric over and sew the top edge.
③
Machine sew 0.3 cm (⅛") inside from the edge.
Sew the partition.
Pocket
Outer fabric (RS)
Basting
Backing fabric (WS)
Flip the fabric so the right side of the backing fabric is facing out, then stitch along the top edge. Baste along the edges to secure temporarily, then sew the partition of the pocket.
④
Machine sew 1 cm (⅜") inside the edge.
Inside pocket: one piece
Gusset (RS)
Gusset (RS)
Fold the gusset in half right side out, then insert the edge of the zippered pocket and sew.
⑤
Snap
Align gusset with the mouth of the case.
4 cm (1⅝") wide bias tape (WS)
Gusset (RS)
Bottom edge of the gusset is not sewn down.
Outer fabric (RS)
Blind stitch
With the right side out, align the gusset and the outer fabric. Sew side edges, then sew piping all around the seam. Attach snap
Flap
Position of pocket
Outer fabric back
50% scaled down pattern
* Enlarge 200% to use.

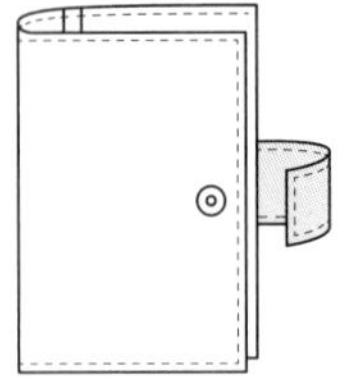

6.5 x 11.5 cm (6½" x 4½")
Design: Yumi Ishida

34 Case with Fabric Flap

Materials

Outer fabric, Lining fabric, Interfacing: each 30 x 25 cm (11⅞" x 9⅞") / Pocket-A: 25 x 20 cm (9⅞" x 7⅞") / Pocket-B: 40 x 15 cm (15¾" x 5⅞") / Pocket-C: 30 x 10 cm (11⅞" x 4") / One zipper: 15 cm (6") / 2 cm (⅞") wide fabric tape: 20 cm (7⅞") / Leather for the flap: 20 x 5 cm (7⅞" x 2") / 1.4 cm (⅝") diameter magnetic snap: one set

Key points

- Unless otherwise specified, add 1 cm (⅜") seam allowance.
- Interfacing is applied on the fabric under the magnetic snap for reinforcement.

Instructions

1 Make pocket-A, then sew on one side of the zipper tape along the zipper opening.
2 Sew the other side of the zipper tape to the lining fabric. Then, baste pocket-A to the lining fabric to hold temporarily.
3 Make pocket-B and -C, then assemble them together. Bind fabric tape along the top edge.
4 Lay assembled pocket-B and -C flat on the lining fabric and baste them to hold temporarily.
5 Attach magnetic snap and make leather flap.
6 Fuse interfacing on wrong side of the outer fabric, then attach magnetic snap.
7 With right sides together, sew the outer and lining fabric together.
8 Turn the fabric right side out. Tack seam allowance along the inside opening. Then, machine sew the opening to close.

Outer fabric: one piece

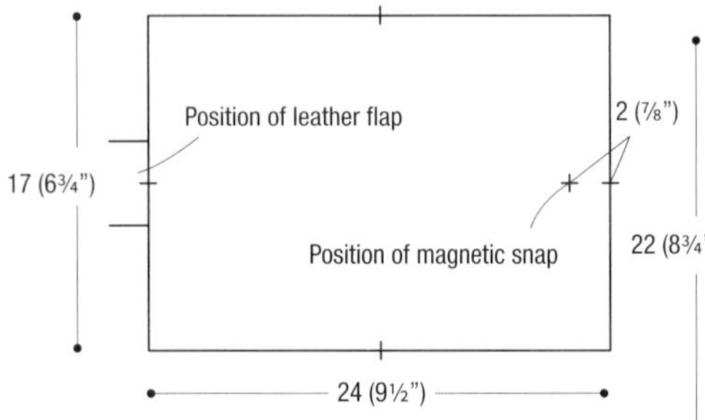

Position of leather flap
2 (⅞")
17 (6¾")
Position of magnetic snap
24 (9½")

* Prepare the lining fabric as indicated above.

Pocket-A: one piece

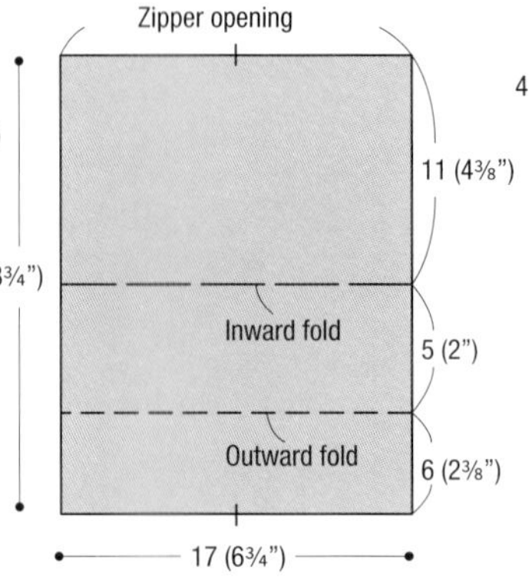

Zipper opening
11 (4⅜")
22 (8¾")
Inward fold
5 (2")
Outward fold
6 (2⅜")
17 (6¾")

Leather flap: one piece

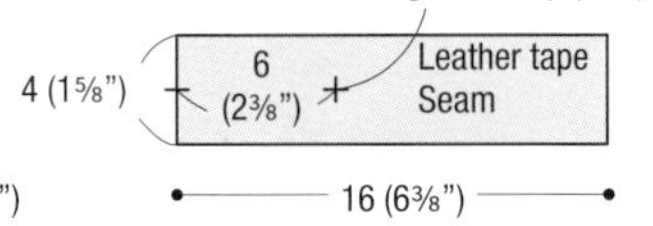

Position of magnetic snap (stud)
4 (1⅝")
6 (2⅜")
Leather tape
Seam
16 (6⅜")

How to Make Leather Flap

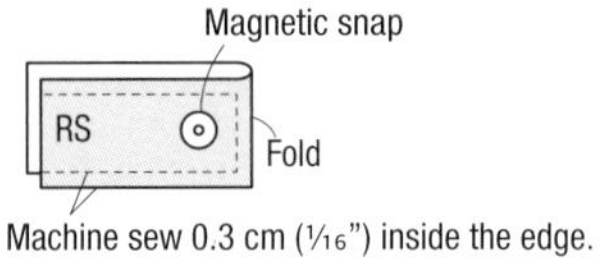

Magnetic snap
RS
Fold
Machine sew 0.3 cm (1/16") inside the edge.

Attach magnetic snap, then fold in half lengthwise. Machine sew the top and the bottom edge.

Pocket-B: one piece

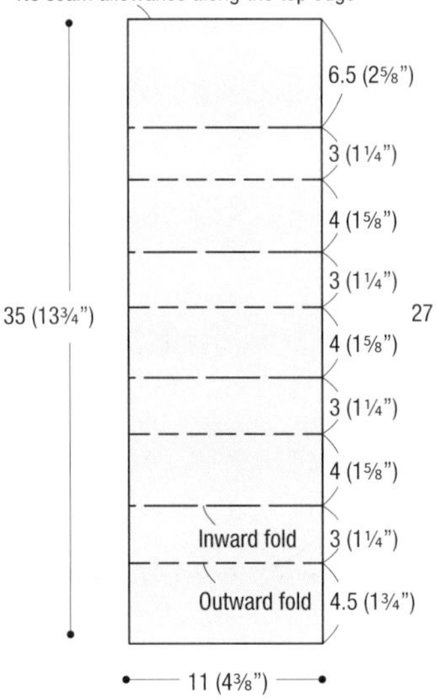

No seam allowance along the top edge
6.5 (2⅝")
3 (1¼")
4 (1⅝")
3 (1¼")
35 (13¾")
4 (1⅝")
3 (1¼")
4 (1⅝")
Inward fold
3 (1¼")
Outward fold
4.5 (1¾")
11 (4⅜")

Pocket-C: one piece

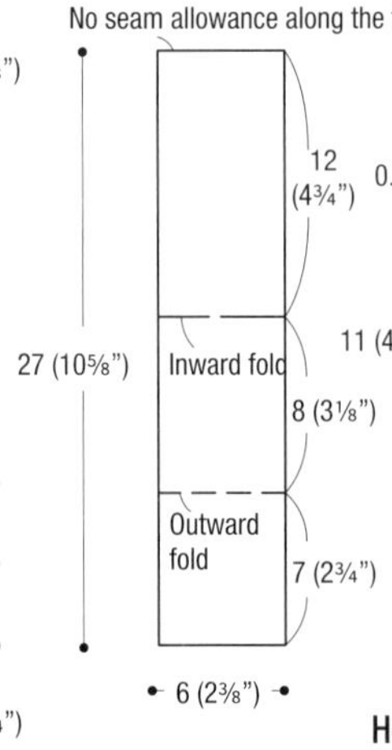

No seam allowance along the top edge.
12 (4¾")
27 (10⅝")
Inward fold
8 (3⅛")
Outward fold
7 (2¾")
6 (2⅜")

How to Make Pocket-A

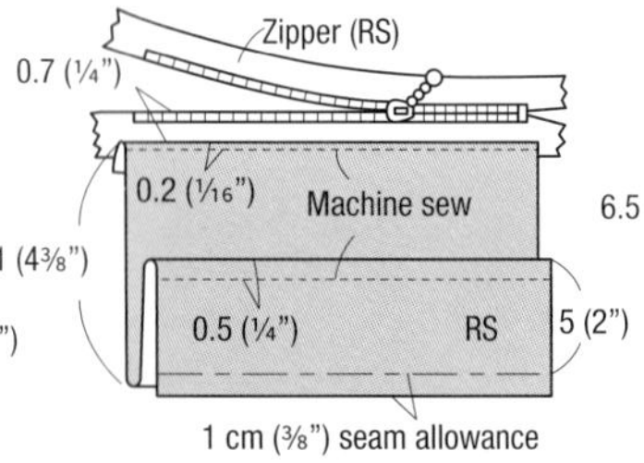

Zipper (RS)
0.7 (¼")
0.2 (1/16")
Machine sew
11 (4⅜")
0.5 (¼")
RS
5 (2")
1 cm (⅜") seam allowance

Fold the fabric along the folding lines. Machine sew along the top and bottom edge of the pocket. Sew one side of the zipper tape along the zipper opening.

How to Make Pocket-B

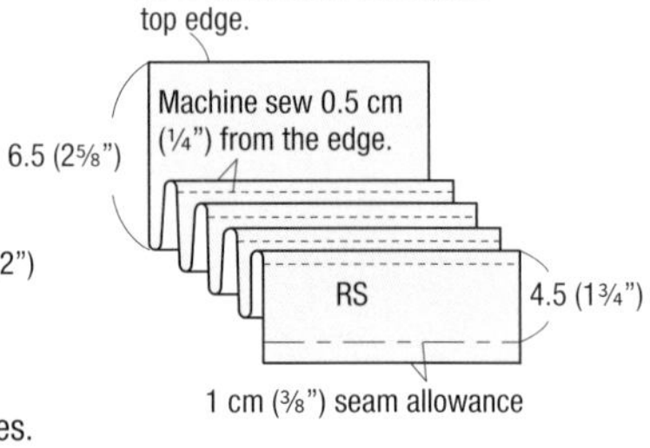

No seam allowance along the top edge.
Machine sew 0.5 cm (¼") from the edge.
6.5 (2⅝")
RS
4.5 (1¾")
1 cm (⅜") seam allowance

As you fold the fabric along the folding lines, machine sew the folded edge.

How to Make Pocket-C

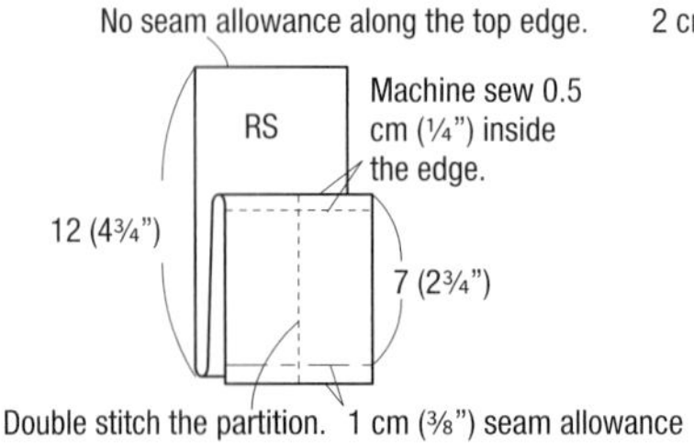

No seam allowance along the top edge.
RS
Machine sew 0.5 cm (¼") inside the edge.
12 (4¾")
7 (2¾")
Double stitch the partition.
1 cm (⅜") seam allowance

Fold the fabric along the folding lines. Machine sew the folded edge, then the partition.

How to Assemble Pocket-B and -C

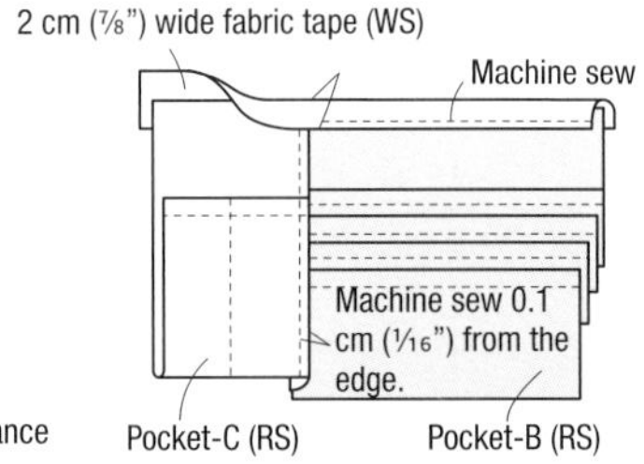

2 cm (⅞") wide fabric tape (WS)
Machine sew
Machine sew 0.1 cm (1/16") from the edge.
Pocket-C (RS)
Pocket-B (RS)

With the right sides together, join pocket-B and -C. Then, with the right sides facing out, machine sew the joined seam. Bind the fabric tape along the top edge.

How to Assemble Lining Fabric

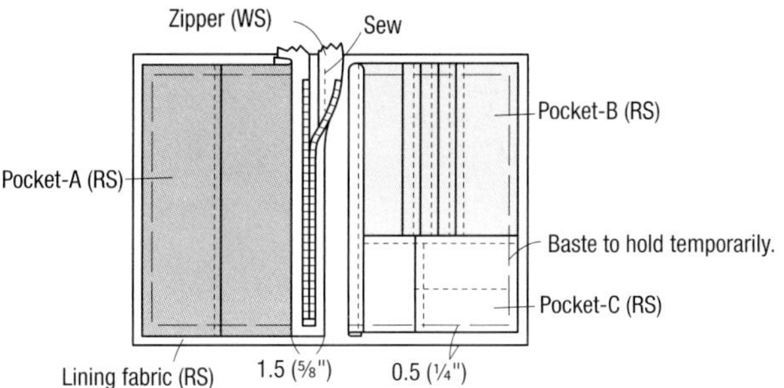

Sew loose zipper tape on the lining fabric. Turn right side out. Lay pocket-A flat and assemble -B and -C on the lining fabric. Baste the edges to hold temporarily.

Instructions

①

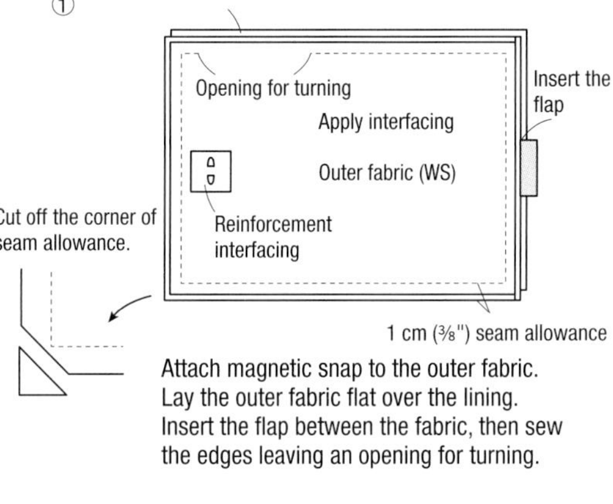

Attach magnetic snap to the outer fabric. Lay the outer fabric flat over the lining. Insert the flap between the fabric, then sew the edges leaving an opening for turning.

②

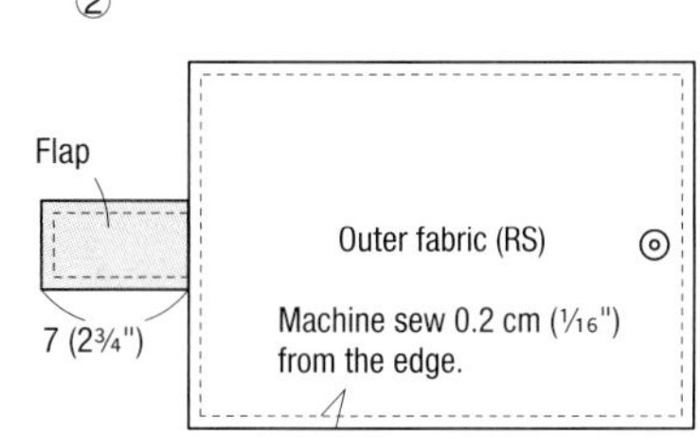

Turn the fabric right side out, tack seam allowance of the opening inside, then machine sew the edges all the way around.

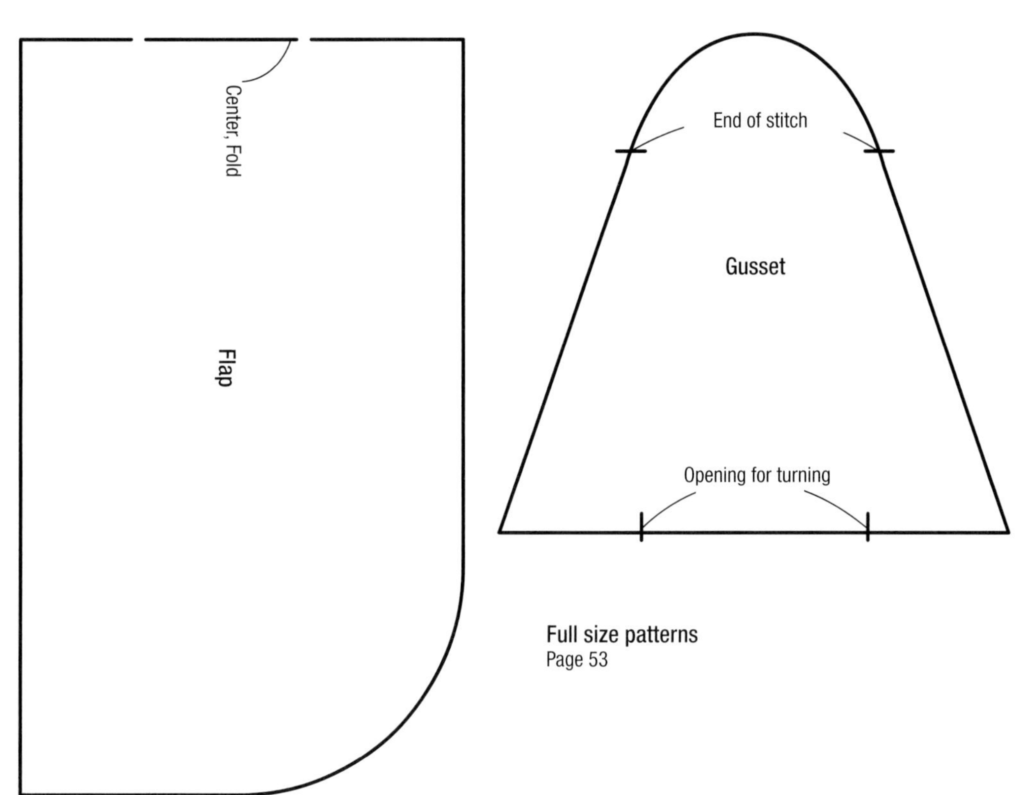

Full size patterns
Page 53

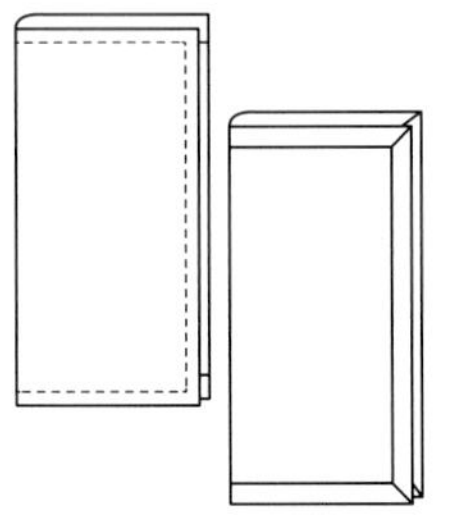

22 x 11 cm (8¾" x 4⅜")
Design: Yuko Nishijima

35 Oblong Passport Case

Materials

Outer fabric (include piping for regular fabric case): 50 x 30 cm (19¾" x 11⅞") / (laminated fabric case) 25 x 25 cm (9⅞" x 9⅞") / Lining fabric: 25 x 25 cm (9⅞" x 9⅞") / Pocket-A: 45 x 25 cm (17¾" x 9⅞") / Pocket-B: 20 x 25 cm (7⅞" x 9⅞") / Pocket-C: 20 x 20 cm (7⅞" x 7⅞") / Firm interfacing: 40 x 25 cm (15¾" x 9⅞") / Interfacing: 25 x 25 cm (9⅞" x 9⅞") (used only for regular fabric case) / 0.3 cm (⅛") wide double-sided tape as necessary (used only for laminated fabric cases)

Key points

- Apply firm interfacing to half of the wrong side of the pocket fabric.
- If you are making a case using regular fabric, apply interfacing to the wrong side of the outer fabric.

Instructions

1 Make the pocket-A, -B, and -C.
2 Layer the outer fabric, the pockets, and the lining fabric.
3 Bind piping all the way along the edges. For a laminated fabric case, instead of piping, fold the edges of the outer fabric (laminate) down and sew.

Outer fabric: one piece

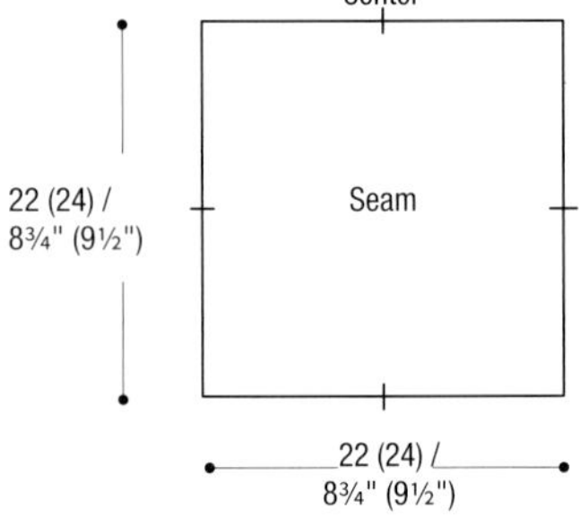

Center
22 (24) / 8¾" (9½")
Seam
22 (24) / 8¾" (9½")

* Measurements inside parentheses are for laminated fabric.

Lining fabric: one piece

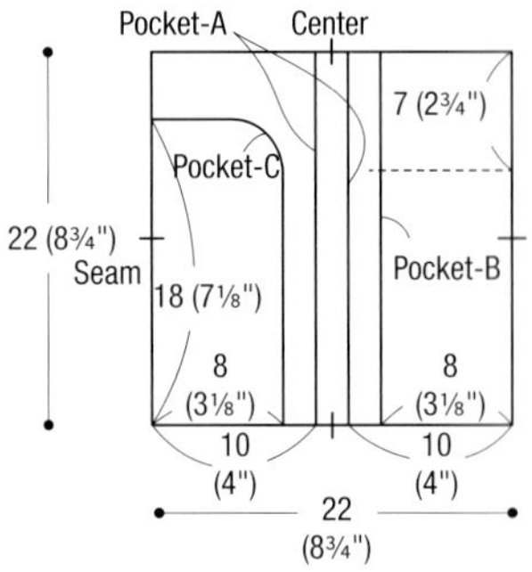

Pocket-A
Center
7 (2¾")
Pocket-C
Pocket-B
22 (8¾")
Seam
18 (7⅛")
8 (3⅛")
8 (3⅛")
10 (4")
10 (4")
22 (8¾")

Pocket-A: two pieces

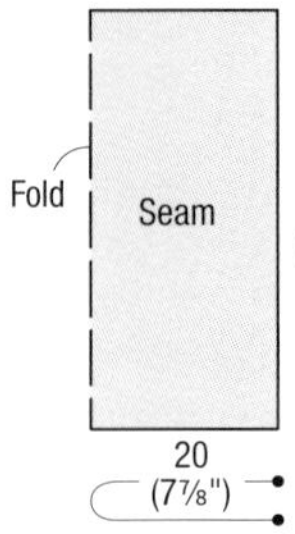

Fold
Seam
22 (8¾")
20 (7⅞")

Pocket-B: one piece

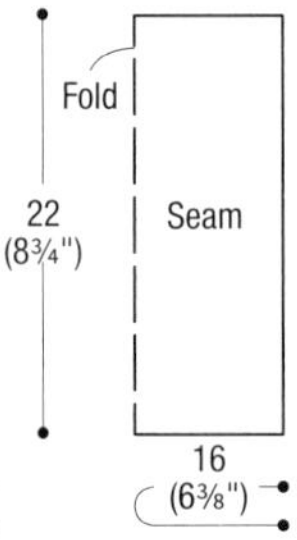

Fold
Seam
16 (6⅜")

Pocket-C: one piece

Add 1 cm (⅜") seam allowance only for the curved edge.
18 (7⅛")
Fold
Seam
16 (6⅜")

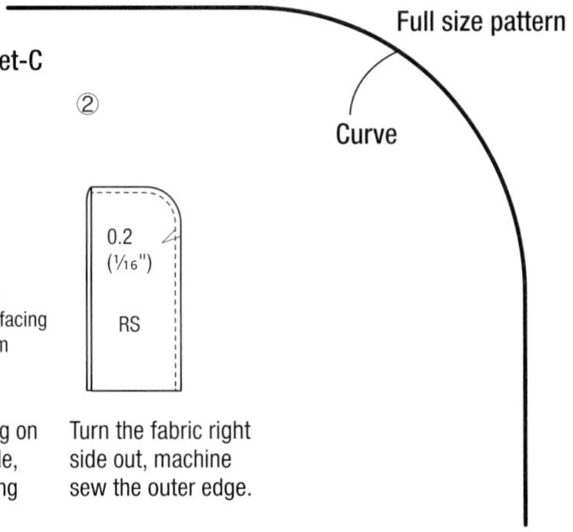

Full size pattern

Curve

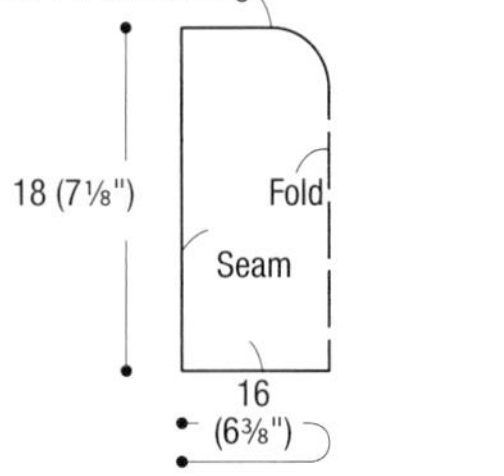

How to Assemble Pocket-A and -B

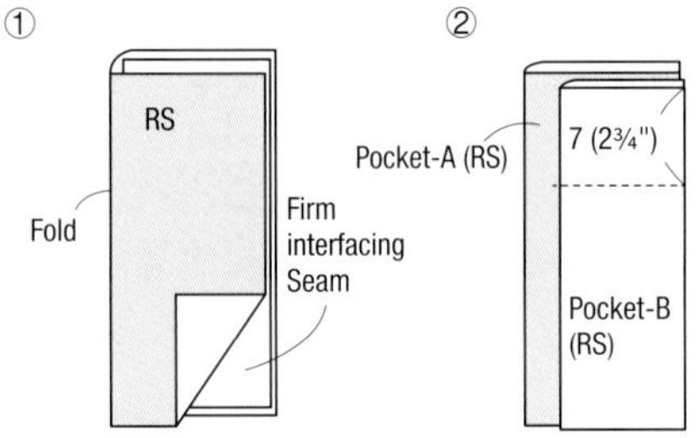

① RS
Fold
Firm interfacing
Seam

② Pocket-A (RS)
7 (2¾")
Pocket-B (RS)

Apply firm interfacing on half of the wrong side, then fold in half with the right sides out (pocket-A, -B same instruction).

How to Make Pocket-C

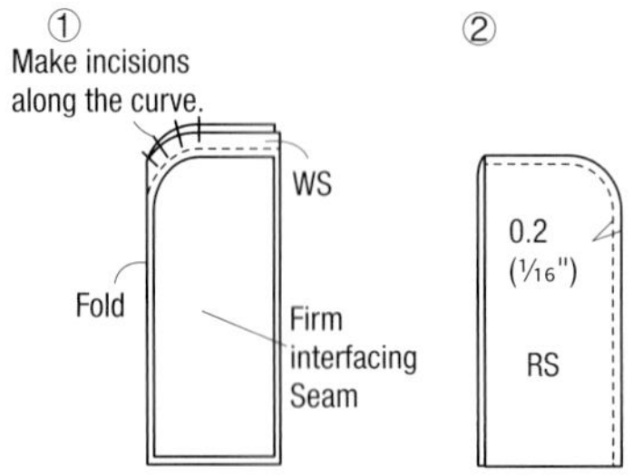

① Make incisions along the curve.
WS
Fold
Firm interfacing
Seam

Apply firm interfacing on half of the wrong side, then fold in half facing with the right sides together. Sew the curve.

② 0.2 (1/16")
RS

Turn the fabric right side out, machine sew the outer edge.

Instructions

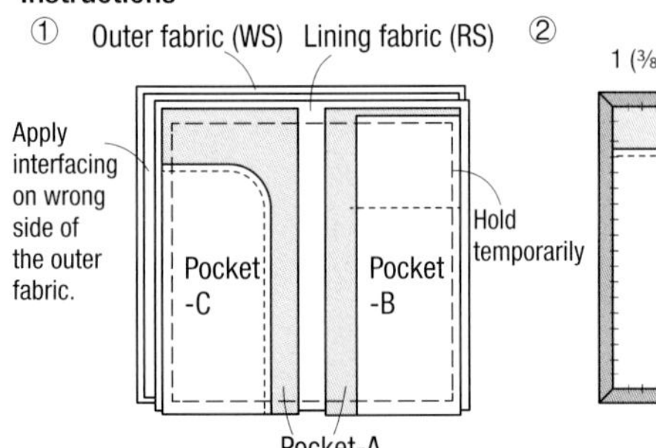

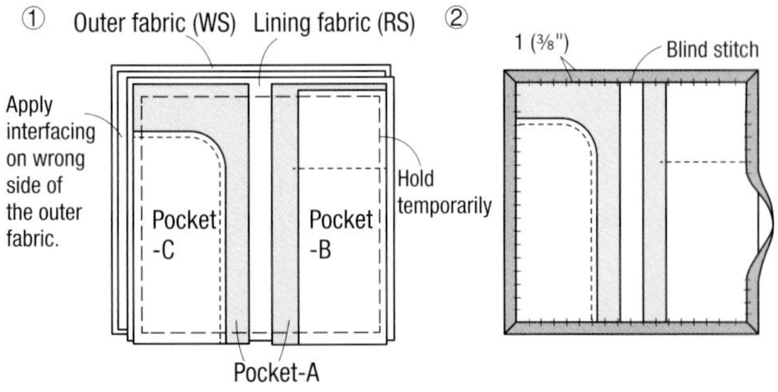

Layer the outer fabric, the lining fabric, and the pockets, then baste them together to hold temporarily.

Bind piping all the way along the edges.

How to Make a Case Using Laminated Fabric

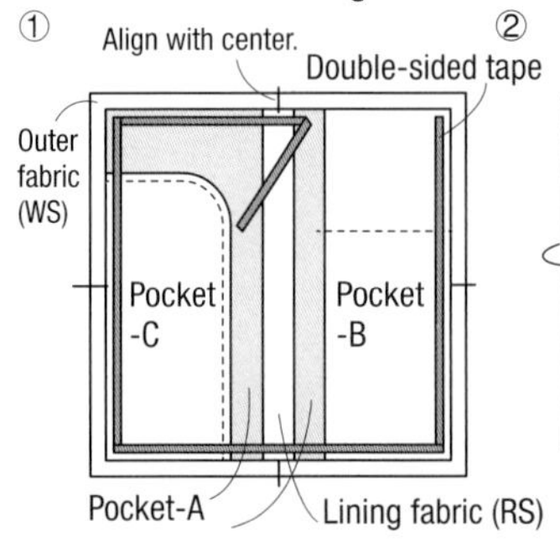

Place the pockets over the lining fabric. Apply double-sided tape along the outer edges. With the right sides out, place the pockets and the lining over the outer fabric (laminated fabric).

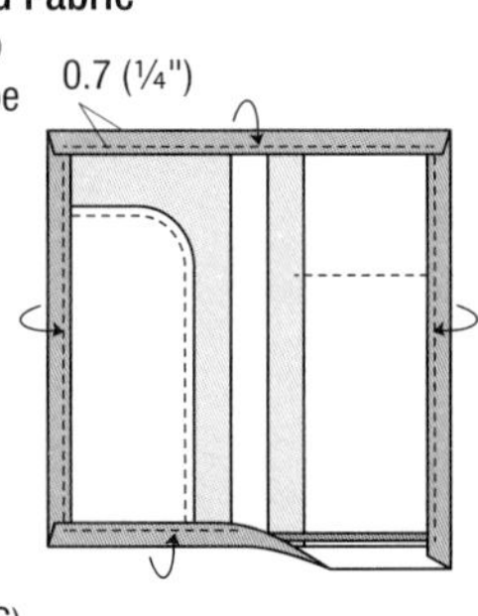

Fold down the seams along the outer edges of the outer fabric, sew down the seams while avoiding the double-sided tape.

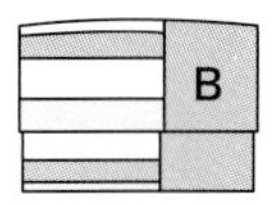

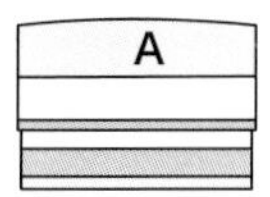

10 x 15 cm (4" x 7⅞")
Design: Mitsuko Ito

36 Bellowed Card Case – Easy to Find, Easy to Remove

Materials

Various fabrics for pressed quilts / Backing fabric (including pocket): 100 x 35 cm (39⅜" x 13¾") / Fusible batting: 30 x 20 cm (11⅞" x 7⅞") / 2 cm (⅞") diameter sew-on magnetic snaps: one set

Key points

- The outer fabric is pressed quilt on fusible batting (or batting).
- See p. 57 for making the bellowed pocket.

Instructions

1 Used pressed quilt to assemble the outer fabric.
2 Make the pocket, then sew it on the lining fabric.
3 With the right sides together, sew the outer and lining fabric along the edges leaving an opening for turning.
4 Turn the fabric right side out. Sew the opening to close. Then, attach magnetic snap.

Be Careful!

Do not store any magnetic stripe card like a credit card in this pouch. The magnet button could damage the magnetic stripe and render the card useless.

A-outer fabric: one piece

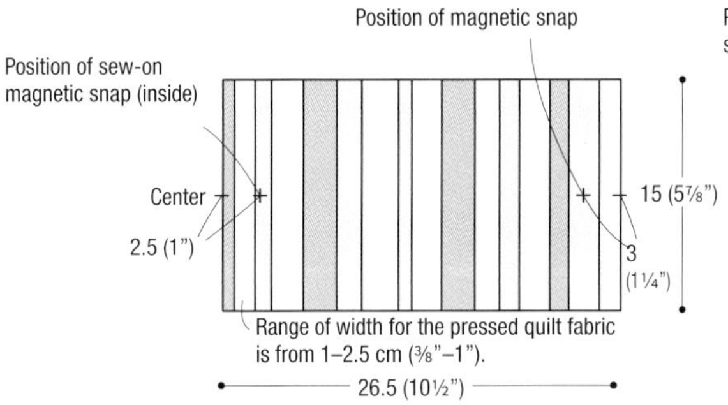

Position of magnetic snap
Position of sew-on magnetic snap (inside)
Center
2.5 (1")
15 (5⅞")
3 (1¼")
Range of width for the pressed quilt fabric is from 1–2.5 cm (⅜"–1").
26.5 (10½")

B-outer fabric: one piece

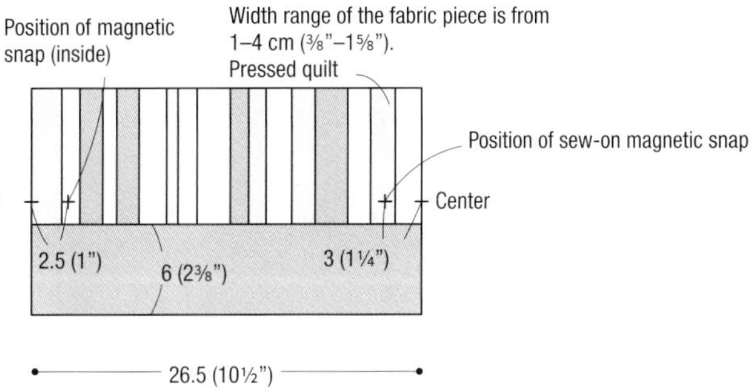

Position of magnetic snap (inside)
Width range of the fabric piece is from 1–4 cm (⅜"–1⅝").
Pressed quilt
Position of sew-on magnetic snap
Center
2.5 (1")
6 (2⅜")
3 (1¼")
26.5 (10½")

Pocket-A: one piece

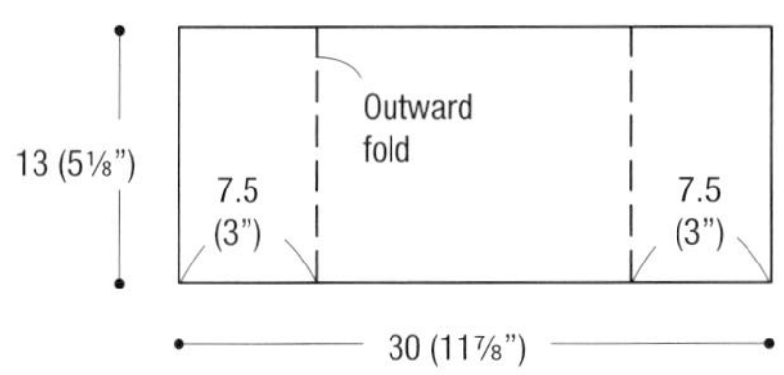

13 (5⅛")
Outward fold
7.5 (3")
7.5 (3")
30 (11⅞")

Pocket-B: one piece

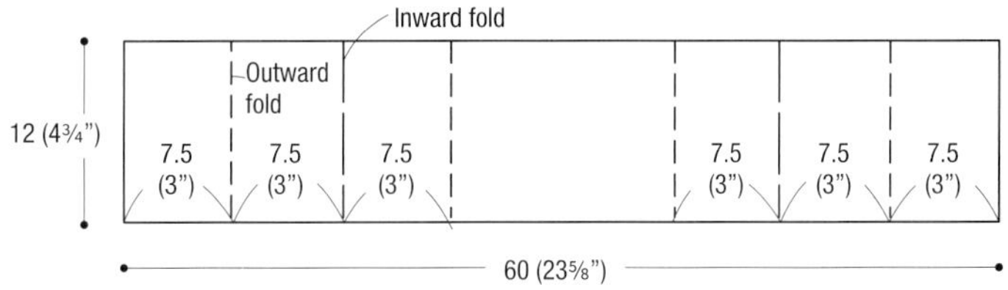

Inward fold
Outward fold
12 (4¾")
7.5 (3")
7.5 (3")
7.5 (3")
7.5 (3")
7.5 (3")
7.5 (3")
60 (23⅝")

Pocket-C: one piece

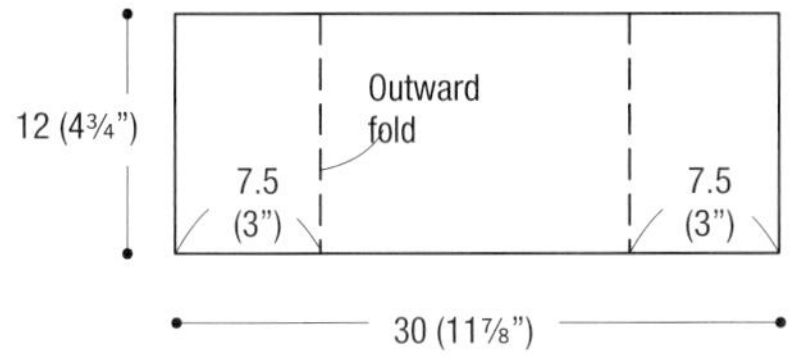

12 (4¾")
Outward fold
7.5 (3")
7.5 (3")
30 (11⅞")

Lining fabric: one piece

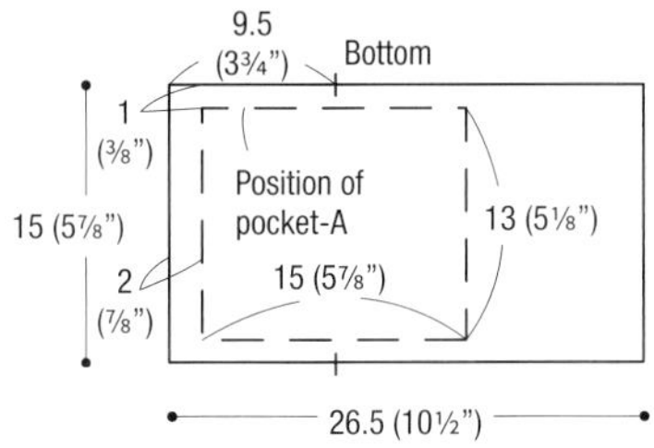

9.5 (3¾")
Bottom
1 (⅜")
Position of pocket-A
13 (5⅛")
15 (5⅞")
15 (5⅞")
2 (⅞")
26.5 (10½")

How to Pressed Quilt

①
Fusible batting
Step 1: fabric (RS)
Step 2: fabric (WS)

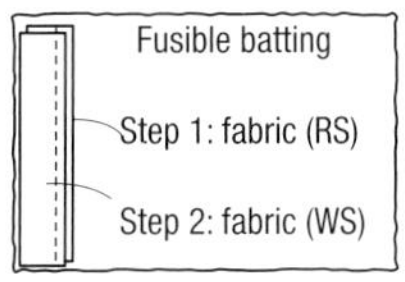

Lay the first piece flat on the batting, with the right sides together, then join the second piece to the first piece.

②
Step1: fabric (RS)
Step3: fabric (WS)
Step3: fabric (RS)
Step2: fabric (RS)

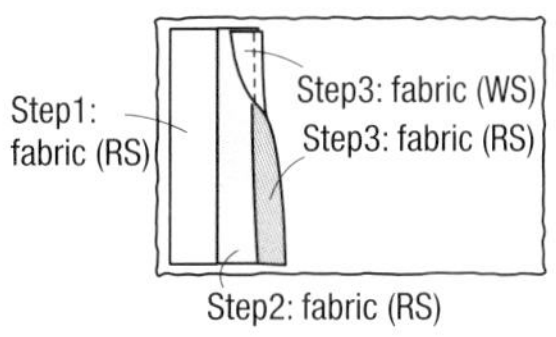

Turn the second piece right side out, right sides together, and then join the third piece to the second. Turn the third piece right side out and join the next piece with the right sides together. Repeat.

Instructions

①
Outer fabric (RS)
Fusible batting
Lining fabric (WS)
10 cm (4") opening for turning

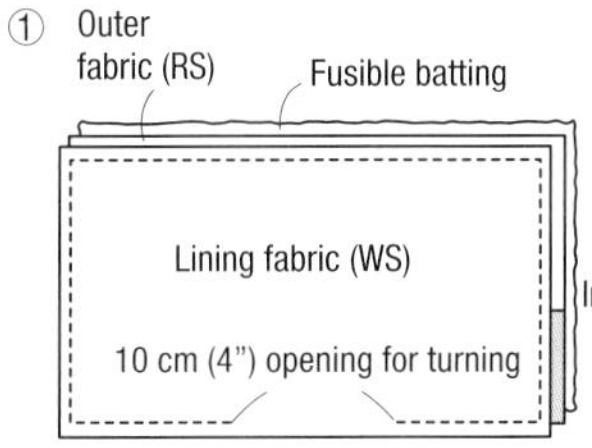

Assemble the outer fabric by pressed quilt technique. With the right sides together, lay the lining fabric that has the pocket attached flat over the outer fabric. Sew along the edges, leaving an opening for turning.

②
Attach magnetic snap.
Inside
2.5 (1")
3 (1¼")
Blind stitch

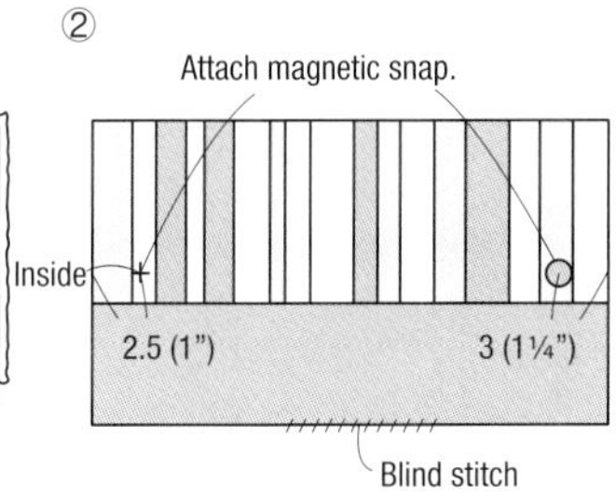

Turn the fabric right side out, then close the opening. Attach magnetic snap.

37 Simple Compact Pouch with Flap

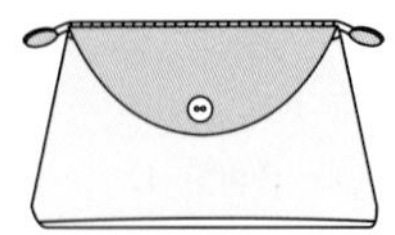

9 x 14 cm (3⅝" x 5½")
Design: Hiroko Fukuda

- Full size patterns are on page 119.

Materials

Fabric for self-covered buttons as necessary / Outer fabric (include bottom gusset, lining of pocket, two self-covered button): 40x35 cm (15¾" x 13¾") / Lining fabric: 20 x 30 cm (7⅞" x 11⅞") / Pocket: 40 x 15 cm (15¾" x 5⅞") / Fusible batting: 40 x 35 cm (15¾" x 13¾") / 1.8 cm (¾") diameter button for self-covered buttons: four pieces / 1.5 cm (⅝") diameter buttons: two pieces / 1 cm (⅜") diameter snap rings: two sets / One zipper: 12 cm (4¾")

Key points

- When joining the side edges of the outer fabric whip stitch with right sides of both fabrics together.
- See p. 61 for installing snap ring.

Instructions

1 Make the pocket.
2 Lay the pocket flat over the outer fabric, then sew on the bottom gusset with right sides together. Do the same for the other side.
3 Fuse batting on the outer fabric and, with the right sides together, sew the outer fabric and the lining along the edges while leaving an opening for turning.
4 Turn the fabric right side out and close the opening.
5 Fold the outer fabric along the folding line as indicated in the diagram. Install the zipper. Make self-covered buttons and attach them to the end of the zipper tape.
6 Whip stitch the side edges of the outer fabric, then sew the bottom gusset.
7 Attach snap ring and button.

Outer fabric: two pieces

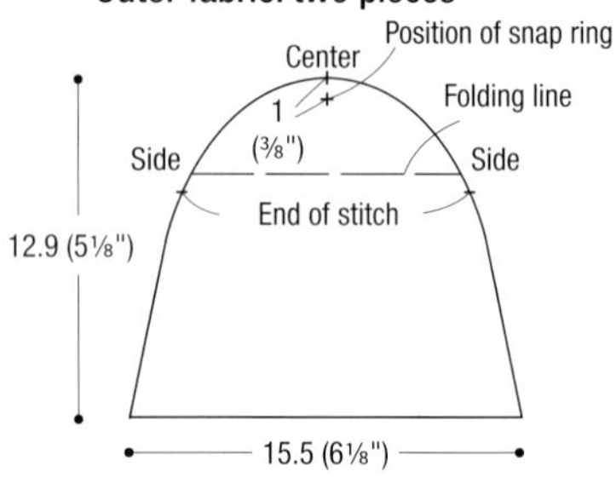

Position of snap ring
Center
1 (⅜")
Folding line
Side
Side
End of stitch
12.9 (5⅛")
15.5 (6⅛")

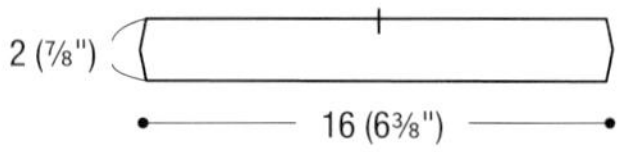

Lining fabric: one piece

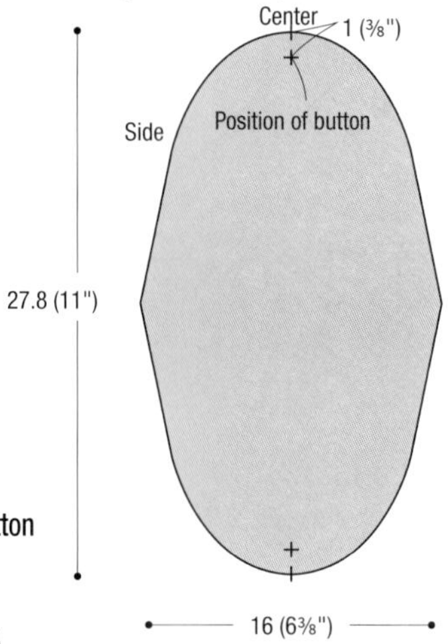

Center
1 (⅜")
Side
Position of button
27.8 (11")
16 (6⅜")

Pocket: two pieces

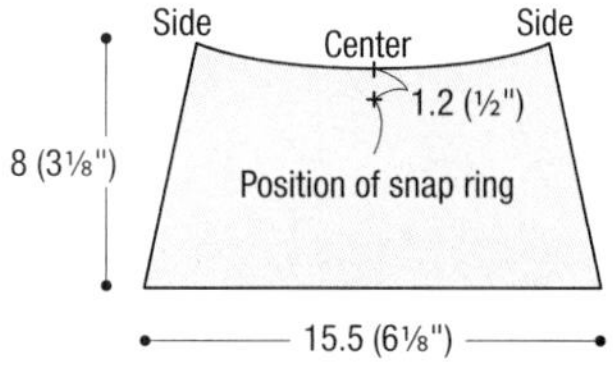

Side
Center
Side
1.2 (½")
8 (3⅛")
Position of snap ring
15.5 (6⅛")

* Prepare lining fabric indicated above.

Bottom gusset: one piece

2 (⅞")
16 (6⅜")

Self-covered buttons: four pieces

3.5 (1⅜")
Seam

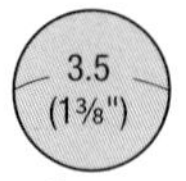

How to Make a Self-covered Button

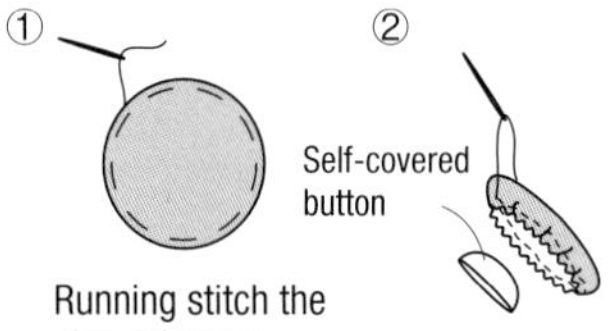

① Running stitch the circumference

② Self-covered button

Pull the thread to gather the fabric, then cover the button.

How to Make Pockets

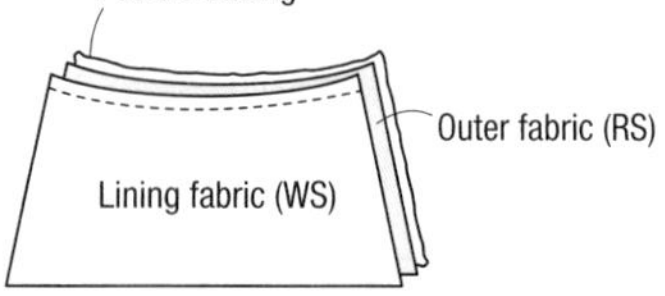

Fusible batting
Outer fabric (RS)
Lining fabric (WS)

Fuse batting on the outer fabric with the right sides together. Sew the outer and lining fabric along the top edges.

Instructions

① Outer fabric (RS)
Pocket (RS)
Bottom (RS)

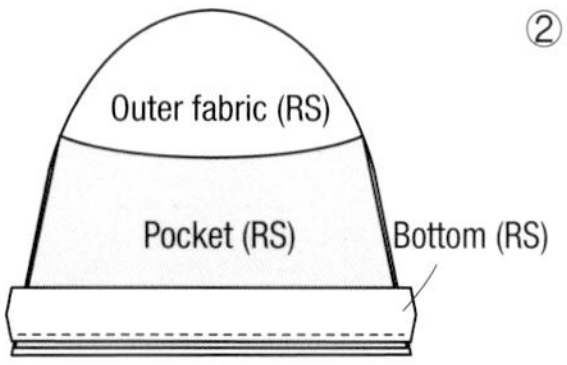

Lay the pocket flat over the outer fabric, then sew on the bottom gusset with the right sides together.

② Outer fabric (RS)
Pocket
Bottom gusset (RS)
Pocket
Outer fabric (RS)

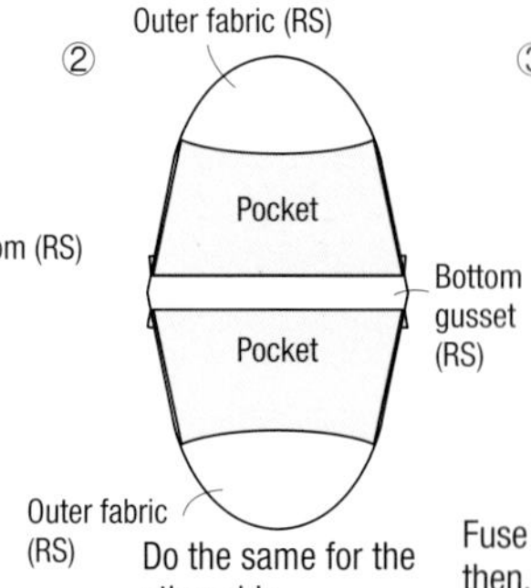

Do the same for the other side.

③ Lining fabric (RS)
Fusible batting
Opening for turning

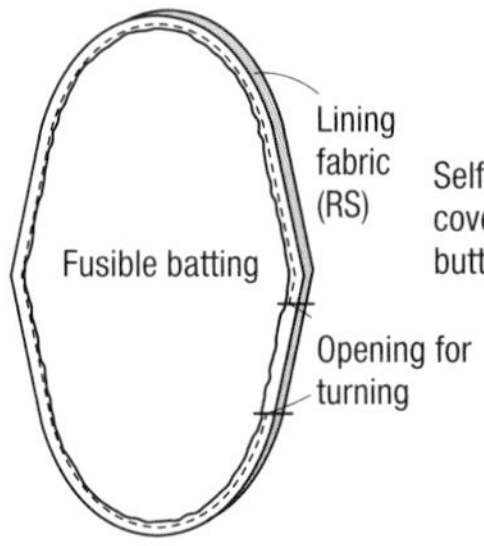

Fuse batting on the outer fabric, then, with the right sides together, sew the lining and the outer fabric along the edges while leaving an opening for turning. Turn the fabric right side out and sew the opening closed.

④ Zipper (WS)
Blind stitch
Self-covered buttons
0.5 (¼")
Blind stitch

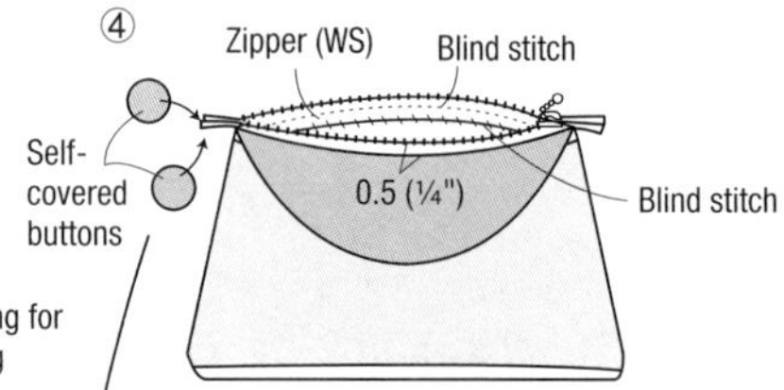

Fold the outer fabric as indicated in the diagram, then install the zipper with the teeth protruding from the opening. Sandwich both ends of the zipper tape with self-covered buttons.

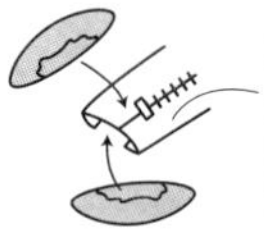

Fold ends of the zipper tape, then sandwich with self-covered buttons. Stitch circumference of the buttons.

⑤ End of stitch
Side
2 (⅞")
Outer fabric (WS)
Whip stitch

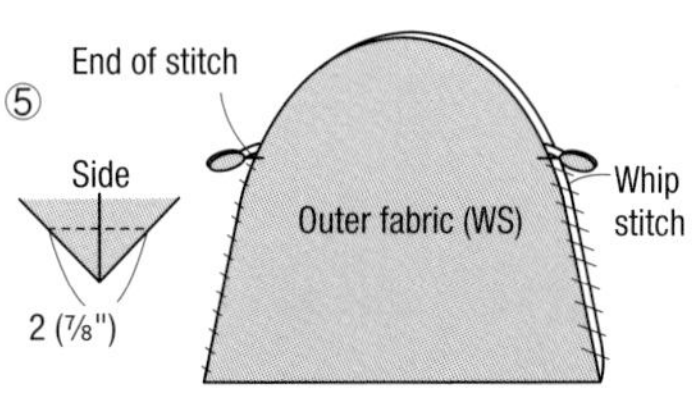

Fold the outer fabric in half with the right sides together. From the bottom to the end of the stitch indicated above, whip stitch the side edges and sew on the bottom gusset.

⑥ Buttons
Snap ring

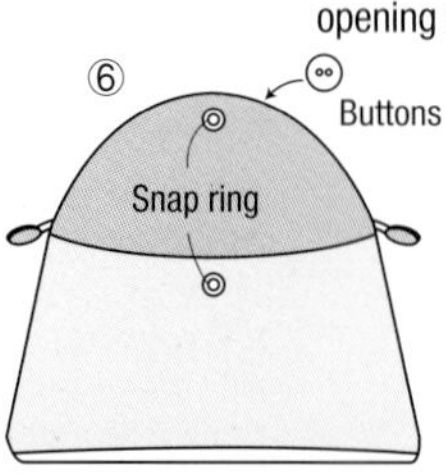

Attach snap rings on the outer fabric and the pocket. Attach a button to the front of the flap.

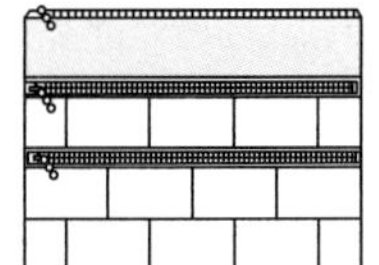

17.5 x 25 cm (6⅞" x 9⅞")
Design: Yasuko Hara

38 Triple Pocket Pouch

Materials
Various fabrics for piecing / Outer fabric-A (including outer fabric-C): 30 x 25 cm (11⅞" x 9⅞") / Lining fabric: 65 x 50 cm (25⅝" x 19¾") / Batting: 30 x 45 cm (11⅞" x 17¾") / Three zipper: 25 cm (9⅞")

Key points
- For the outer fabric, you can use piecing or plain fabric.

Instructions
1 Use piecing to assemble quilt top of the outer fabric-B and -C. The outer fabric-A is plain fabric.
2 Lay the quilt top flat over the batting and baste. Quilt as desired.
3 Install the zipper on outer fabric-C and lining fabric-C.
4 Install the zipper on lining fabric-C and outer fabric-B.
5 Install the zipper on outer fabric-B and lining fabric-B.
6 4 Install the zipper on lining fabric-B and outer fabric-A.
7 Install the zipper on outer fabric-A and lining fabric-A.
8 Install the zipper on lining fabric-A and outer fabric-C.
9 Turn the lining fabric-A right side out. Sew both side edges.
10 Bind fabric tape along the seam.

Outer fabric-A: one piece
Side 2 (⅞") Side 4 (1⅝")
26 (10¼")

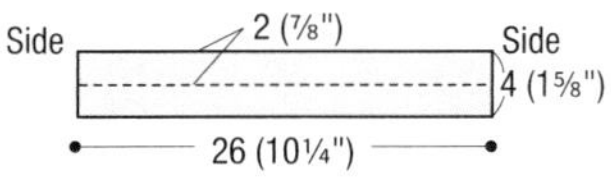

Outer fabric-B: one piece
3.25 (1¼") 2 (⅞") 6.5 (2⅝") Side
Side 4 (1⅝")
26 (10¼")

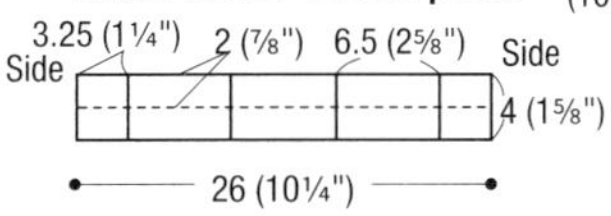

Outer fabric-A: one piece
Side 2 (⅞") 6.5 (2⅝") 4 (1⅝") Side
4 (1⅝")
26 (10¼") 3.25 (1¼") 6 (2⅜")
6.5 (2⅝") 4 (1⅝")
Outline quilting 8 (3⅛")
26 (10¼")
* •= (⅞")

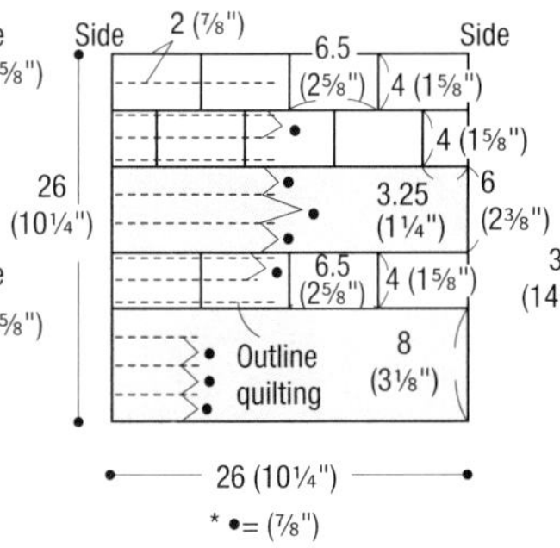

Lining fabric-A: one piece
Side Side
36 (14¼")
26 (10¼")

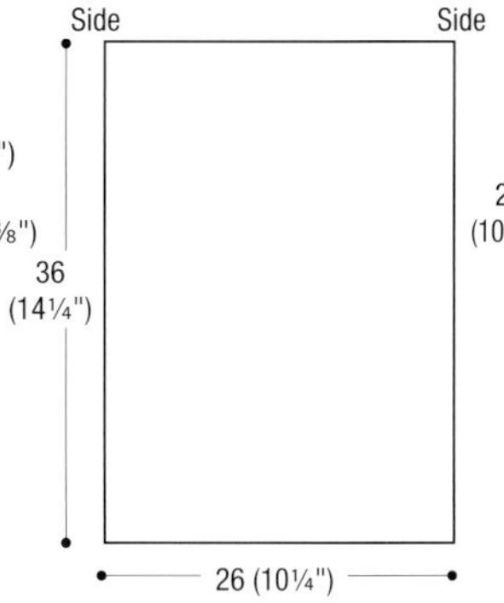

Lining fabric-B: one piece
Side Side
27 (10⅝")
26 (10¼")

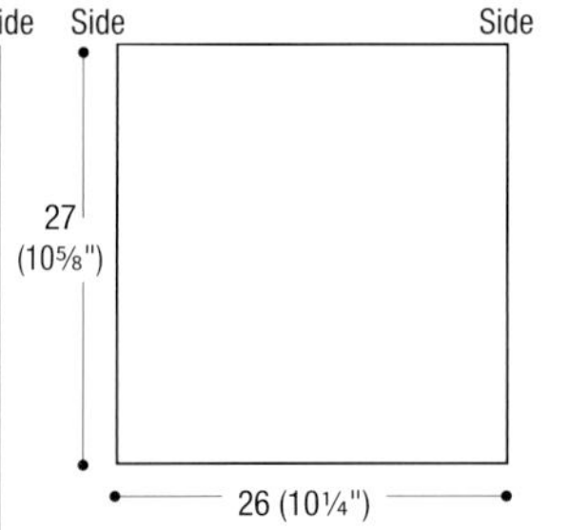

Lining fabric-C: one piece 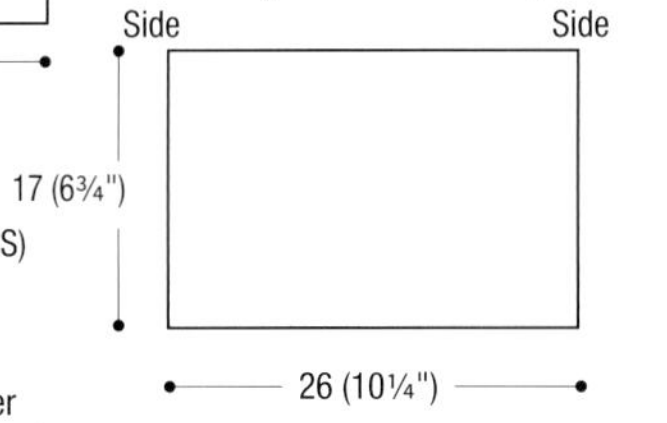
Side Side
17 (6¾")
26 (10¼")

Instructions

① Lining fabric-C (RS) / Outer fabric-C (WS) / Zipper (RS)
With the right sides together lay outer fabric-C flat over lining-C. Insert the zipper, then sew.

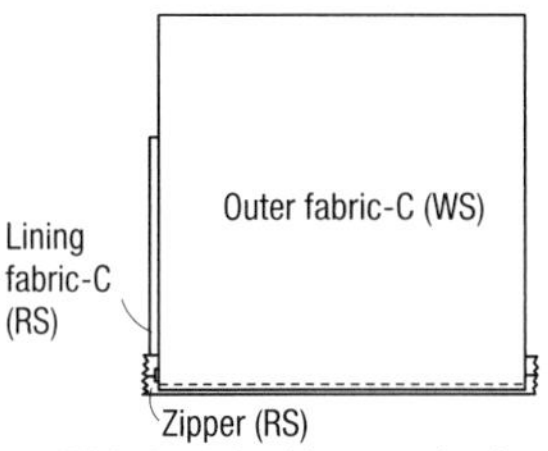

② Stitch / 0.2 (1⁄16") / Outer fabric-C (RS)
Flip right side out, then stitch.

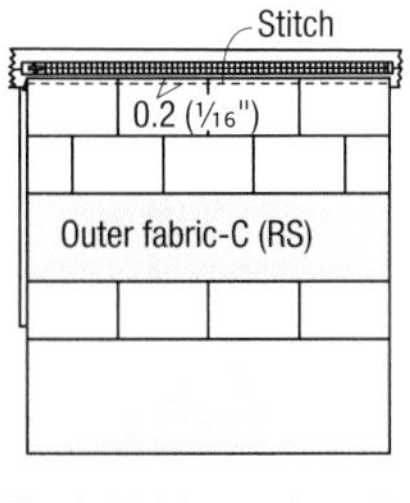

③ Baste to hold temporarily. / Lining fabric-C (RS) / Outer fabric-B (WS) / Fold / Outer fabric-C (RS)
Fold lining fabric-C, with the right sides together, then baste onto the other side of the zipper tape to hold temporarily. With right sides together, sew outer fabric-B. Turn outer fabric-B right side out and stitch in the same manner as ②.

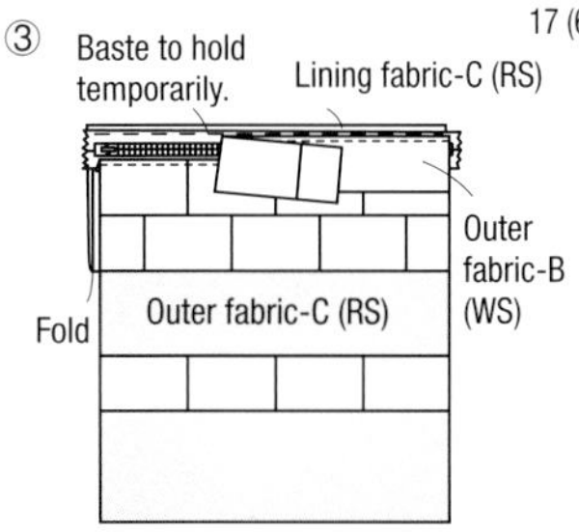

④ Zipper (WS) / Outer fabric-B (RS) / Lining fabric-B (WS)
Align the zipper with outer fabric-B, with the right sides together, then lay lining fabric-B over and sew. Flip the fabric right side up.

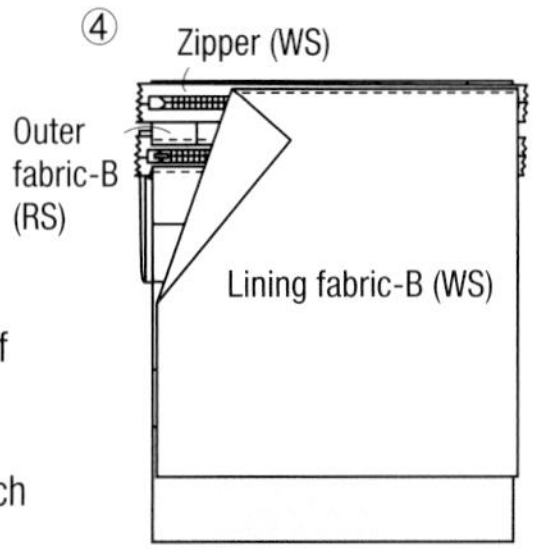

⑤ Baste to hold temporarily. / Lining fabric-B (RS) / Outer fabric-A (WS) / 1 (⅜") / Fold
Fold lining fabric-B, with the right sides together, then baste onto the other side of the zipper tape to hold temporarily. Sew outer fabric-A with the right sides together. Flip outer fabric-A right side up and stitch.

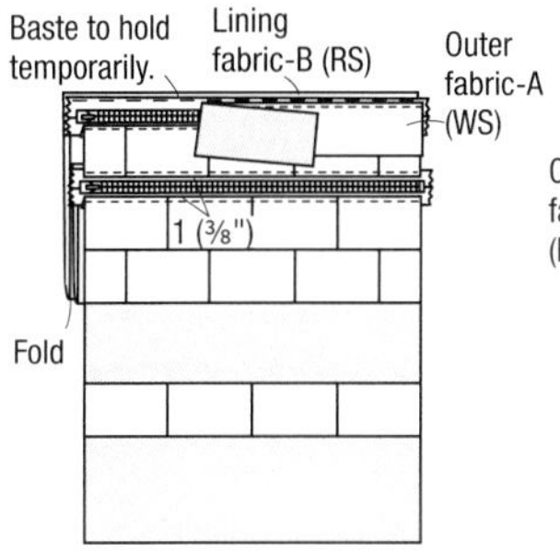

⑥ Zipper (WS) / Outer fabric-A (RS) / Lining fabric-A (WS)
Align the zipper with outer fabric-A, right sides together. Lay lining fabric-A over and sew. Flip the fabric right side up.

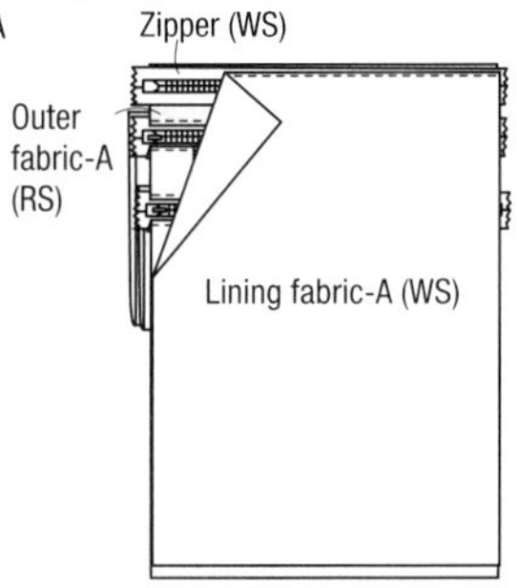

⑦ Leave the zipper open. / Lining fabric-A (RS) / Outer fabric-C (WS) / Fold
Fold lining fabric-A, with the right sides together, then baste onto the other side of the zipper tape to hold temporarily. Sew outer fabric-C with the right sides together. Flip lining fabric-A right side up.

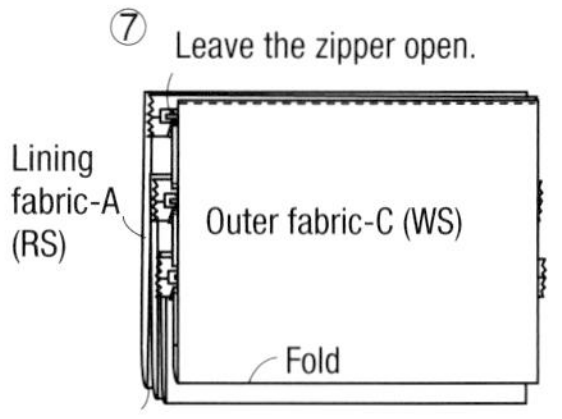

⑧ Lining fabric-A (RS) / Fold
Adjust the shape of the pouch with the zipper-side facing up. Sew both side edges. Bind fabric tape along the seam.

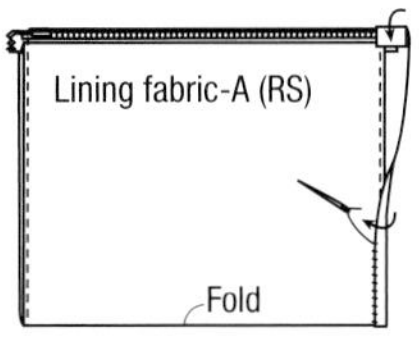

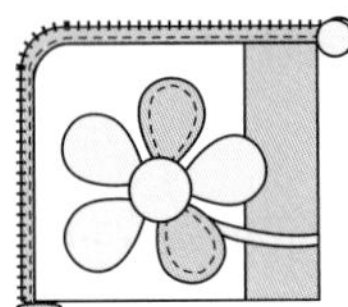

10 x 11.5 cm (4" x 4½")
Design: Chizuko Kojima

- Full size patterns are on page 119.

39 Flower Appliqué Small Wallet

Materials

Fabric for appliqué, outer fabric, and self-covered buttons / Lining fabric: 30 x 15 cm (11⅞" x 5⅞") / Pocket: 45 x 15 cm (17¾" x 5⅞") / Interfacing: 100 x 15 cm (39⅜" x 5⅞") / Double-sided fusible batting: 40 x 15 cm (15¾" x 5⅞") / One zipper: 20 cm (7⅞") / 2 cm (⅞") diameter button: two pieces / 1.8 cm (¾") diameter button: one piece / 0.7 cm (¼") wide wavy tape: 20 cm (7⅞") / #8 needlework thread

Key points

- Add 1 cm (⅜") seam allowance.
- Apply appliqué on the pouch using double-sided iron-on, then zig-zag stitch edges of the appliqué.

Instructions

1 Assemble the outer fabric with piecing, appliqué, and needlework.
2 Apply double sided iron-on on the lining fabric. With right sides together, sew the lining and the outer fabric. Turn the fabric right side out, iron-on to fuse the layer.
3 Make the pocket, then sew on the lining fabric.
4 With the right sides together, fold the outer fabric in half. Whip stitch the bottom edge.
5 Install the zipper on the outer fabric.
6 Make a set of self-covered buttons, then sandwich the end of the zipper tape.
7 Bind the other end of the zipper tape onto the wallet, then sew a button over it.

Outer fabric: one piece

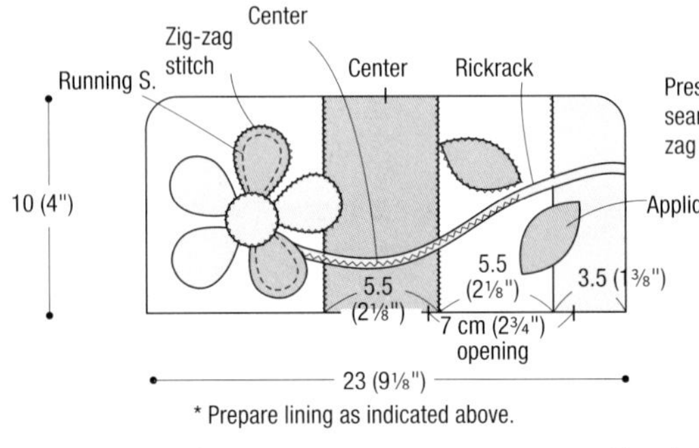

* Prepare lining as indicated above.

How to Make Outer Fabric

Press open the seam, then zig-zag stitch over.

After applying interfacing on each piece, join them together.

Outer fabric (WS)

Interfacing

After piecing is done, apply interfacing over the entire joined surface. Apply appliqué on the front.

Self-covered button: two pieces

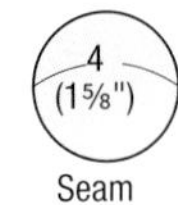

Seam

Pocket: one piece

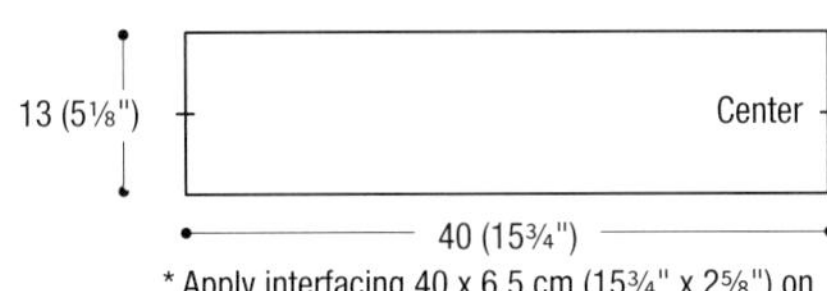

* Apply interfacing 40 x 6.5 cm (15¾" x 2⅝") on wrong side.

How to Make Pocket

①

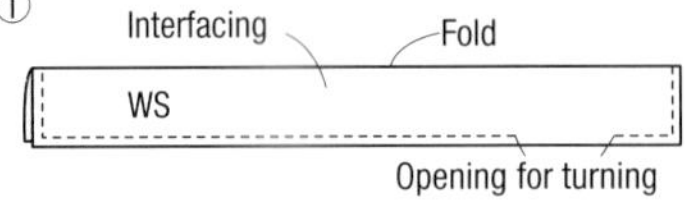

Apply interfacing to half of the wrong side. With the right sides together, fold in half lengthwise. Sew the edges while leaving an opening for turning.

②

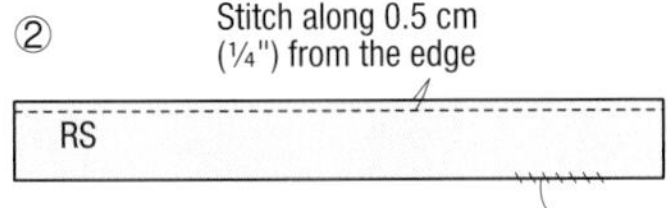

Turn the fabric right side out, sew the opening to close. Stitch along the folded edge.

Instructions

①

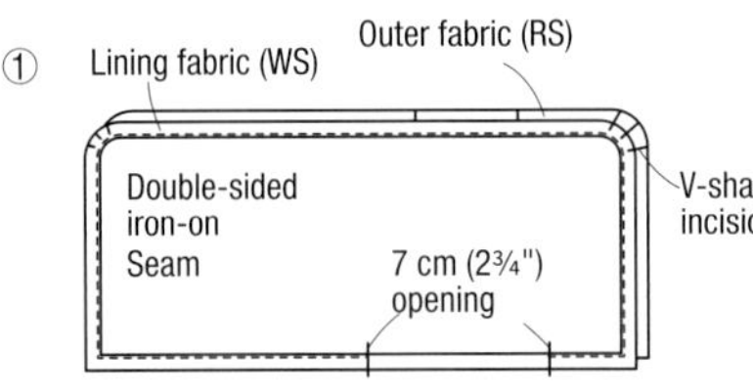

Apply double sided iron-on to the lining fabric. Sew the outer and the lining fabric along the edges, with the right sides together, leaving an opening for turning.

②

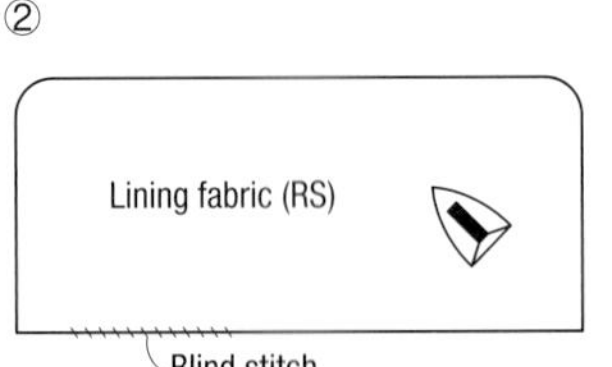

Turn the fabric right side out and sew the opening to close. Iron the surface to fuse the double-sided iron-on.

③

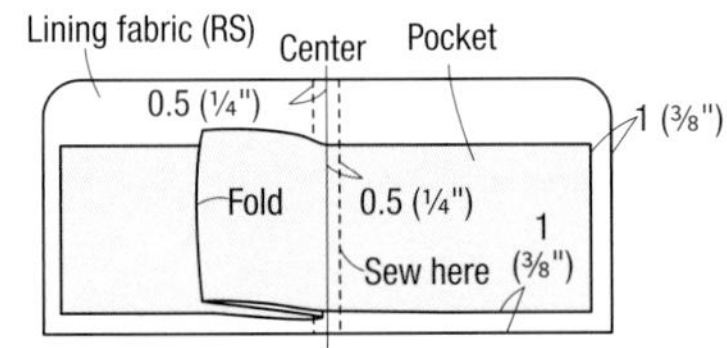

Align the center and lay the pocket flat over the lining fabric. Machine sew 0.5 cm (¼") from the left side of center. Similarly, machine sew 0.5 cm (¼") from the right side of center.

④

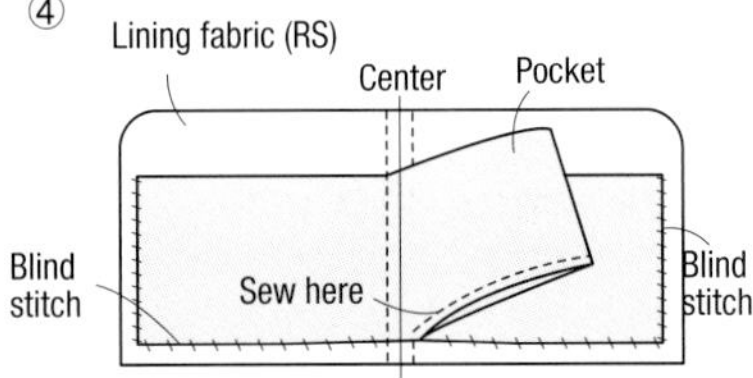

Sew the bottom and both side edges of the pocket, then sew the bottom of the overlapped edge to make a pocket.

⑤

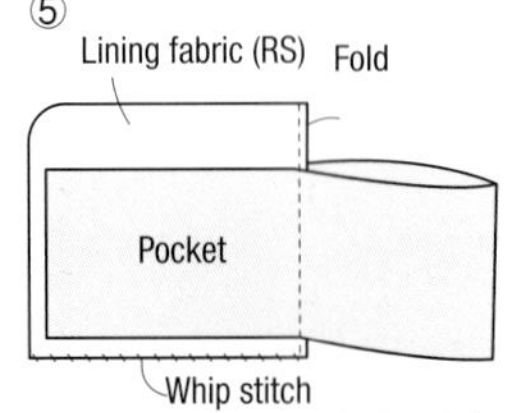

Fold the wallet in half with the right sides together. Whip stitch the bottom of the wallet body. Whip stitch the bottom of the lining fabric.

How to Install Zipper

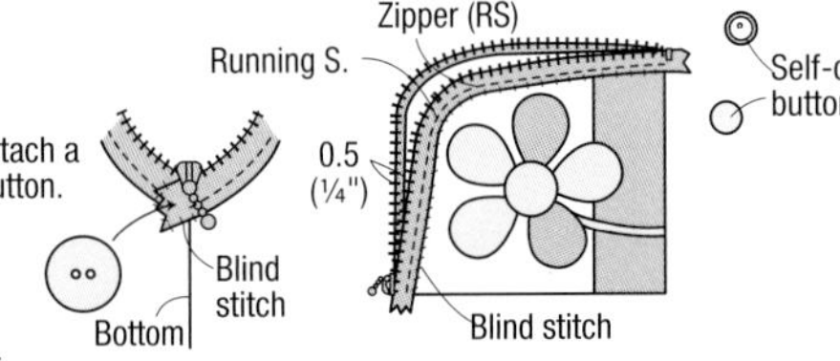

Install the zipper such that the teeth protrude from the edge of the wallet. Sandwich the end of the zipper tape with a set of self-covered button. Bind the other end of the zipper tape onto the wallet, then attach a button over it.

Full size patterns

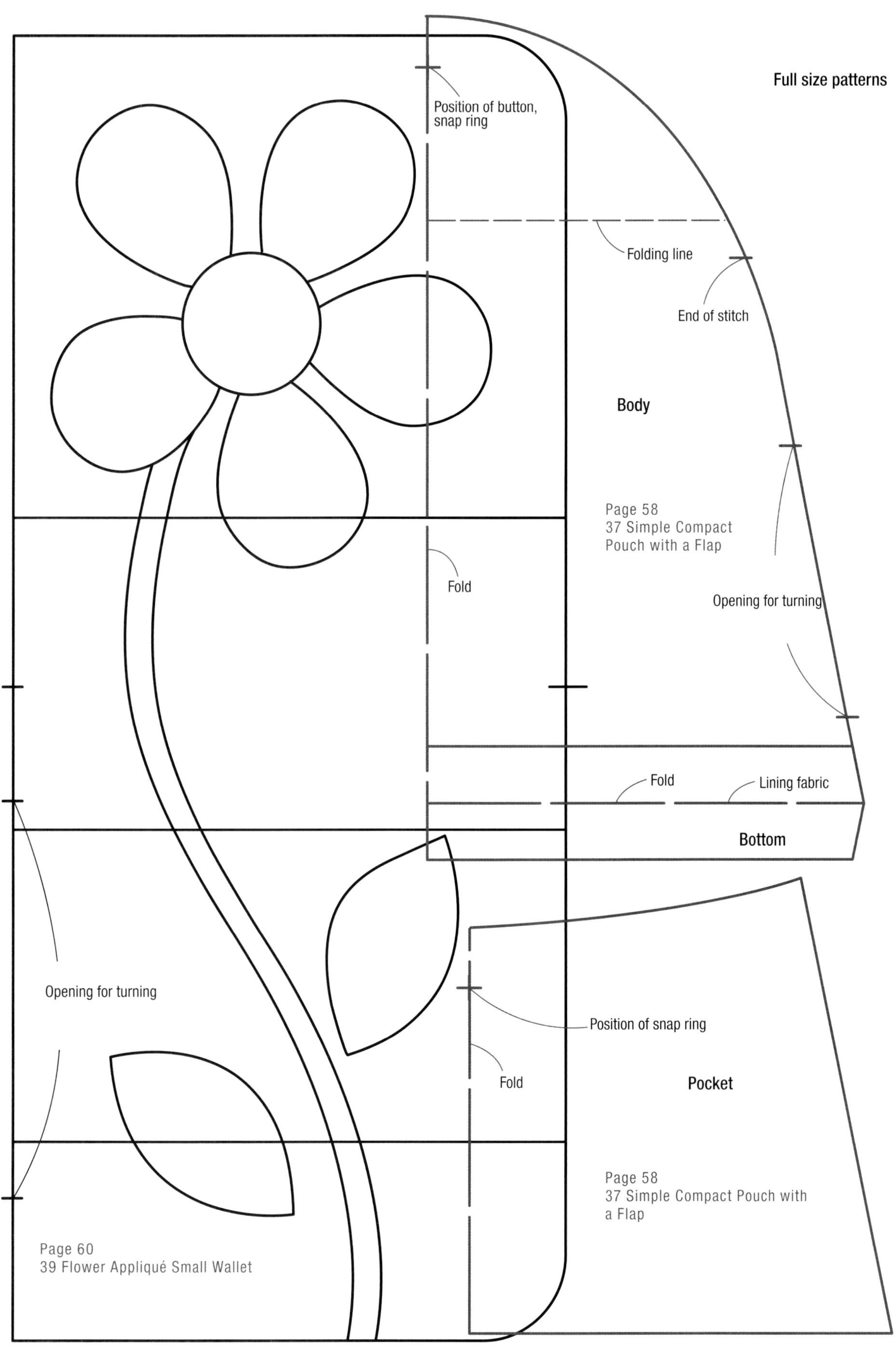

9 x 13 cm (3⅝" x 5⅛")
Design: Mariko Hayasaki

43 Timeless Standard, Metal Clasp Pouch

Materials
Various fabrics for piecing / Fusible batting, Lining fabric: each 35 x 15 cm (13¾" x 5⅞") / Fabric for piping cord: 20 x 20 cm (7⅞" x 7⅞") / 0.2 cm (1⁄16") width cord: 30 cm (11⅞") / One metal clasp: 11.5 x 4 cm (4½" x 1⅝") / 1.5 cm (⅝") wide lace trim: 20 cm (7⅞") / Tag: one piece /

Key points
- Fusible batting does not need seam allowance.
- Add 0.5 cm (¼") seam allowance and make small incisions along the curved edges.
- See p. 69 for installing a metal clasp.

Instructions
1 Assemble the outer fabric by piecing.
2 Fuse batting to the wrong side of the outer fabric and quilt as desired.
3 Attach lace trim and tag. Sew the dart.
4 Make piping cord.
5 Lay two pieces of the outer fabric flat, with the right sides together, and insert the piping cord in between. Sew.
6 Do the same for the lining. Be sure to leave an opening for turning.
7 Sew along mouth of the outer and lining fabric with the right sides together.
8 Turn the fabric right side out, close the opening. Stitch along mouth of the pouch.
9 Attach the metal clasp.

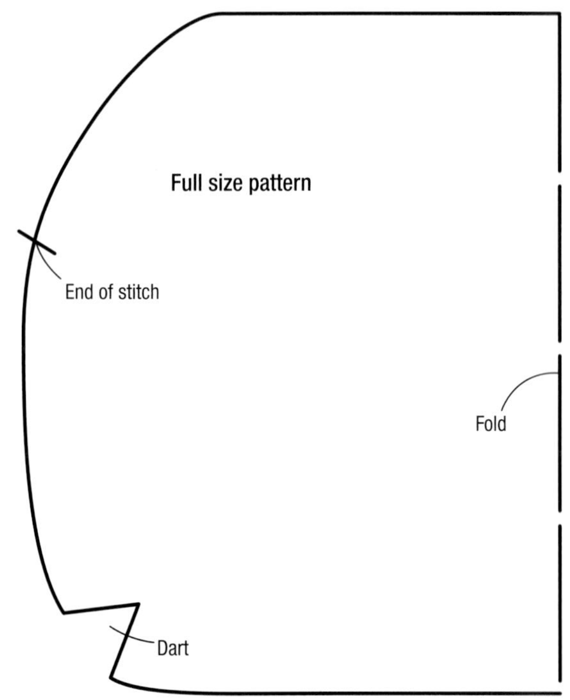

Outer fabric: two pieces

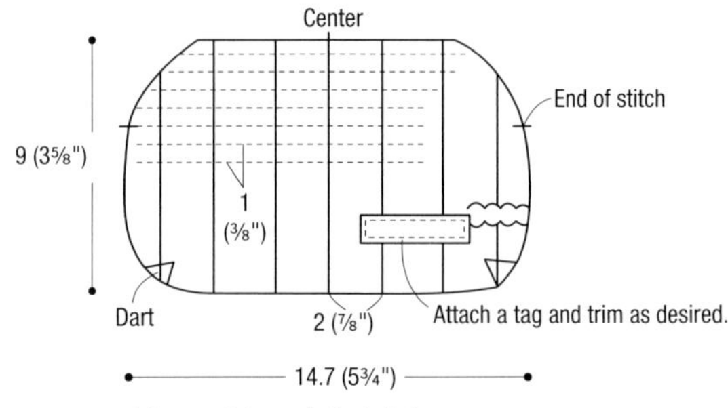

* Prepare lining as indicated above.

How to Make Piping Cord

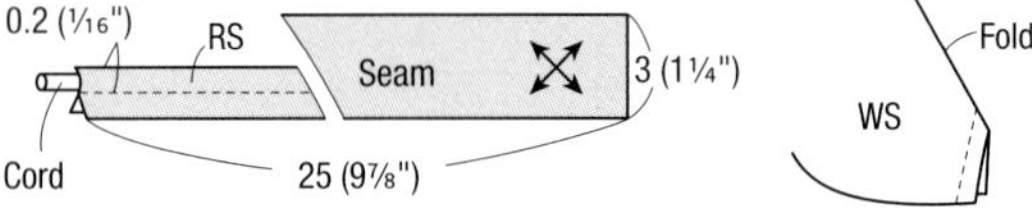

Insert cord and fold the fabric in half with the right side out. Then sew along the edge of the cord.

How to Sew Darts

Sew the dart with the right sides together.

Instructions

①

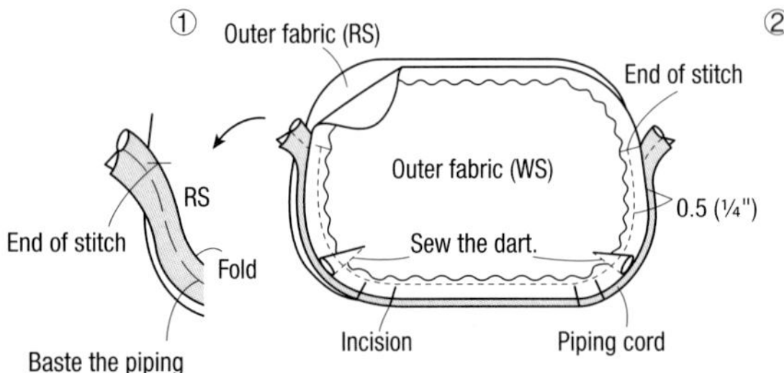

Baste the piping on one side to hold temporarily.

Lay the back and front of the outer fabric flat with the right sides together. Insert the piping cord, then sew together to the end of the stitch position. Do the same for the lining fabric and leave an opening.

②

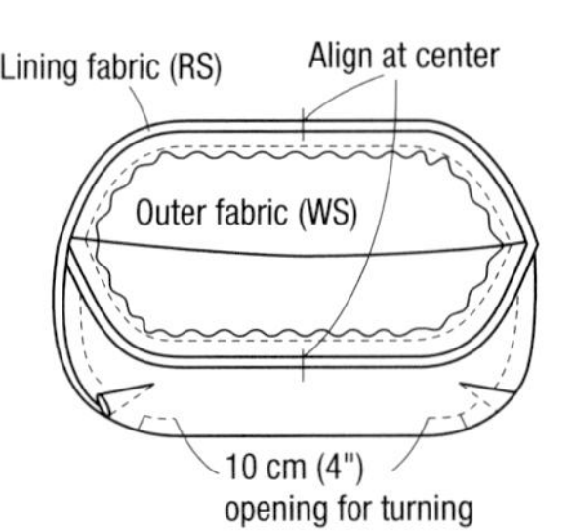

Sew the lining fabric and the outer fabric, with the right sides together, along the mouth of the pouch. Turn the fabric right side out through the opening in the lining. Blind stitch the opening to close.

③

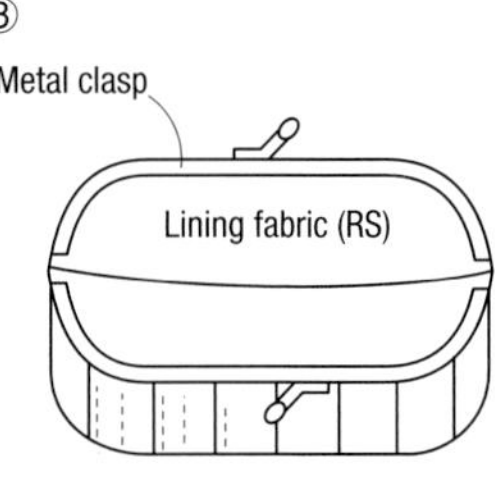

Stitch down along the mouth of the pouch, then install the metal clasp.

9 x 13 cm (3⅝" x 5⅛")
Design: Mika Ohatake

45 Soft Flex Frame Pouch with a Pleat

Materials
Outer fabric (including flex frame casing): 40 x 20 cm (15¾" x 7⅞") / Fusible batting, Lining fabric: each 25 x 20 cm (9⅞" x 7⅞") / One flex frame: length 10 cm (4") / One sequin: 0.4 cm (⅛") wide / #25 needlework thread

Key points
- Add 1 cm (⅜") seam allowance.
- See p. 79 for installing a flex frame.

Instructions
1 Fuse batting on the wrong side of the outer fabric. Apply needlework on the front and attach a sequin.
2 Pleat fabric separately to both the outer and lining fabric. Baste it to hold temporarily.
3 With the right sides together, sew the casing of the flex frame on the outer fabric. Then sew the lining onto the casing with the right sides together.
4 With the right sides together, fold the outer and the lining separately. Sew the side edges while leaving an opening for installing the flex frame. Create some boxed corners.
5 Turn the fabric right side out and insert the lining inside the outer fabric. Sew the casing of the flex frame.
6 Install the flex frame.

Outer fabric: one piece

Side
Center
Side
2.5 (1")
16 (6⅜")
Needlework
3.5 (1⅜")
Bottom center
Pleat 4 cm (1⅝")
8 (3⅛")
18 (7⅛")

* Prepare the lining fabric as indicated above.

Flex frame casing: two pieces

Center
Folding line
6.5 (2⅝")
Opening
32.5 (12⅞")
1 (⅜")
14 (5½")
End of stitch

How to Pleat

2 (⅞")
Basting
RS

Pleat the fabric, then baste to hold temporarily.

Instructions

①
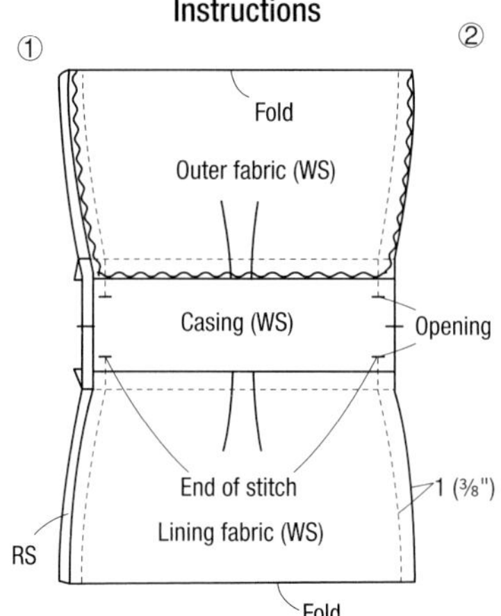

With the right sides together, align the casing with the outer and lining and sew on the casing. Separately fold the outer fabric and the lining fabric with right sides together, then sew the side edges from the end of stitch position down.

②
Side
WS
4 (1⅝")

Separately sew boxed corners on both the outer and the lining fabric.

③
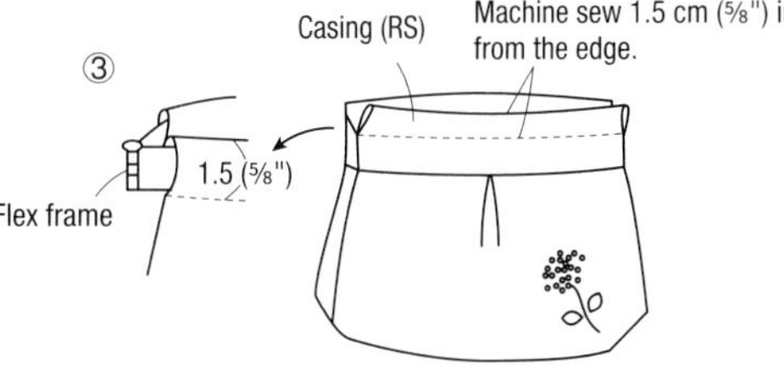

Turn the fabric right side out and insert the lining inside the outer fabric. Sew the casing. Install the flex frame.

How to Stitch a Colonial Knot

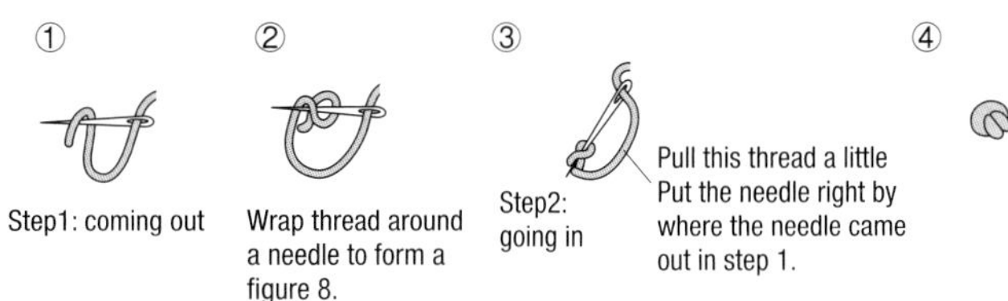

How to Satin Stitch

How to Outline Stitch

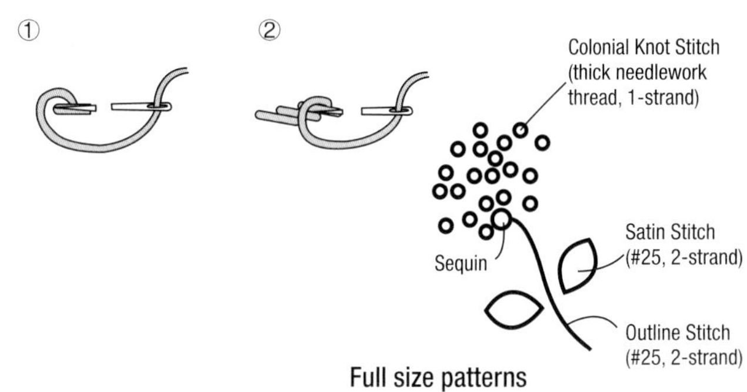

Full size patterns

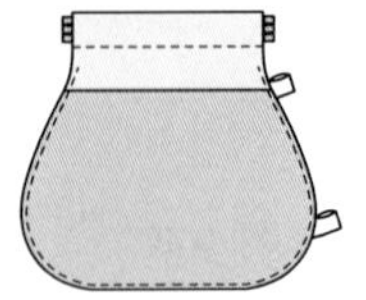

12 x 13.5 cm (4¾" x 5⅜")
Design: Chizuko Kojima

46 Modern and Pop-style Flex Frame Pouch

Materials

Fabric-A: 20 x 20 cm (7⅞" x 7⅞") / Fabric-B, Double-sided fusible batting: 20 x 25 cm (7⅞" x 9⅞") / Lining fabric: 35 x 20 cm (13¾" x 7⅞") / One flex frame: length 10 cm (4") / Fabric for tags

Key points

- Before turning the outer fabric right side out, trim the seam to 0.5 cm (¼") and make small incisions along the curved edge.
- You can use ribbon for the tag.
- When joining the front and back of the outer fabric, with the right sides together, you can whip stitch along the side edges.
- See p. 79 for installing a flex frame.

Instructions

1 Join fabric-A and -B and assemble the front and back of the outer fabric.
2 Apply double-sided batting on wrong side of fabric-B, then quilt as desired.
3 Lay the outer fabric flat over the lining with the right sides together. Sew along the outer edges.
4 Turn the right side out and stitch the top and side edges of fabric-A.
5 Fold fabric-A to make the casing for the flex frame.
6 Make the tags.
7 With right sides out, lay the back and front of the outer fabric flat. Insert the tags. Sew the outer edge from the end of the stitch mark to the other side.
8 Install the flex frame.

Outer fabric: two pieces

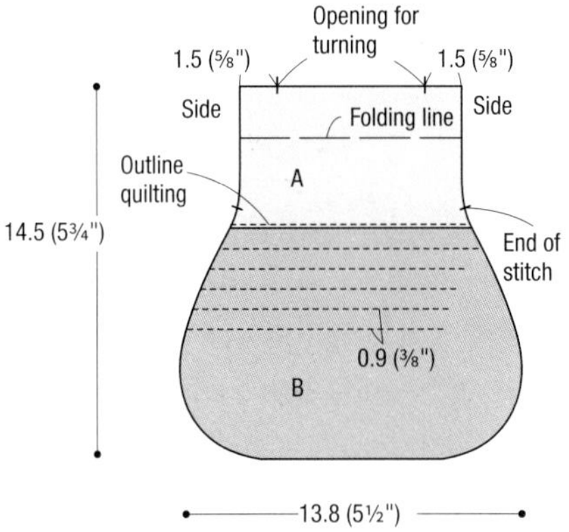

Opening for turning
1.5 (⅝")
1.5 (⅝")
Side
Folding line
Side
Outline quilting
A
14.5 (5¾")
End of stitch
0.9 (⅜")
B
13.8 (5½")

* Apply fusible batting on the wrong side of fabric-B.
* Prepare lining as indicated above.

Instructions

① Lining fabric (RS)
Opening for turning
Outer fabric (WS)
Incision
Double-sided fusible batting

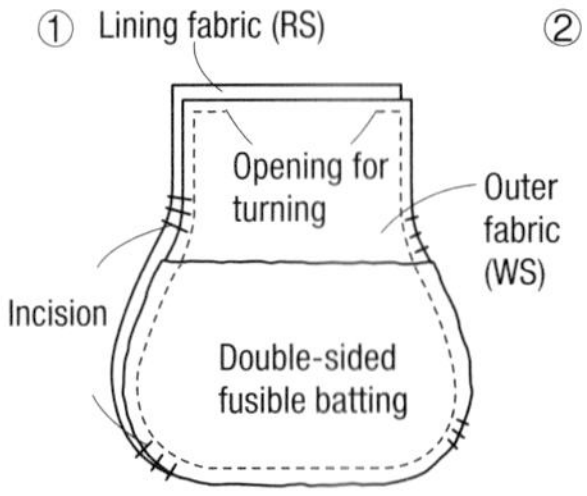

Apply double-sided fusible batting only on fabric-B. With the right sides together, lay the outer fabric flat over the lining fabric. Sew along the outer edges leaving an opening for turning.

② Stitch along 0.2 cm (1/16") from the edge
Tack seam allowance along the inside opening.
Outer fabric (RS)

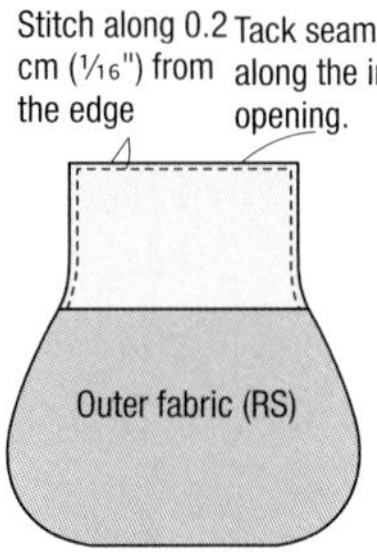

Turn the fabric right side out. Fold down seam allowance, then fuse fabric-B with batting. Stitch along only the outer edges of fabric-A.

③ 1.8 (¾")
Folding line
Outer fabric (RS)

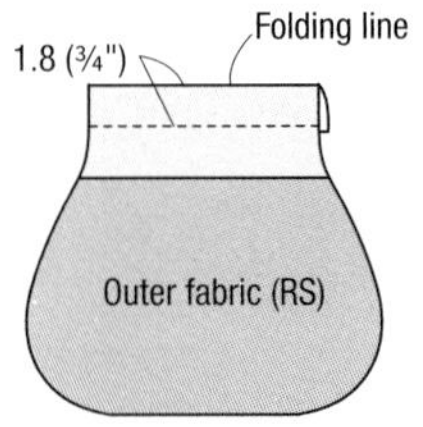

Fold fabric-A along the folding line to make the casing for the flex frame. Make casing at the front and back of the outer fabric.

Tag: two pieces

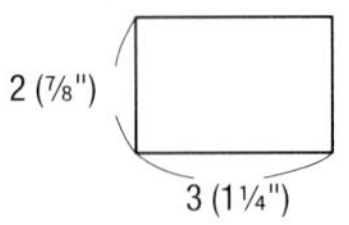

2 (⅞")
3 (1¼")

How to Make Tag

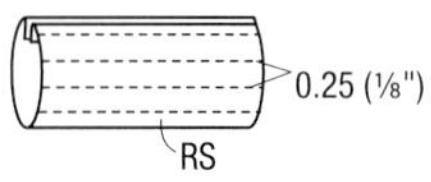

0.25 (⅛")
RS

Fold seam allowance, then stitch.

④ End of stitch
Outer fabric (RS)
Tag
0.2 (1/16")

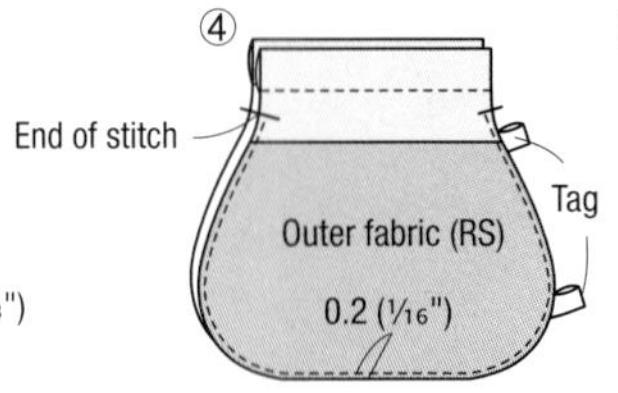

With right sides out, lay the back and front of the outer fabric flat. Insert the folded tags between the fabric. Sew the outer edge from the end of the stitch mark to the other side.

⑤ Flex frame

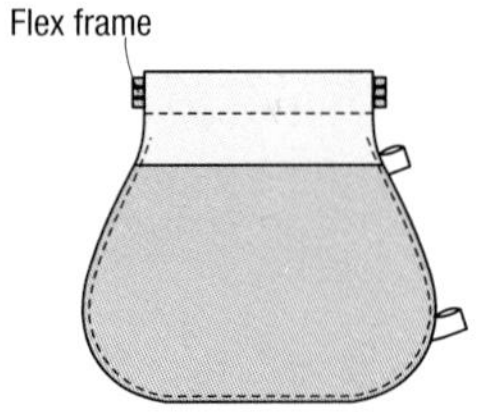

Install the flex frame.

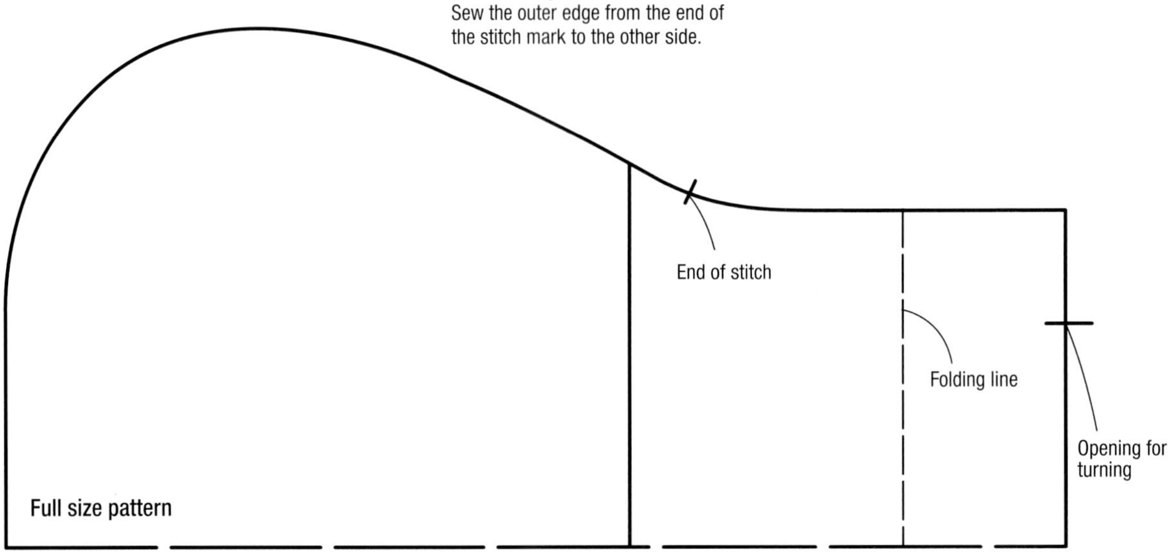

End of stitch
Folding line
Opening for turning
Full size pattern

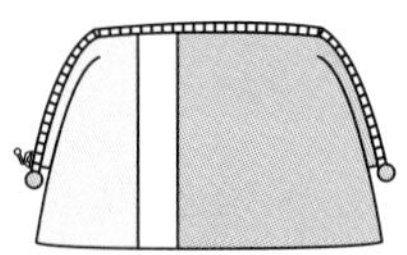

7 x 12 cm (2¾" x 4¾")
Design: Noriko Sakurai

47 Wide Mouth Pouch

Materials
Fabric for making yo-yos: 10 x 10 cm (4" x 4") / Fabric-A: 10 x 25 cm (4" x 9⅞") / Fabric-B: 5 x 25 cm (2" x 9⅞") / Fabric-C: 15 x 25 cm (5⅞" x 9⅞") / Backing, Lining, Batting: each 25 x 25 cm (9⅞" x 9⅞") / One zipper: 20 cm (7⅞") / 10 cm (4") wide wire frame: one set

Key points
- Machine quilt as desired.

Instructions
1. Join the fabric-A, -B, and -C. Assemble the outer fabric.
2. Fuse batting on the wrong side of the outer fabric, then layer with the backing fabric. Baste together and machine quilt as desired.
3. With the right sides together, lay the outer fabric flat over the lining fabric and insert the zipper between them. Sew together.
4. Do the same for the other side.
5. Fold the outer fabric and the lining fabric separately with the right sides together. Sew the side edges and the boxed corners.
6. Turn the fabric right side out, then close the opening. Sew the casing for the wire frame and install the frame.
7. Make yo-yos, sandwich the end of the zipper tape, and bind.

Outer fabric: one piece

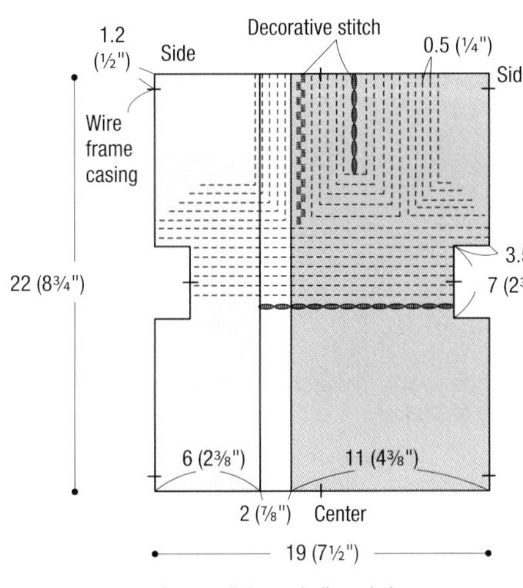

* Prepare lining as indicated above.

Instructions

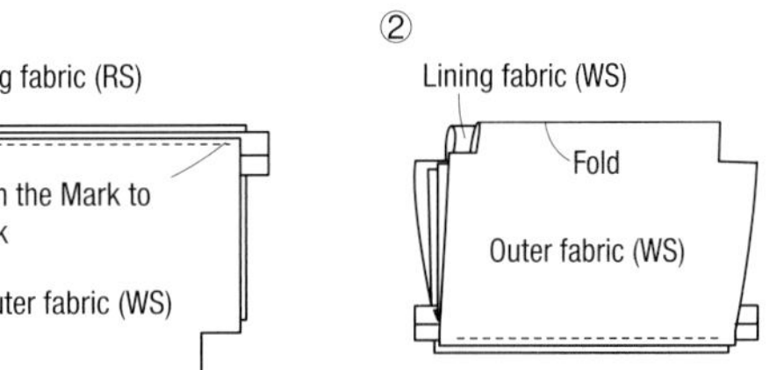

① Lay the outer fabric flat over the lining fabric with the right sides together. Insert the zipper and sew along the dotted line.

② Do the same for the other side.

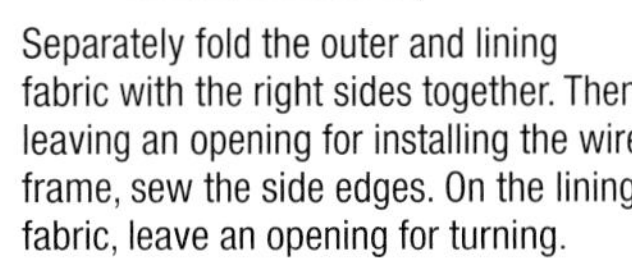

③ Separately fold the outer and lining fabric with the right sides together. Then, leaving an opening for installing the wire frame, sew the side edges. On the lining fabric, leave an opening for turning.

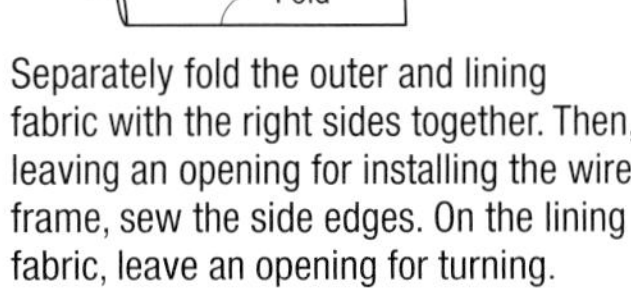

④ Make a boxed corner for each corner.

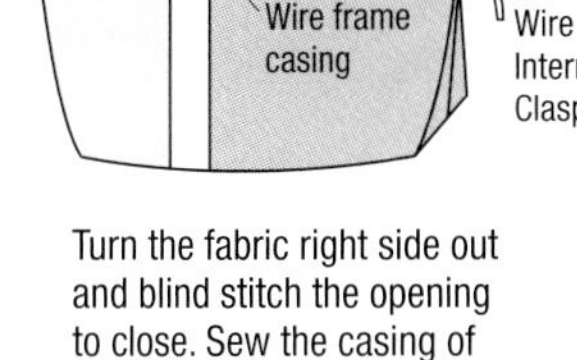

⑤ Turn the fabric right side out and blind stitch the opening to close. Sew the casing of the wire frame, then install the wire frame.

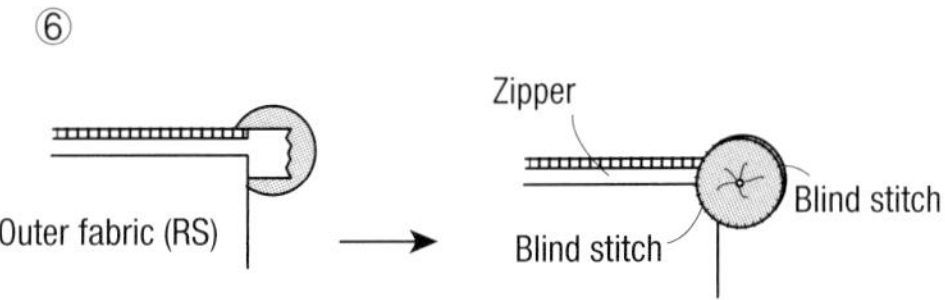

⑥ Sandwich the end of the zipper tape with a set of yo-yos then bind.

Yo-yo: four pieces

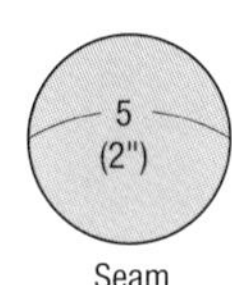

How to Make a Yo-yo

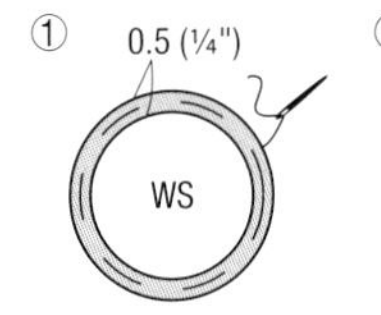

① Press down seam allowance and running stitch along the circumference.

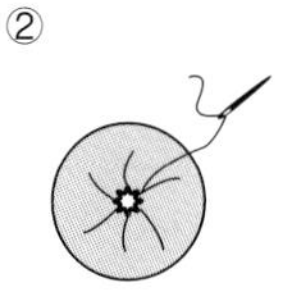

② Pull thread to gather fabric.

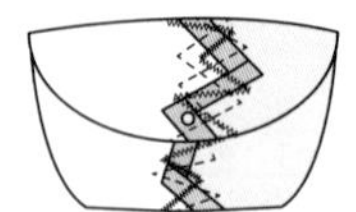

8.5 x 16 cm (3⅜" x 6⅜")
Design: Noriko Sakurai

48 Metal Snap Pouch with Design Showcasing Materials

Materials
Two types of fabric: each 15 x 30 cm (5⅞" x 11⅞") / Lining, Interfacing: each 20 x 30 cm (7⅞" x 11⅞") / 1 cm (⅜") diameter metal snap: one set / 1.5 cm (⅝") wide organdy ribbon as necessary

Key points
- Attach ribbon and stitch as desired.
- See p. 79 for installing metal snap.

Instructions
1 Join fabric to make the outer, then apply interfacing on wrong side.
2 Lay ribbon on the right side of the outer fabric, then stitch it down.
3 With the right sides together, lay the lining fabric flat over the outer fabric. Sew along the straight edges leaving an opening for turning.
4 Fold the bottom outward between the lining and the outer fabric. Sew along the outer edges.
5 Sew the boxed corners.
6 Turn the fabric right side out, close the opening and stitch along mouth of the pouch and flap.
7 Attach metal snap.

Outer fabric: one piece

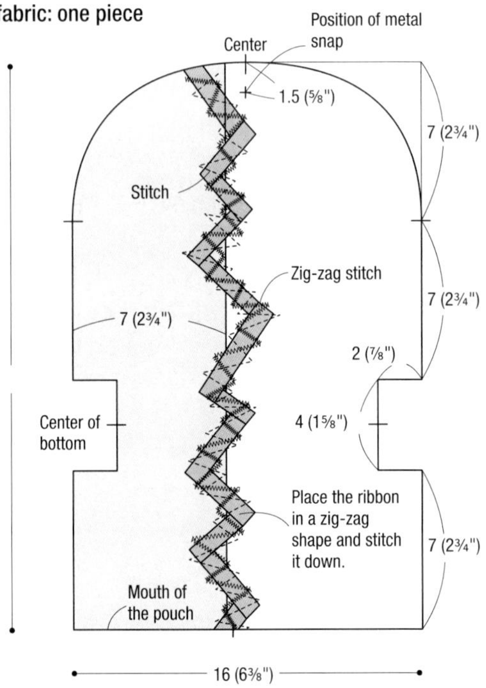

Position of metal snap
Center
1.5 (⅝")
7 (2¾")
Stitch
Zig-zag stitch
7 (2¾")
7 (2¾")
2 (⅞")
Center of bottom
4 (1⅝")
Place the ribbon in a zig-zag shape and stitch it down.
7 (2¾")
Mouth of the pouch
16 (6⅜")

* Prepare lining as indicated above.

Instructions

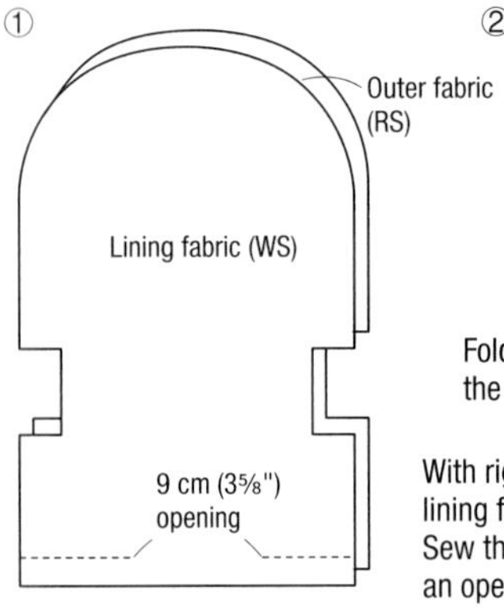

①
Outer fabric (RS)
Lining fabric (WS)
9 cm (3⅝") opening

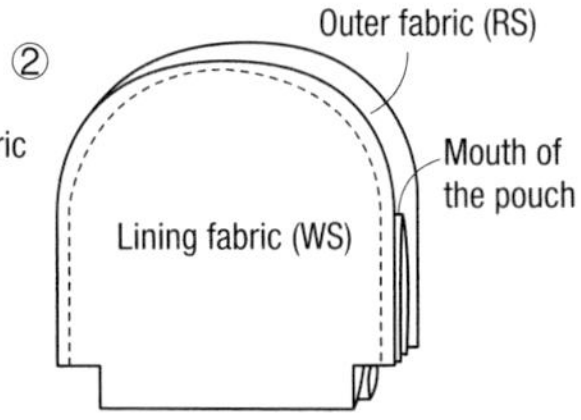

With right sides together, lay the lining fabric flat over the outer fabric. Sew the bottom edge while leaving an opening for turning.

②
Outer fabric (RS)
Mouth of the pouch
Lining fabric (WS)

Fold the bottom outward between the fabrics, then sew the outer edges.

③
Outer fabric (WS)
Side
Lining fabric (WS)
Center of bottom

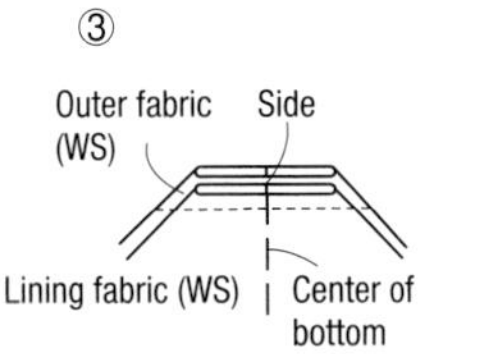

Align side seam with center of bottom, sew the boxed corner on the lining and outer fabric.

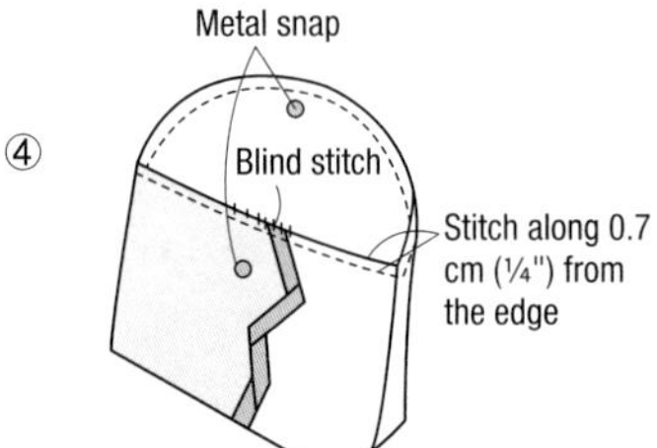

④
Metal snap
Blind stitch
Stitch along 0.7 cm (¼") from the edge

Turn the fabric right side out, blind stitch the opening to close. Stitch along mouth of the pouch and flap. Attach metal snap.

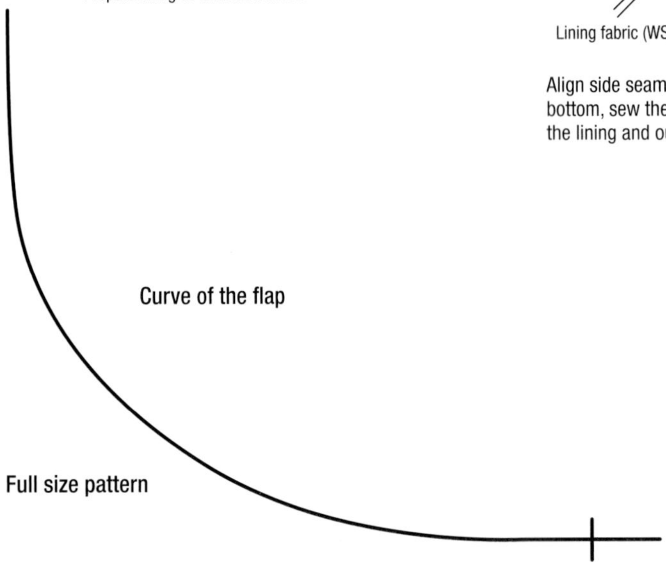

Curve of the flap

Full size pattern

49 Pouch with a Rickrack Flower 1: Zippered 2: Pocket

10 x 22 cm (4" x 8¾")
Design: Noriko Hosoo

Materials

Two types of outer fabric front: 30 x 15 cm (11⅞" x 5⅞") / Outer fabric back: 30 x 30 cm (11⅞" x 11⅞") / Lining, Double-sided fusible batting: each 55 x 30 cm (21⅝" x 11⅞") / One zipper: 15 cm (6") / 2.5 cm (1") wide rickrack: approx. 90 cm (35½")

Key points

- Add 0.7 cm (¼") seam allowance along zipper opening, 1 cm (⅜") for other edges.
- Leave the zipper open when joining front and back of the outer fabric.
- See p. 78 for making rickrack flower.

Instructions

1 Fuse batting on wrong side of the outer fabric front. Quilt as desired.
2 With the right sides together, lay the lining flat over the outer fabric front and sew the top edges together. Turn the fabric right side out.
3 Sew on one side of the zipper tape along top edge of the outer fabric front.
4 Fuse batting on wrong side of the outer fabric back. Sew it onto the fabric you put together in the above step with the right sides together.
5 On the outer fabric front, lay the lining of the outer fabric back flat with the right sides together. Sew the outer edges while leaving an opening for turning.
6 Turn the fabric right side out, and close the opening.
7 Make a rickrack flower and sew it on the pouch.

Outer fabric front: two pieces

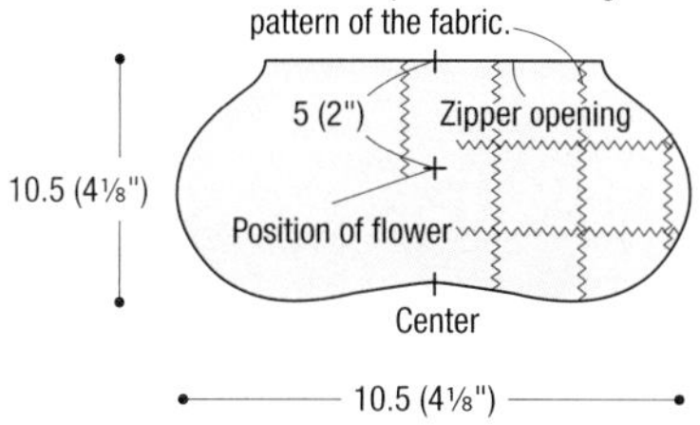

* Prepare lining as indicated above.

Outer fabric back: one piece

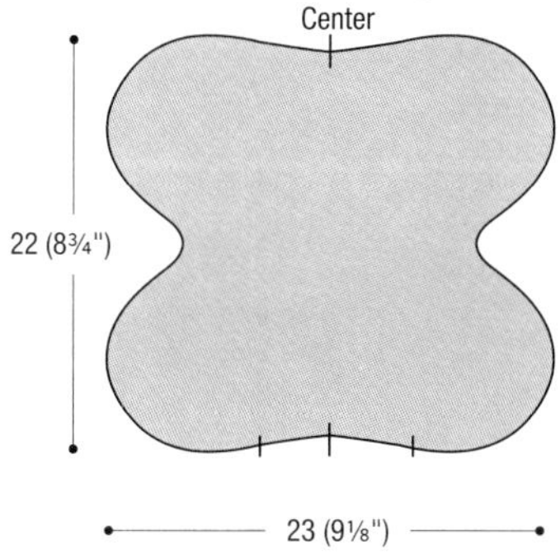

* Prepare lining as indicated above.

How to Make Rickrack Flowers

①

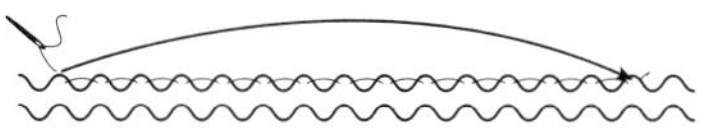

Stitch fifteen top edges, then stitch the first and the last top edge again. Secure them while making a circle of the tape.

②

Pull thread to gather tape, then tie off and adjust the shape.

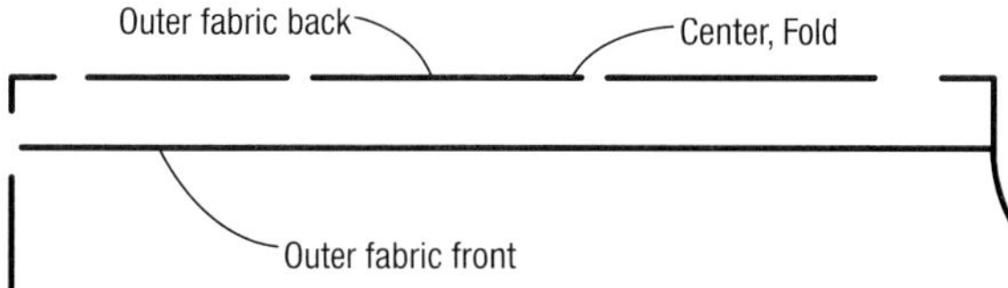

Instructions

①

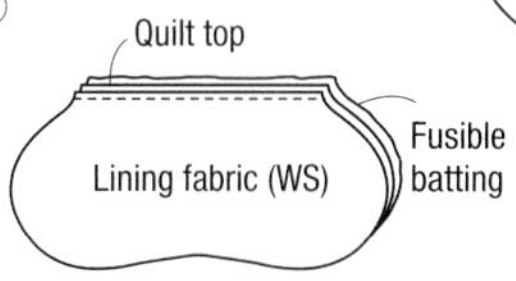

With the right sides together, lay the outer fabric front and the lining fabric flat. Sew top edges and turn the fabric right side out.

②

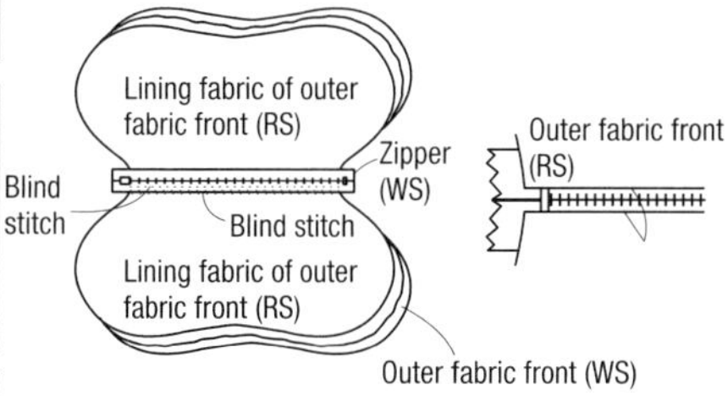

Install the zipper along the straight edges of both outer fabric fronts.

③

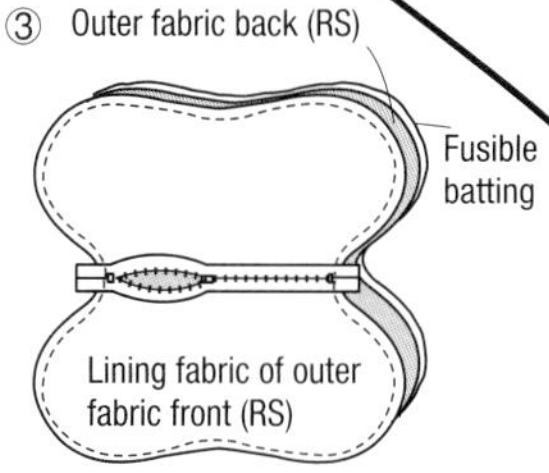

With the right sides together, sew the outer fabric back to the front.

④

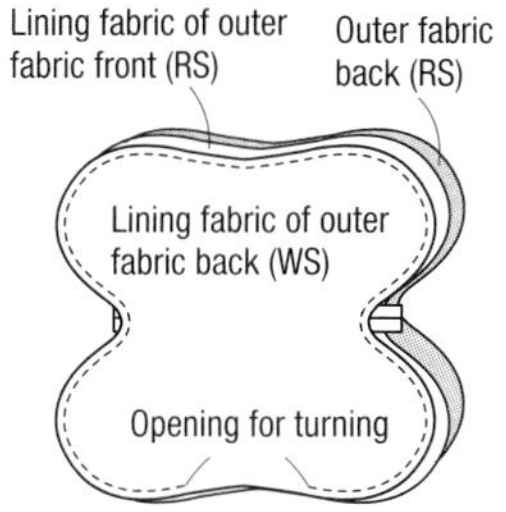

Lay the lining fabric of outer fabric back flat over the lining of the outer fabric front with the right sides together. Sew the outer edges while leaving an opening for turning. Turn the fabric right side out, blind stitch the opening to close.

⑤

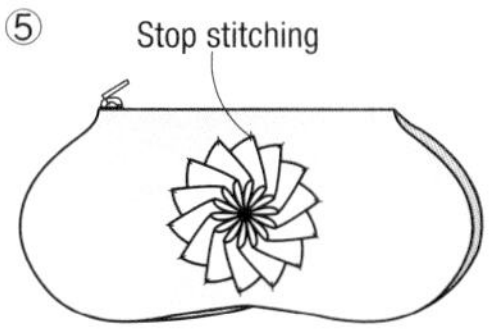

Blind stitch the outside of the flower onto the pouch.

Full size pattern

17.5 x 23 cm (6⅞" x 9⅛")
Design: Noriko Sakurai

50 Hook-and-loop Fastener Pouch

Materials
Outer fabric: 30 x 40 cm (11⅞" x 15¾") / Bottom fabric (incl. tab): 30 x 20 cm (11⅞" x 7⅞") / Outer fabric: 30 x 40 cm (11⅞" x 15¾") / 1.5 cm (⅝") wide hook-and-loop fastener: 20 cm (7⅞")

Key points
- Machine sew the hook-and-loop fastener on the pouch.

Instructions
1. Join the fabrics together and attach the hook-and-loop fastener to assemble the outer fabric.
2. With the right sides together, sew the outer and lining fabric together.
3. Make the tab.
4. Refold the outer and lining fabric separately, with the right sides together, then insert the tab on the left side and sew the side edges.
5. Sew the boxed-corners.
6. Turn the fabric right side out. Stitch along the side seams.

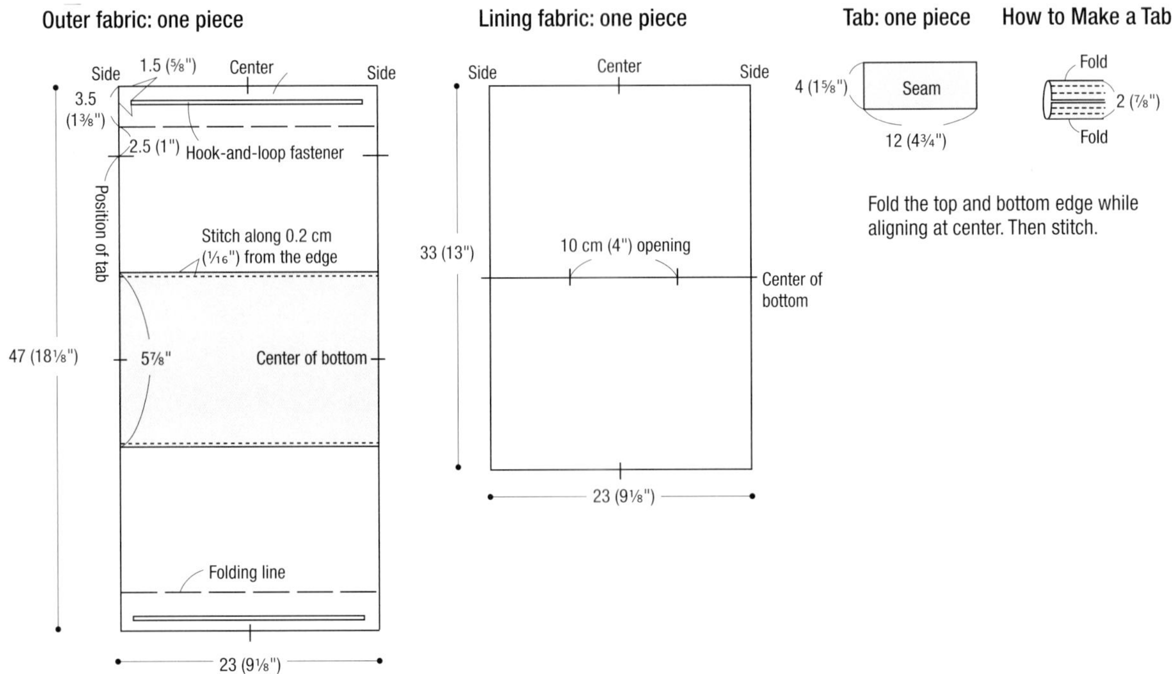

Instructions

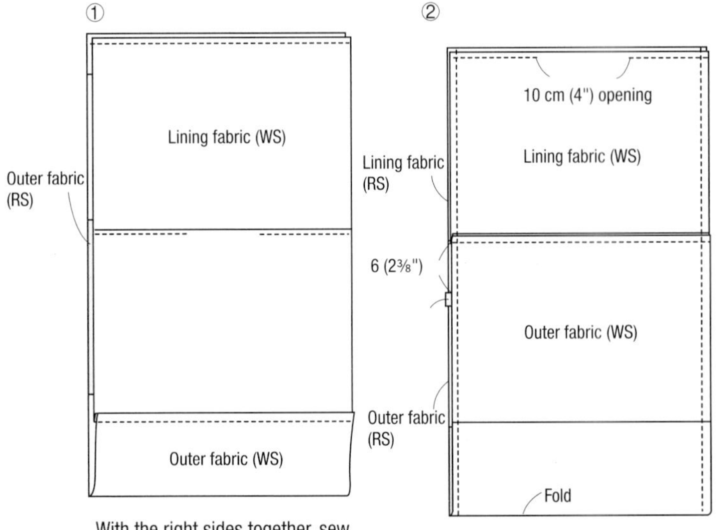

With the right sides together, sew the outer and the lining fabric together.

Refold the outer and the lining fabric separately with the right sides together. Then insert the tab on the left side and sew the side edges.

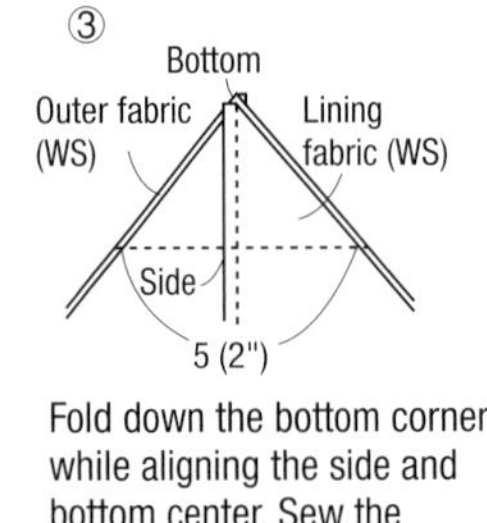

Fold down the bottom corner while aligning the side and bottom center. Sew the boxed corner.

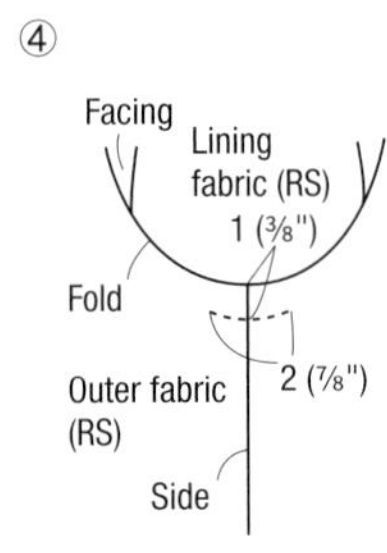

Turn the fabric right side out and close the opening using a blind stitch. Fold the edges along the folding line as specified in the diagram, then stitch the edge.

Full size patterns

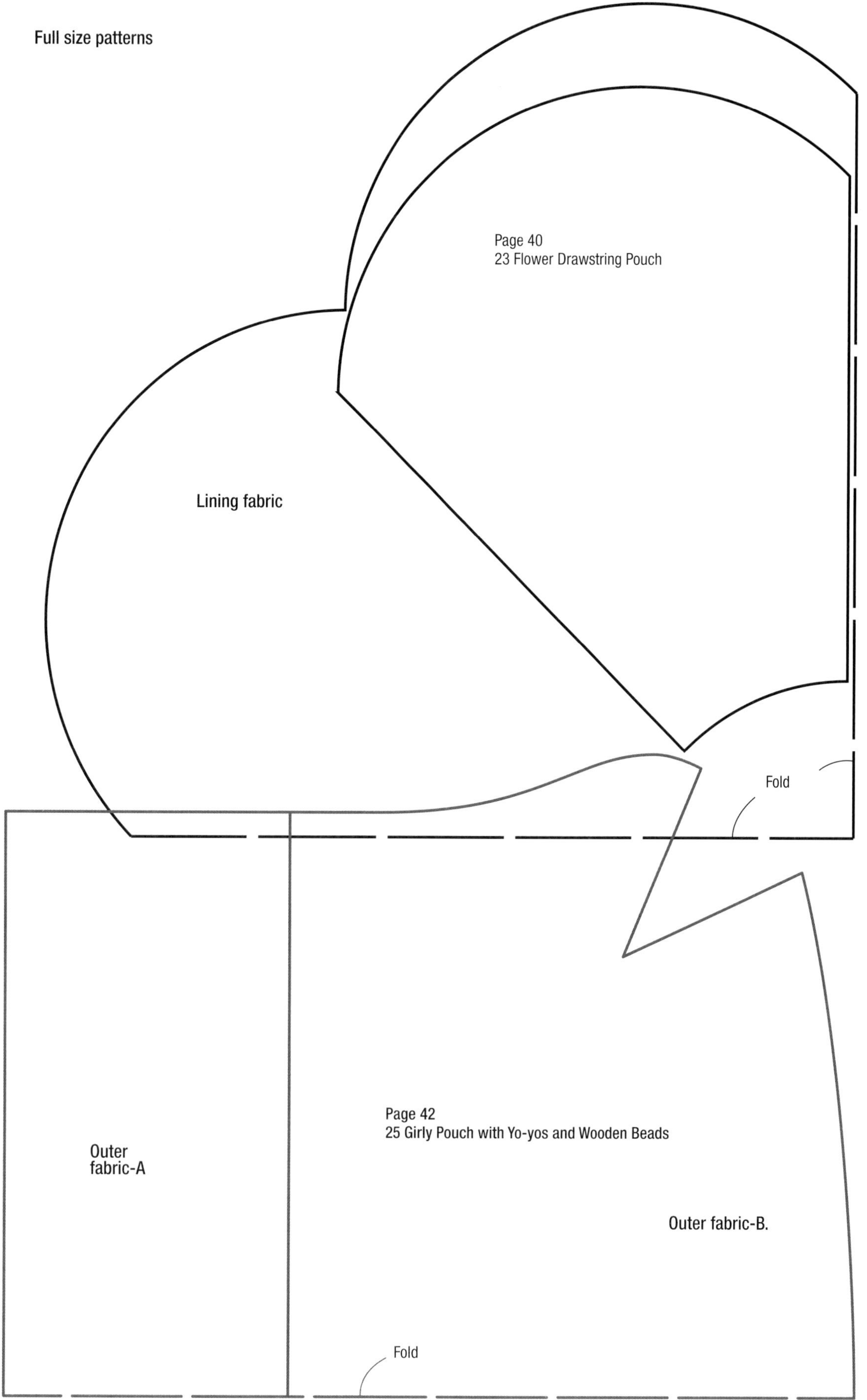

Other Schiffer Books on Related Subjects:

Welcome to Weaving: The Modern Guide, Lindsey Campbell, ISBN 978-0-7643-5631-5

Threads Around the World: From Arabian Weaving to Batik in Zimbabwe, Deb Brandon, ISBN 978-0-7643-5650-6

The Painted Word: Mixed Media Lettering Techniques, Caitlin Dundon, ISBN 978-0-7643-5647-6

Edited by Graphic-sha Publishing Editorial Dept. Text and images copyright © 2016 Graphic-sha Publishing Co., Ltd. First designed and published in Japan in 2016 by Graphic-sha Publishing Co., Ltd. English edition published in the United States of America in 2019 by Schiffer Publishing, Ltd.

Library of Congress Control Number: 2019935798

ISBN 978-0-7643-5809-8

Printed in China

Published by Schiffer Publishing, Ltd.
4880 Lower Valley Road
Atglen, PA 19310
Phone: (610) 593-1777; Fax: (610) 593-2002
E-mail: Info@schifferbooks.com
Web: www.schifferbooks.com

Original edition creative staff:

Photos:	Kazumasa Yamamoto
Book design:	Satomi Nakata
Illustrations:	Makiko Ochi
Instruction pages:	Yuki Oshima, Tomoko Yusa
Editing:	Ayako Enaka (Graphic-sha Publishing Co., Ltd.)

English edition creative staff:

English translation:	Kevin Wilson
English edition layout:	Shinichi Ishioka
Production and management:	Kumiko Sakamoto (Graphic-sha Publishing Co., Ltd.)